THE
WORD

THE
WORD

MYSTICAL REVELATIONS OF JESUS CHRIST
THROUGH HIS TWO WITNESSES

VOLUME 5 | (1981–1984)

ELIZABETH CLARE PROPHET

SUMMIT UNIVERSITY PRESS®

Gardiner, Montana

THE WORD
Mystical Revelations of Jesus Christ through His Two Witnesses
Volume 5 (1981–1984)
by Elizabeth Clare Prophet
Copyright © 2022 The Summit Lighthouse, Inc. All rights reserved.

For information, contact
The Summit Lighthouse, 63 Summit Way, Gardiner, MT 59030 USA
Tel: 1-800-245-5445 or 1 406-848-9500
info@SummitUniversityPress.com
SummitLighthouse.org

Library of Congress Control Number: 2022951156
ISBN: 978-1-60988-424-6 (softbound)
ISBN: 978-1-60988-425-3 (eBook)

Summit University 🕊 Press®

25   24   23   22   1   2   3   4

CONTENTS

FOREWORD

Two thousand years ago, Jesus Christ appeared in the Middle East—an event of such import that we divide history into the epochs before and after his coming. He walked the Holy Land performing miracles, preaching to the multitudes, and imparting an inner teaching to the Apostles and the Holy Women.

After three short years, he ascended from Bethany's Hill. Yet that was not the end of Jesus' mission—nor the end of his teaching.

Paul proclaimed that he received his knowledge of Jesus' teaching *not* from the Apostles, but directly "by the revelation of Jesus Christ."[1]

John received "the Revelation of Jesus Christ"[2] while in a cave on the island of Patmos fifty years after Bethany's Hill.

In fact, Jesus has *never* ceased teaching. Through all the centuries since his departure from that scene, Jesus has spoken directly to the heart of his disciples.

Some, like Francis of Assisi and Catherine of Siena, were empowered by the Master for a very public mission. They were true spiritual revolutionaries.

Others found their lives transformed by his very personal impartation of the keys to their spiritual path. They have kept the flame by their profound inner communion with the Master.

Today, once more Jesus brings a new public revelation of his Truth. For more than forty years, he released his teachings through Mark L. Prophet and Elizabeth Clare Prophet, messengers for the ascended masters. And along with this new revelation, he also brings a torch of responsibility that he would pass to those who are ready to receive it.

Two thousand years ago, he told us that "the kingdom of God is within you."[3] Today he brings a more profound understanding of what this really means.

He told us then of the time of judgment that must come at the end of the age.[4] He tells us now that we are living through the fulfillment of that prophecy. He tells us that we have a key role to play in that judgment, and he tells us how to pass through it unscathed.

He demonstrated miracles then as proof of the promises he made. Today he explains the spiritual science behind those miracles. And he shows us how we can also work the "greater works"[5] that he promised those who follow in his footsteps.

The image in many churches is of Jesus on the cross—as if that were the defining moment of his mission. Jesus himself has reminded us that he was on the cross only a few brief hours. In fact, his life was not one of suffering but of great joy and a profound communion with God.

He bids us experience that communion.

He bids us experience the resurrection—a gift intended for the many, not the few.

He bids us embrace our sacred labor and become on earth, as he was, an agent of the Cosmic Christ.

And he offers the full cup of joy that he experienced, the abundant life promised to all who follow in his footsteps.

THE EDITORS

CHAPTER 1

You are the messengers going before the One Sent who
is the Word incarnate. You are the disciples who go into
every city and town wheresoever the Word should come.
You are the Marys and the Marthas. . . .
You are clearing the way.

CHAPTER 1

THE MYSTERY OF THE MOTHER FLAME WITHIN THEE: THE WOMAN CRUCIFIED WITHIN THE CHAMBER OF THY HEART… AND HER RESURRECTION

Standing upon the hill of eternal life, I behold the sheep of my flock scattered abroad throughout this land and over the whole earth. I behold them without the true shepherds who are my own.[1]

I come on this weary day as elementals portray the weariness of heart and soul of my own blessed Mother, who has chosen not to be resurrected with me on this commemorative morning but rather to remain upon the cross in the mourning of those whose crucifixion does not end the slaughter of the holy innocents, the taking of life by force. This abortion of life continues. And the effect thereof continues to press in upon all of nature when there ought to be rejoicing of angels, elementals, and sons of God!

There is yet the deliberation of the Three-and-Thirty of the council of the Lord of the World. And the twelve legions of angels of the Father, who would have delivered me from the cross had I summoned them,[2] are here in this hour for the deliverance of those who have been placed upon that cross—not by God, but by the fallen angels who once stood in his Presence but who have long gone out from him to persecute his children, to take his flame as the essential element of heaven—and to take it by force.[3]

The stealing of the light is ever attempted as they pursue it unto their own consuming. For that which they have ill-gotten will turn and rend them, even as they determined to rend the holy garment of the one who went before me—my own beloved master, my own friend of light. Unto him I pay homage in this hour!

NOT I ALONE WOULD GIVE MY LIFE THAT YOU MIGHT SEE

Behold John Baptist! Behold him—fully the avatara of the age, fully the incarnate Word. Behold him as he shines in the darkness. Behold him as he rebukes the very darkness of noncomprehension. Behold him as he rebukes the Pharisees, the Sadducees who come seeking to steal his light, even as they would have stolen it at our birth had they been able to find us and tear us from our mother's breast![4]

Thus, when you see the fullness of the man of God incarnate and you read the Word I gave to the poet whom I sponsored,[5] there is portrayed before your eye the awfulness of this hell itself into which our spirits are flung for a season. Not I alone would live to give my life to atone that you might see—and, having eyes, see the presence of the Evil One in your midst.

Oh, the foul tongue of Herod, mouthing friendliness in the very hour of his murder of the Son of God—not once, but twice. Therefore, as the heavens opened wide and the master and his disciple descended—the one preceded by the other, as it is written[6] —even so, the heavens opened wide for the fallen ones to have their hour and the power of darkness,[7] that they might be seen against the backdrop of the holiness of the Lord, Sanat Kumara, who sent us forth on a mission *for ye all!*

It is for *you* that we have come! It is for you that we have worn these bodies of flesh, knowing our own end written before our descent—the beheading of John Baptist, my own hanging [on the cross] by the fallen ones.[8]

THE RALLYING POINT AND THE STUMBLING BLOCK

Our fervent cry: Father, O Father, we are willing! Promise us if thou wilt, O Father, that these thy children, these our chosen ones, these our disciples, will never, never forget that we come, that we came in the name of the One Sent to dwell in the tabernacle of their own dwelling place, even the temple of the living God.[9] Let them not forget, lest all forget, the message of our life: that that which is done unto us will be done unto you,[10] unless with our ascent to the heart of God and the descent of the Holy Spirit there might be a communion of saints upon earth—oh, such a communion as the world has never known!

Therefore, we have said: Let their rallying be around the stone that the angel parted from the tomb and rolled away—the cleavage of the rock by the lightning and the thunder![11] Let that rock be the rallying point. I AM the Rock.[12] There is another. It is the stumblingblock[13]—the point of pride of Herod and his henchmen. Thus, may they rally round that cross as the sign of victory and the sign of judgment.

How oft have we desired, we two together, for you to know the fullness of that glory!

With what contempt has the LORD God spoken through John the Baptist unto Herod, "It is not lawful for thee to take thy brother Philip's wife!"[14] Thus, with the full fury—with the full fury of the Lord Sanat Kumara!—he thus spoke, knowing full well it was the signal of his own end and the knell of death, even the ultimate expiring of the sacred fire breath unto God.

Blessed hearts, behold the man. Behold this man of God who before me went—because he is and was the messenger sent.[15]

Behold this man of God! Had he not come with his rebuke and the invocation of the judgment, I could not have come to be baptized of him in Jordan. He held the balance for my fasting in the wilderness, lo, forty days! See the compassion of my Father who placed one, the God-man in incarnation, before me—holding the balance of my life, holding it even through the hour of the temptation of that archdeceiver of the Woman and her seed for whose namesake I AM come.[16]

Blessed hearts, even as our messengers today have gone "before your face" proclaiming your personal Christhood throughout the land and the continents, so I AM come to give you the understanding of the purpose of the messenger in every age. No Christ can be born or rise in the midst of the people save the messenger come.

Think on this. What has the messenger brought? First and foremost, the delineation of your own incarnation of the Word, that you might remember that you are come in my name as Bethlehem babes born of Mary to rise and shine in the name of Sanat Kumara, to be stars in the firmament of God's being in earth, in heaven.[17]

The messengers have brought the message of the judgment, fearlessly proclaiming it, publicly denouncing those leaders in Church and State—who have done what? Who have failed to lead you in the path of your own Christhood! Thus, the teaching is set. The judgment is set. And the messengers, by cosmic law, have been and are the incarnate Word before you.

RECEIVE MY MANTLE BODILY INTO YOUR TEMPLE

As John Baptist was my Guru—even Elijah, as I served him as Elisha[18]—so behold the Guru! Behold, the God-man/-woman as the androgynous Father-Mother God have appeared to you in these twin flames—*for a purpose,* I say! for a *mighty purpose!*—not for you to consider that their mission is the end of it, but the beginning.

Receive my mantle and know that your hour is come when you receive me bodily into your temple. Therefore, beloved hearts, these roles must be fulfilled. As the golden scrolls descend, as rolls of parchment, so read the handwriting of God.

You are messengers going before the One Sent who is the Word incarnate. You are the disciples who go into every city and town wheresoever the Word should come. You are the Marys and the Marthas who establish the home of Bethany[19] in each teaching center, in every city wheresoever I would go through my messenger and through the Mother whose time is come. Therefore you are the clearing of the way, even as the Mother has cleared the way before you, even as the ascended messenger so cleared the way before her.

Thus, in the mighty figure eight of this decade of the eighties —at any hour and day—you may be called upon to fulfill the light of John the Baptist and to retire that the incarnate Word might speak. And then again, you know that the messengers have established the platform for your denunciation of the fallen ones, for your calling of the disciples unto the Lord Sanat Kumara.

Hear our cry! For I have said to you that many John the Baptists are needed. And it is true that many shepherds coming in my name are needed. Understand the roll call and the calling of your role. And do not miss your cues upon this foundation of life. For it is the foundation of the crystal white, dazzling pyramid of life, which ye are!

This is the hour of the Guru becoming the chela and of the chela becoming the Guru. Who therefore is crucified? Is it not when the Greater enters the heart of the lesser by love that there be the crucifixion? And by that shedding of blood, is there not the transmutation of karma—the "remission of sin"?[20] Is there not the becoming unto Christhood through the eternal Christus by those who stand at the foot of the cross and receive the drops of blessed agony?

RECEIVE THE MOTHER DOWN FROM THE CROSS
CHOOSE WHOM THOU WILT SERVE

For those who share the resurrection morn, I come. I come that there might be resurrected within you the person of Guru,

John the Baptist—and of chela, my own name and heart. I come for the resurrection of the holy office of chela within you, as you are God-fearing the man of God manifest before you. It is the hour of the entering of this messenger into your own heart's chamber, there to be the replica of the image of Mother Mary as she is upon the cross.

You have heard it said: "Christ died for your sins." So, beloved, the eternal Christus manifest in the heart of the messenger is upon the cross upon the hill of life in your heart—and will so be there until you take her down, having forsaken every jot and tittle of your waywardness, your *ignore-ance* of the flame, your lack of sensitivity to the needs of the Christed One.

This focus is in a sealed chamber of those chosen. And those chosen for this focus are those whose names have been written in the Book of Life for this initiation. Therefore, my beloved, the ever-present witness within you of the Mother of life upon the cross is intended to bring out within you your most intense compassion, fulfilling every element of the Law, in order that thou mayest receive the Mother down from the cross and hold her in thine arms that the world, too, might receive the grace and the benediction of life.

The presence of the Mother crucified within is an irritant to every stain of sin and sinfulness and withholding of thy life unto God. Therefore, juxtaposed as thou art, O soul, twixt the crucified Mother and thine own self-will, I say: *Choose ye this day whom thou wilt serve*[21]—and serve well!

As I was upon the cross for the appointed hours, let me say, there is the coming of the Woman upon the cross and there is the resurrection. Mother Mary represents the macrocosmic wonder of Woman crucified! And therefore, this manifestation is the intimate and most personal initiation of those who are the devout chelas of the Mother of the World throughout this planetary body. Known or unknown, it matters not. It is by the measuring of the heart.

Realize, then, that the hour will come when the stone (if it be there) of the hardness of thy heart will be rolled away and the Mother will come forth from the chamber of your heart in the full garb of the resurrection. In that hour is the opportunity for thy resurrection. See to it that thou art prepared to ascend with the Woman in glory.

Therefore, the sign of the cross within thy heart—which I now establish as the cross upon the hill—is the sign of the four quadrants of thy being and of the divisions of the lines of the circumference of Self. It is the sign of Christhood, thy very own, within the four Matter spheres at the four points of the foundation of thine own pyramid of life. Understand, then, that with the establishment of the cross there is a giant hand that moves and measures the time and time, time again, and the half a time again[22] for that crucifixion, which is for the atonement of thy karma.

I have revealed to you a mystery of Christus. For this is the ancient ceremony of the laying down of the life of Christ[23] that that Christ might increase within each chosen disciple—mind you, the *chosen* disciple.

Thus, with the shedding of each drop of blood there shall be the increase of the Christ consciousness within those who approach the sacred heart of my very own God flame with reverence, who perceive the beyond and the beyond the veil, that as the Woman be crucified within you—so is your own Christ Self, so am I, so is Lord Maitreya, so is Lord Buddha. Therefore, we lay down the life of our Christhood for you—*for you* each one to whom it is given, to whom it is given to drink of the nectar of the essence of our own crown of glory! Therefore, behold the receding. We must decrease, thou must increase.[24]

Summon the will in love to accept the scepter of our wisdom. Be the messengers of the Guru within. Go before the blessed inner Guru into all of the cities and the nations of the earth—while Christ be in the tomb preparing, unfolding the leaves of the Book of the Law for thee.

Proclaim, *proclaim* our coming and the coming of the World Mother! For when the Blessed Mary and her blessed one be taken down from that cross, you will see a period of the resurrection spiral—the going forth of Mother Mary and this messenger, proclaiming the mysteries of the resurrection flame throughout all the land and the world itself. And those forty days[25] may be forty weeks, forty years, forty centuries—as cycles of life. The hour will come when the Mother flame will focus in the earth a resurrection fire on behalf of the new birth of all souls whom you will now kindle with the violet fire, with the sacred fire of our anointing.

Blessed hearts, be thou anointed now for this the opportunity of thy life.

UNDERSTAND THIS MYSTERY OF THE CHRISTUS

I have taken you into the very heart of Luxor. I have taken you into the heart of the Great Pyramid of Life that you might understand this mystery of the Christus.

Understand thy role. Understand the keeping and the guarding of the tomb while a Mother's heart—above and below thee—work, work to solve the problem of being for a planet and an evolution. Understand the guarding of thy heart. For thou art messengers in the fiery orb of John the Baptist! Understand the guarding of the heart for all that is in it. Understand the intensity of this sacred fire and this experience, which will continue day and night, day and night.

And if perchance, in the quietude of your meditation, you experience the agony and the ecstasy of this Person upon the cross, I bid you welcome. Welcome, my beloved. For your hour will also come, as the one who is chela one day becomes the teacher. Thus it is in the ever-expanding spirals of life—we came and we come that all might know that the path of initiation is surely the abundant life[26] to all here below. Abundant light. Abundant love. This is the story of our Father's love.

Thus, I would recite for you the prayer that I spoke unto the Father in the hour of this glory. Understand the glorification as the beatification, as the descent of light unto you—each and every one.

Father, the hour is come; glorify thy Son, that thy Son also may glorify thee: as thou hast given him power over all flesh, that he should give eternal life to as many as thou hast given him.

And this is life eternal, that they might know thee the only true God, and Jesus Christ, whom thou hast sent.

I have glorified thee on the earth: I have finished the work which thou gavest me to do.

And now, O Father, glorify thou me with thine own self with the glory which I had with thee before the world was.

I have manifested thy name I AM THAT I AM unto the men which thou gavest me out of the world: thine they were, and thou gavest them me; and they have kept thy word.

Now they have known that all things whatsoever thou hast given me are of thee.

For I have given unto them the words which thou gavest me; and they have received them, and have known surely that I came out from thee, and they have believed—*they have believed* that thou didst send me.

I pray for them: I pray not for the world, but for them which thou hast given me; for they are thine.

And all mine are thine, and thine are mine; and I AM glorified in them.

And now I AM no more in the world, but these are in the world, and I come to thee. Holy Father, keep through thine own name those whom thou hast given me, that they may be one, as we are.

While I was with them in the world, I kept them in thy name: those that thou gavest me I have kept, and none of them is lost, but the son of perdition; that the scripture might be fulfilled.

And now I come to thee; and these things I speak in the world, that they might have my joy fulfilled in themselves.

I have given them thy word; and the world hath hated them, because they are not of the world, even as I AM not of the world.

I pray not that thou shouldest take them out of the world, but that thou shouldest keep them from the evil.

They are not of the world, even as I AM not of the world.

Sanctify them through thy truth: thy word is truth.

As thou hast sent me into the world, even so have I also sent them into the world.

And for their sakes I sanctify myself, that they also might be sanctified through the truth.

Neither pray I for these alone, but for them also which shall believe on me through their word—through thy Word in them, O Lord, my God;

That they all may be one; as thou, Father, art in me, and I in thee, that they also may be one in us: that the world may believe that thou hast sent me.

And the glory which thou gavest me I have given them; that they may be one, even as we are one: I in them, and thou in me, that they may be made perfect in one; and that the world may know that thou hast sent me, and hast loved them, as thou hast loved me.

Father, I will that they also, whom thou hast given me, be with me where I AM; that they may behold my glory, which thou hast given me: for thou lovedst me before the foundation of the world.

O righteous Father, the world hath not known thee: but I have known thee, and these have known that thou hast sent me.

And I have declared unto them thy name, and will declare it: that the love wherewith thou hast loved me may be in them, and I in them.[27]

MY COMFORT UNTO THE FATHER
AND TO MOTHER MARY

My most blessed disciples, I address you as I addressed the Father. If you will hear this prayer of my heart that I have spoken unto him, you will know that it is my soul's comfort unto the Father. In the hour of my own crucifixion, it was and is my desire to comfort the Father himself that his little ones will be safe because I will dwell in them—because I send the call perpetually that my glory will be fulfilled in them.

It is the will of the Son of God. It is the will of our heart.

As the Lamb passes through the gate to the slaughter,[28] so our Father must know that these little ones will be held safe and secure, will be kept from the temptations of the Evil One—how else than by the dwelling in the innermost heart of these precious lambs.

My admonishment to Peter "Feed my lambs!"[29] is given to you as you go forth. But my admonishment to Mother Mary, then and now, is this:

O my Mother, I take my leave of thee.
Guard thou the heart of my disciples.
O thou bride of the Holy Spirit,
Come into the heart of my lambs.
Be there the keeper of the flame of the Holy Spirit.
Be there, O thou most blessed Virgin,
The keeper of the Mother flame.
Tarry with them, blessed Mother,
Until I come again,
Until I come to receive my own
Unto the realm celestial.

Thus I speak to you, dear hearts.

The embrace of the Mother and the Son—the master, the disciple—the love of this eternal union can never be broken. Never is there an altercation between the Mother and the Son but only the alteration, worlds without end, of the inbreathing and the out-breathing of the mighty figure-eight flow of the mighty flow of life!

Now we see the face of the chela beholding the face of God. Now we behold the face of the Mother peeping through the heart of the chela. Thus the rhythmic equation of life is seen. And as you are humble of heart, lo, great things of our God will come unto thee. It is the hour.

It is the hour of our coming and of the judgment of all who oppress the poor in Spirit who have not yet but are soon to receive the fullness of that Spirit within the heart. Yes, the poor in Spirit are those who are waiting for the coming of the Spirit, even the mighty one of God. Their hearts purified, they weep. And their tears wash my feet. They anoint my feet with a holy oil. And thus their coming, beloved heart, is the sign just before the descent, *filling, then*—filling, then, the heart with joy!

THE JOYOUS PRESENCE OF MOTHER MARY WITHIN YOU

After all of this—for joy I AM come! that your joy might be full because it is the fullness of the joyous presence of my Mother, Mary, within you.

Joyful are the angels! Joyful are the heavens! Joyful are the bells that peal to announce the day of thy own resurrection! Joyful is the heart of the one in whom the flame of Christus burns so brightly! For in that hour of the fullness of our cup, we must run to be crucified in the heart of the disciple, lest that cup run over and spill upon the ground when it is every precious drop for the fulfilling of the cycles of life within our own!

Lo! I AM come. *Lo!* I AM come. *Lo!* I AM come into your temple. For I AM the messenger of the Mother in this hour and in this age. Her light is victorious within ye all. Accept my message of the salvation of the Saviouress and be thou made whole! And let the wholeness of our love be for this two-thousand-year dispensation, that Saint Germain might reveal the Woman of Aquarius, even the Woman crowned with the twelve stars of light.[30]

Thus may the mystery unfold that yet has not been told. May it come. And when it comes, may it be the mystery of the light of Mother flame within thee.

HOLY COMMUNION:
BREAKING THE BREAD OF MY LIFE

Children of the Sun, East and West, I shall now deliver unto you my Body and my Blood that is blessed by the qualification of the body and the blood of Mother. Come and receive the Communion of saints.

Bring me the chalice of the bread that we may begin. Please rise. Let the wine be brought and let the wine be served quickly. Come forward.

[Communion is served through the messenger to over 1200 people (66 minutes).]

What I have done, I have done.

Understand the purpose of the breaking of the bread of my life. Understand that on the path of life there is the partaking of the bread of forgiveness and the wine of communion. But when I give to you, as I have done, my flesh and my blood, then know that a portion of myself has entered into you. And I also perceive that virtue is gone out of me[31]—but for a holy purpose.

Depart from me, ye despisers of the Word! You have no part with me. I have no part with thee. Come closer, then, my own. For my life is for the atonement of the many and the few.

As our Father has said, even beloved Alpha, the hour is come for those who have gone out of the way, following the Watchers in the stead of the sons of God, to come to the center of Reality.[32] May it be so is my prayer for you.

This bread of my life is as a white-hot coal of angels.[33] It is for that light in you to be the fullness of myself, that you might become who you really are.

BE AWARE OF THE PASSAGE OF CYCLES

When you think that I was with you but three short years, consider that in the life of any one of the ones who are sent, there is the apportioning of the hours and the cycles. The opportunities for certain of the teachings are past. By the mercy of God, they have been recorded—and, by your free will, may be published and studied and read. There are teachings I have given through the messengers that are finished. Though you come today for the first time into my presence, yet much has gone before. And you can recapitulate the sand that has already fallen in the hourglass.

For some, you hear of the mystery—the eternal mystery of Christ crucified in the heart—for the first time, without preparation. For you it is the vision of the future. For others it is the reality of the present. For still others it shall become the sign of an opportunity lost.

Thus, be aware of the passage of cycles. Understand the wave of light. Move with the wave—and let it move thee. For thou canst not turn aside the wave of light nor impel its course but only choose to be with it in the bursting of the foam of the crystal fire mist.

BEGIN THE ACTION OF LOVE, INCREASE THE FIRE OF THE HEART

There is the inner retreat of the heart—your heart—to which the Mother retreats. In a way, it is comforting to know. In a way, it is not. For those who live on the surface of their own world, it is a hard saying. But for those who live in the heart who have already prepared her room, there is the welcome and the rejoicing.

So it is for our Inner Retreat. Therefore, let us preserve the here and the there, the past, the present, and the future that all may come in life and take up that fruit at the feast of my Father's table, which is meet for them to eat in the hour of their coming. Let no man judge another's fruit! Let no man judge another's initiation. Let the tender hearts, as tender grapes, be received.

I AM cutting off from the flow of life those who have been sustained by the very presence of the messenger's heart in this octave, whose hour is come to swim in the cosmic sea on their own light. It is a dark night, if you will. But not of the crucifixion but of the severance that the individual might find the thread of contact and begin—begin the action of love and only that love that can increase the fire of the heart.

Therefore, there is a shifting of worlds as there is the union, which this one cannot, if she would, resist. It is the powerful union of my own with the heart of the Mother flame to which she has long ago given her life. This free will has been given. Therefore, in the sweet surrender, it is complete. And wherever I lead her, she will go. Thus, beloved, it is as though all had been done before your arrival at this conference. Nothing could be changed or mitigated, but you yourself have set the jewel of self in the years of opportunity of thy life.

Let those who feel that they are now on their own, recognize that all can weave a crystal thread out of the light that beats the heart. All can release that thread of light and cast it in the cosmic sea and hope that some angel of starry bands, some avatar with outstretched hand, might extend the arm of succor and safety and take that thread that is woven and fasten it again to the heart, the flaming heart of the Mother. Let there be the multiplication of life because of this union.

I have come for a massive release of light! I have personally touched you, each one. According to your faith, I say: Be thou made whole. For that which I have given to you in this hour, my beloved, is more than a grain of mustard seed![34] It is flesh of my very flesh and blood of my blood.

I send you forth to be as I AM—conquerors of death and hell. Until they be bound and cast into the lake of fire,[35] we have yet to be in our Father's service here below.

Go forth, empowered as thou art. Receive as thou hast been given.

Waste not the glad commission of angels. For you do not know if or when or where 'twill be given to you again.

I, Jesus, speak to you in your very heart of hearts. Take care! Take care of my life that I have given you. Take care of Mother. Take care of sweetest child that you now bear in your arm and in your heart.

I AM always Jesus—always come to start a new fire for the burning, a new fire for your reconsecration to the next rung of life.

O hallowed spiral, *here we come!*

April 19, 1981
Camelot
Los Angeles County, California
Elizabeth Clare Prophet (ECP)

CHAPTER 2

Come, souls of light! Come, brides of Christ!
Be united with the King of kings and Lord of lords. . . .
Let the meeting of heaven and earth be in the very heart
of hearts within the secret sanctuary of each one's being.

CHAPTER 2

O LORD, RECEIVE THY BRIDE
IN PERFECT LOVE!

Messenger's Invocation:

O Lord, our light, Sanat Kumara, vitalize and infill the temple of the soul with thy kindling light. Ancient of Days, preside now over the marriage of the Lamb and the Lamb's wife.

In the name of Gautama Buddha, Lord Maitreya, and Lord Jesus, we invoke the presence of the ascension flame. Beloved Serapis Bey, let this light, this kindling light—this white fire of our souls' love for the Bridegroom—be fused in the victory of our Lord and Saviour Jesus Christ.

Come, souls of light! Come, brides of Christ! Be united with the King of kings and Lord of lords.

Come, seraphs! Come, legions of light! Attend the wedding of the soul unto God. O purity of the heart of every living saint, O universal Christ, beloved Christ Self of each one: Behold, the Bridegroom cometh! Behold, the Lamb's wife!

Let the soul of the starry body of God now appear, wed unto the Spirit. Let thy kingdom come, O God, on earth as it is in heaven. And let the meeting of heaven and earth be in the very heart of hearts within the secret sanctuary of each one's being.

O Lord, receive thy bride in perfect love!

In the name of the Father and of the Mother, of the Son and of the Holy Spirit, Amen.

"Say Ye to the Daughter of Zion,
Behold, Thy Salvation Cometh!"

Isaiah

I will greatly rejoice in the LORD, my soul shall be joyful in my God; for he hath clothed me with the garments of salvation, he hath covered me with the robe of righteousness, as a bridegroom decketh himself with ornaments, and as a bride adorneth herself with her jewels.

For as the earth bringeth forth her bud, and as the garden causeth the things that are sown in it to spring forth; so the Lord GOD will cause righteousness and praise to spring forth before all the nations.[1]

Thou shalt also be a crown of glory in the hand of the LORD, and a royal diadem in the hand of thy God.

Thou shalt no more be termed Forsaken; neither shall thy land any more be termed Desolate: but thou shalt be called Hephzibah,[2] and thy land Beulah:[3] for the LORD delighteth in thee, and thy land shall be married.

For as a young man marrieth a virgin, so shall thy sons marry thee: and as the bridegroom rejoiceth over the bride, so shall thy God rejoice over thee.

I have set watchmen upon thy walls, O Jerusalem, which shall never hold their peace day nor night: ye that make mention of the LORD, keep not silence,

And give him no rest, till he establish, and till he make Jerusalem a praise in the earth.

The LORD hath sworn by his right hand, and by the arm of his strength, Surely I will no more give thy corn to be meat for thine enemies; and the sons of the stranger shall not drink thy wine, for the which thou hast laboured:

But they that have gathered it shall eat it, and praise the

LORD; and they that have brought it together shall drink it in the courts of my holiness.

Go through, go through the gates; prepare ye the way of the people; cast up, cast up the highway; gather out the stones; lift up a standard for the people.

Behold, the LORD hath proclaimed unto the end of the world, Say ye to the daughter of Zion, Behold, thy salvation cometh; behold, his reward is with him, and his work before him.

And they shall call them, The holy people, The redeemed of the LORD: and thou shalt be called, Sought out, A city not forsaken.[4]

"FRIENDS OF THE COMMUNITY"
A Reading from Maitreya

The community, being a fellowship first of all, sets as a condition for entrance two conscious decisions: labor without limit and acceptance of tasks without rejection. It is possible to eliminate faintheartedness by means of a twofold organization.

As a result of unlimited labor there may be a broadening of consciousness. But many people, not bad otherwise, do not envision the results, being frightened by incessant labor and enormous tasks. And yet they have accepted basically the idea of the community.

It would be harmful to include these yet weak people in the community; but in order not to extinguish their striving, one should not cast them out.

For this it is useful to have a second organization— friends of the community. Herein, without forsaking the customary order of life, these newcomers can become more deeply conscious of the community.

Such a twofold organization permits the preservation of a far more concentrated sincerity in the work.

If, however, a formal entrance into the community itself

be allowed, one will be obliged periodically to eject the unfit ones. In other words, the community will cease to exist altogether. It will be simply an institution under a false label, beside which the Sanhedrin of the Pharisees would be a highly righteous establishment.

Friends of the community provide the possibility of having a reservoir without danger of betraying the bases of the Teaching. Friends of the community do not conceal their weaknesses, and this gives the possibility of successfully strengthening them.

Indeed, We use the word "friends" because for the Occident this term is more understandable. Among Ourselves We call them disciples of a certain degree, but the West poorly contains Our concept of discipleship. Therefore, let us keep to the better-known designation—friends of the community.

It is absurd for the West not to accept Our simple propositions, fortified by long experience.

Our Communities are old! Have not the best people understood the community, not proposing any other form? From the community to the far-off worlds![5]

"The Marriage of the Lamb Is Come,
and His Wife Hath Made Herself Ready"
Revelation

Let us be glad and rejoice, and give honour to him: for the marriage of the Lamb is come, and his wife hath made herself ready.

And to her was granted that she should be arrayed in fine linen, clean and white: for the fine linen is the righteousness of saints.

And he saith unto me, Write, Blessed are they which are called unto the marriage supper of the Lamb. And he saith unto me, These are the true sayings of God.[6]

And I saw a new heaven and a new earth: for the first heaven and the first earth were passed away; and there was no more sea.

And I John saw the holy city, new Jerusalem, coming down from God out of heaven, prepared as a bride adorned for her husband.

And I heard a great voice out of heaven saying, Behold, the tabernacle of God is with men, and he will dwell with them, and they shall be his people, and God himself shall be with them, and be their God.

And God shall wipe away all tears from their eyes; and there shall be no more death, neither sorrow, nor crying, neither shall there be any more pain: for the former things are passed away.

And he that sat upon the throne said, Behold, I make all things new. And he said unto me, Write: for these words are true and faithful.

And he said unto me, It is done. I am Alpha and Omega, the beginning and the end. I will give unto him that is athirst of the fountain of the water of life freely.

He that overcometh shall inherit all things; and I will be his God, and he shall be my son.

But the fearful, and unbelieving, and the abominable, and murderers, and whoremongers, and sorcerers, and idolaters, and all liars, shall have their part in the lake which burneth with fire and brimstone: which is the second death.

And there came unto me one of the seven angels which had the seven vials full of the seven last plagues, and talked with me, saying, Come hither, I will shew thee the bride, the Lamb's wife.

And he carried me away in the spirit to a great and high mountain, and shewed me that great city, the holy Jerusalem, descending out of heaven from God,

Having the glory of God: and her light was like unto a stone most precious, even like a jasper stone, clear as crystal.[7]

And I saw no temple therein: for the Lord God Almighty and the Lamb are the temple of it.

And the city had no need of the sun, neither of the moon, to shine in it: for the glory of God did lighten it, and the Lamb is the light thereof.

And the nations of them which are saved shall walk in the light of it: and the kings of the earth do bring their glory and honour into it.

And the gates of it shall not be shut at all by day: for there shall be no night there.

And they shall bring the glory and honour of the nations into it.

And there shall in no wise enter into it any thing that defileth, neither whatsoever worketh abomination, or maketh a lie: but they which are written in the Lamb's book of life.[8]

THE SEVENTH MANSION
A Reading from *Interior Castle*
by Teresa of Avila

There is the same difference between the Spiritual Betrothal and the Spiritual Marriage as there is between two betrothed persons and two who are united so that they cannot be separated any more.

As I have already said, one makes these comparisons because there are no other appropriate ones, yet it must be realized that the Betrothal has no more to do with the body than if the soul were not in the body, and were nothing but spirit.

Between the Spiritual Marriage and the body there is even less connection, for this secret union takes place in the deepest centre of the soul, which must be where God Himself dwells, and I do not think there is any need of a door by which to enter it. I say there is no need of a door because all that has so far been described seems to have come through the medium of the senses and faculties and this appearance of the Humanity of the Lord must do so too.

But what passes in the union of the Spiritual Marriage is very different. The Lord appears in the centre of the soul, not through an imaginary, but through an intellectual vision (although this is a subtler one than that already mentioned), just as He appeared to the Apostles, without entering through the door, when He said to them: "Pax vobis."

This instantaneous communication of God to the soul is so great a secret and so sublime a favour, and such delight is felt by the soul, that I do not know with what to compare it, beyond saying that the Lord is pleased to manifest to the soul at that moment the glory that is in Heaven, in a sublimer manner than is possible through any vision or spiritual consolation.

It is impossible to say more than that, as far as one can understand, the soul (I mean the spirit of this soul) is made one with God, Who, being likewise a Spirit, has been pleased to reveal the love that He has for us by showing to certain persons the extent of that love, so that we may praise His greatness. For He has been pleased to unite Himself with His creature in such a way that they have become like two who cannot be separated from one another: even so He will not separate Himself from her.

The Spiritual Betrothal is different: here the two persons are frequently separated, as is the case with union, for, although by union is meant the joining of two things into one, each of the two, as is a matter of common observation, can be separated and remain a thing by itself. This favour of the Lord passes quickly and afterwards the soul is deprived of that companionship—I mean so far as it can understand.

In this other favour of the Lord it is not so: the soul remains all the time in that centre with its God. We might say that union is as if the ends of two wax candles were joined so that the light they give is one: the wicks and the wax and the light are all one; yet afterwards the one candle can be perfectly well separated from the other and the candles become two again, or the wick may be withdrawn from the wax.

But here it is like rain falling from the heavens into a river or a spring; there is nothing but water there and it is impossible to divide or separate the water belonging to the river from that which fell from the heavens. Or it is as if a tiny streamlet enters the sea, from which it will find no way of separating itself, or as if in a room there were two large windows through which the light streamed in: it enters in different places but it all becomes one.

Perhaps when St. Paul says: "He who is joined to God becomes one spirit with Him," he is referring to this sovereign Marriage, which presupposes the entrance of His Majesty into the soul by union. And he also says: *Mihi vivere Christus est, mori lucrum.* (Phil. 1:21, "For to me to live is Christ, and to die is gain.") This, I think, the soul may say here, for it is here that the little butterfly to which we have referred dies, and with the greatest joy, because Christ is now its life.[9]

THE THEME
A Reading from *The Spiritual Canticle* by Saint John of the Cross

These stanzas begin with a person's initial steps in the service of God and continue until he reaches spiritual marriage, the ultimate state of perfection. They refer, consequently, to the three states or ways of spiritual exercise (purgative, illuminative, and unitive) [the purging of the soul of sin, the illumination of the soul unto Christ the Lord, and the unitive or uniting of the soul with Christ the Lord] through which a person passes in his advance to this state, and they describe some of the characteristics and effects of these ways.

The initial stanzas treat of the state of beginners, that of the purgative way.

The subsequent ones deal with the state of proficients in which the spiritual espousal is effected, that is, of the illuminative way.

The stanzas following these refer to the unitive way, that of the perfect, where the spiritual marriage takes place. This unitive way of the perfect follows the illuminative way of the proficients.

The final stanzas speak of the beatific state, that sole aspiration of a person who has reached perfection.

STANZAS BETWEEN THE SOUL AND THE BRIDEGROOM

Bride

Where have You hidden,
Beloved, and left me moaning?
You fled like the stag
After wounding me;
I went out calling you, and You were gone.

Shepherds, you that go
Up through the sheepfolds to the hill,
If by chance you see
Him I love most,
Tell Him that I sicken, suffer, and die.

Seeking my Love
I will head for the mountains and for watersides,
I will not gather flowers,
Nor fear wild beasts;
I will go beyond strong men and frontiers.

O woods and thickets
Planted by the hand of my Beloved!
O green meadow,
Coated, bright, with flowers,
Tell me, has He passed by you?

Pouring out a thousand graces,
He passed these groves in haste;
And having looked at them,
With His image alone,
Clothed them in beauty.

Ah, who has the power to heal me?
Now wholly surrender Yourself!
Do not send me
Any more messengers,
They cannot tell me what I must hear.

All who are free
Tell me a thousand graceful things of You;
All wound me more
And leave me dying
Of, ah, I-don't-know-what behind their stammering.

How do you endure
O life, not living where you live?
And being brought near death
By the arrows you receive
From that which you conceive of your Beloved.

Why, since You wounded
This heart, don't You heal it?
And why, since You stole it from me,
Do You leave it so,
And fail to carry off what You have stolen?

Extinguish these miseries,
Since no one else can stamp them out;
And may my eyes behold You,
Because You are their light,
And I would open them to You alone.

Reveal Your presence,
And may the vision of Your beauty be my death;
For the sickness of love

Is not cured
Except by Your very presence and image.

O spring like crystal!
If only, on your silvered-over face,
You would suddenly form
The eyes I have desired,
Which I bear sketched deep within my heart.

Withdraw them, Beloved,
I am taking flight!

Bridegroom

Return, dove,
The wounded stag
Is in sight on the hill,
Cooled by the breeze of your flight.

Bride

My Beloved is the mountains,
And lonely wooded valleys,
Strange islands,
And resounding rivers,
The whistling of love-stirring breezes,

The tranquil night
At the time of the rising dawn,
Silent music,
Sounding solitude,
The supper that refreshes, and deepens love.

Catch us the foxes,
For our vineyard is now in flower,
While we fashion a cone of roses
Intricate as the pine's;
And let no one appear on the hill.

Be still, deadening north wind;
South wind come, you that waken love,
Breathe through my garden,

Let its fragrance flow,
And the Beloved will feed amid the flowers.

You girls of Judea,
While among flowers and roses
The amber spreads its perfume,
Stay away, there on the outskirts:
Do not so much as seek to touch our thresholds.

Hide Yourself, my Love;
Turn Your face toward the mountains,
And do not speak;
But look at those companions
Going with her through strange islands.

Bridegroom
Swift-winged birds,
Lions, stags, and leaping roes,
Mountains, lowlands, and river banks,
Waters, winds, and ardors,
Watching fears of night:

By the pleasant lyres
And the siren's song, I conjure you
To cease your anger
And not touch the wall,
That the bride may sleep in deeper peace.

The bride has entered
The sweet garden of her desire,
And she rests in delight,
Laying her neck
On the gentle arms of her Beloved.

Beneath the apple tree:
There I took you for My own,
There I offered you My hand,
And restored you,
Where your mother was corrupted.

Bride

Our bed is in flower,
Bound round with linking dens of lions,
Hung with purple,
Built up in peace,
And crowned with a thousand shields of gold.

Following Your footprints
Maidens run along the way;
The touch of a spark,
The spiced wine,
Cause flowings in them from the balsam of God.

In the inner wine cellar
I drank of my Beloved, and, when I went abroad
Through all this valley
I no longer knew anything,
And lost the herd which I was following.

There He gave me His breast;
There He taught me a sweet
    and living knowledge;
And I gave myself to Him,
Keeping nothing back;
There I promised to be His bride.

Now I occupy my soul
And all my energy in His service;
I no longer tend the herd,
Nor have I any other work
Now that my every act is love.

If, then, I am no longer
Seen or found on the common,
You will say that I am lost;
That, stricken by love,
I lost myself, and was found.

With flowers and emeralds
Chosen on cool mornings

We shall weave garlands
Flowering in Your love,
And bound with one hair of mine.

You considered
That one hair fluttering at my neck;
You gazed at it upon my neck
And it captivated You;
And one of my eyes wounded You.

When You looked at me
Your eyes imprinted Your grace in me;
For this You loved me ardently;
And thus my eyes deserved
To adore what they beheld in You.

Do not despise me;
For if, before, You found me dark,
Now truly You can look at me
Since You have looked
And left in me grace and beauty.

Bridegroom

The small white dove
Has returned to the ark with an olive branch;
And now the turtledove
Has found its longed-for mate
By the green river banks.

She lived in solitude,
And now in solitude has built her nest;
And in solitude He guides her,
He alone, Who also bears
In solitude the wound of love.

Bride

Let us rejoice, Beloved,
And let us go forth to behold ourselves
    in Your beauty,

To the mountain and to the hill,
To where the pure water flows,
And further, deep into the thicket.

And then we will go on
To the high caverns in the rock
Which are so well concealed;
There we shall enter
And taste the fresh juice of the pomegranates.

There You will show me
What my soul has been seeking,
And then You will give me,
You, my Life, will give me there
What You gave me on that other day:

The breathing of the air,
The song of the sweet nightingale,
The grove and its living beauty
In the serene night,
With a flame that is consuming and painless.

No one looked at her,
Nor did Aminadab appear;
The siege was still;
And the cavalry,
At the sight of the waters, descended.[10]

Messenger Leads a Meditation on the Perfect Love
of Our Beloved Christ Self for Our Soul:

Let us meditate upon the perfect love of our beloved Christ Self
for our soul—the Bridegroom for the bride.

Let us meditate upon the perfect union of our soul with Christ
and, through Christ who is the Lord of this temple, with our beloved
Lord and Saviour Jesus Christ.

THE MARRIAGE OF YOUR SOUL
UNTO THE LAMB OF GOD:
THE PURGING, THE ILLUMINATION, THE UNION

Dictation of Our Lord and Saviour Jesus Christ
to the Messenger Elizabeth Clare Prophet

Souls of my heart, brides-to-be in Christ, I would initiate you within the interior castle into the rites of the marriage of your soul unto the Lamb of God.

This is the true celebration of my ascension upon earth. For if you are taken up in the ascension as the commemoration of the culminating ritual of my life, who then will remain to tell of the path that leads to the consummation of love? Therefore, I propose the pursuit of thy heart for the union with the Bridegroom.

MAKE THYSELF PERFECT FOR THE BRIDEGROOM

Behold, he cometh!—the very Lord of lords of thy life. Welcome him and recognize that, in the very first instance, it is necessary for the Bridegroom to purge the blessed one who would become his very own.

Thus, beloved, in those weeks and months and years of longing for the perfect love of thy life and the sense that now and again thy soul is rejected by thy Lord, understand well that it is necessary to feel the spurning of the very sacred fire of that perfect love that you yourself might reach for the higher manifestation.

The period of the purging is the action of the Holy Spirit. It is indeed the violet flame. Thus, in this period of thy life, the striving for the goal of perfect love takes into account all of the human hardships of manifesting perfect love in this world where there is yet the imperfect human condition and the karma that must first be seen for what it is, be challenged and overcome, that thou might make thyself perfect for the Bridegroom.

Understand, then, that the sorrowing of thy soul in the absence of the Bridegroom is the very necessary chastening—the realization that this is a ritual of perfect love. In order to have perfect love, demands are made of thee by that very love, by the embodiment of that love. For, you see, when in the grand finale of life the Bridegroom cometh and taketh unto himself the beloved, he will take that soul, assimilate it unto himself—to the very Holy of Holies of the throne of God.

THE MOTHER FLAME

Therefore, the goal of assimilation is the reason I have come in this hour and two thousand years ago to set the path of the saints, to initiate you, my disciples, in the way of the Mother flame, which itself is a purging light.

Where the Mother is corrupted, where you have misused her light, there you must come, even under the apple tree—your own tree of life,[11] the mighty I AM Presence. And there you must come in the flame of the Buddha and the Mother to meditate upon the fruit of life and striving and to enter into the crystal stream of the River of Life to be washed, to be made whole—there to come in contact at first as the betrothal where you merge your heart with your beloved Christ Self now and again as in the stage of courtship.

You are courting the Christ. And the Christ is courting you. But you remain separate for the purging, for the illumination. And that illumination is the raising up of the white fire of the Mother unto the crown of perfect wisdom. Thus, the crown of the Woman is also the crown of her Lord's wisdom glorified.

Blessed hearts, I commend you to the study of the intricate explanations that I inspired upon Saint John of the Cross concerning this poem of the bride and the Bridegroom. Each line and each word has a profound meaning for the understanding of thy path on earth.

The perfect love and the way of love is the way of the example whereby, through the consummate love of your own Beloved, you then manifest my own ascension flame. Though I personally may not receive you fully until the hour of the ascension, the union of your soul with your Christ Self will be the example to all of the path of the ascension and of the ruby ray.

Teresa of Avila understood and experienced this path, as did John.

Most blessed hearts, listen then to the teachings of your own messenger on the writings of Saint John of the Cross already recorded[12] and then pursue this perfect love and, ultimately, this perfect marriage. It is the sign of the ascending ones. It will not extinguish you, I promise. But it will give to you joy unspeakable, joy so intense that only perfect silence can contain it! For the secrets of love in the interior castle are truly the very crystallization of Spirit in Matter whereby, through the weight of your devotion, you anchor upon earth such an intense love for God.

In consideration of this hour of my ascension, I have determined to recall for you the teachings of Sanat Kumara[13]—the teachings on the Lamb and ultimately the Lamb who is the Christ incarnate, the sign and the symbol of your own Christ Self.

THE WAY OF PERFECT STRIVING— PERFECT LABOR MUST BE PERFECT LOVE

Through the open door of the Mother, I AM come. I AM also prepared to appear within the temple of thy being, entering not by any door but by the grace of compassion of the heart. There I would receive you into my Sacred Heart. There I would transfer to you, in this blessed union, the essence of my light—expressed as the drop of blood from the heart of Christ.

This transfer of my love to you must surely come if you enter the way of the cross, the way of perfect striving—if you understand community as that place where devotees understand that, in the purging and in the illumination of the soul in preparation for the marriage, incessant labor, sacred labor is the means to the assimilation of Christ.

And in what does that labor consist? Dear heart, truly it is the labor in the field of the LORD's consciousness. Truly it is the preparation of the marriage feast for all who will come and attend the wedding of thy soul to God. It is all of the tasks at hand that are needed to prepare for the Bridegroom who cometh to his own through souls who enter in at the open gate.

It is physical labor but not physical labor alone. It is striving in each of the levels of the mansion of the soul. It is striving in each of the centers of life, which flow until ultimately the perfect labor must be the perfect love.

Therefore, labor not in vain but believe on the One Sent[14] as thy Redeemer—the one who can give to you the light of the ascension flame.

Let those who understand our chastening love of recent weeks realize that all of this is a part of the purging process, even the purging of the very community itself. Be not dismayed at this process, neither within thy members nor within the body of the community.

For we are obliged to find many and diverse ways for each soul to come to the awareness of the supreme longing and the very intense desire for union with Christ. That longing is there, but often it is covered over by outer activities and superficial longings. Often it is polluted and diluted until the soul thinks that it longs for something that it does not, when in reality the deep desiring for wholeness can only be fulfilled by wholeness with Christ.

And therefore, the desiring itself has its beginning and its ending in the cycles of Alpha and Omega that perpetually flow, as a mighty caduceus, through the soul chakra and the soul desiring in those intervals, intervals between the undulating currents of life. In those moments of the sense of aloneness, that *all-oneness* is truly the object of the experience of being alone—and then one.

Realize that in all of the cycles of life, our Father has provided almost microscopic intervals that there might register upon all life in the Matter spheres the remembrance that the soul is not yet complete and not yet whole until it has entered into the fullness of Christ. And therein is no interval in the cyclings of perfect love. This is a scientific principle that scientists may one day understand to a greater degree.

WALK WITH THE SAINTS
UNTO THE MARRIAGE OF THE LAMB

Blessed ones, this temporary absence of the light itself is the impelling force that impels pilgrims and disciples to pass through the fiery trial in order to gain admittance into the very heart of the Beloved. This has been the way of all saints in every walk, in every century. Those who are truly the saints of all ages have experienced this desiring for the perfect love of the Lamb of God.

I come this year to set a cycle in the very midst of Serapis Bey's dispensation of love.[15] As you are walking this fourteen-month rosary with Serapis, realize that it is a walk with the saints unto the marriage of the Lamb.

Now then, by my presence, by the light with which I hold you in the divine embrace, I seek to impress upon you the memory of your original union with and as the Son of God. And I am determined—if you will also be determined—that you will not so often lose the memory or the longing of your First Love.

It is ordinate to love the successive representatives of the universal Christ as thou lovest thine own Beloved. And therefore, as I am the translator of thy love unto Maitreya, so Maitreya is the translator of thy love unto Gautama, and Gautama is the translator of thy love unto Sanat Kumara.

Therefore, seek the joy of Christ who is with thee. Seek the joy of union with the messenger who represents and is that Christ. And know that the hour is come truly unto thine own house for the marriage of the Lamb. The hour is come wherever thou might appear on this most sacred ritual and discipline—the purging, the illumination, the union.

Take each step carefully, for it leads to the next. Let thy foot be secure on the spiral staircase. For within thy being is that spiral. Mounting it is thy soul. And thy soul will assimilate the very genius of God—even the light, even the moments of far-off worlds.

Let there be a homing. And let there be a holy order of those who are the true mystics of the Holy Grail.

Let us understand that once the marriage has taken place, even in the heart of one in your midst—that union itself is the magnet for the New Jerusalem to descend out of heaven. The bride adorned for her husband becomes the Holy City. And what is the Holy City? It is the place where heaven and earth meet.

LET THIS PLACE OF WORSHIP AND TEACHING PROVIDE THE WAY

As you know, this city of my Mother is dedicated as the very soul of America and the earth and the place for the outpicturing of that path of the New Jerusalem. At inner spheres, the Holy City is seen as the coordinate of the city over Jerusalem. But, my beloved, we have chosen to consecrate the Inner Retreat for your individual realization of the New Jerusalem, because karmic law requires that the conditions now prevalent and present in Los Angeles be expiated in many ways in time and space ere the fullness of that city may appear here on earth.

Thus, let us consecrate Los Angeles to this ultimate victory. Let us draw here the faithful of the heart of Christ. Let them feel our presence, as we truly contain within our auras—each one so ascended as I AM—the matrix of the City Foursquare.[16]

Let this Camelot and this place of worship and of teaching provide the way, so long as it is ordained by God, for souls to enter the path of perfect love. And let those who reach the levels of illumination and preparing for that union understand that, at that level of discipleship, there is an Inner Retreat where one may continue the work of community at other levels, latitudes, longitudes, in an accelerated time and space.

Thus the Inner Retreat, celebrating the ascension of my own Mother,[17] becomes in itself for you the place of the interior castle, the place where I may enter thy temple—not through the door but, because you have assimilated my body and my blood, you are Self-realized and sealed in the marriage of the Lamb.

A MIGHTY MAGNET OF LOVE, HEART BY HEART

What I am proposing is a mighty magnet of love—a magnet consisting, heart by heart, of those who dare to study this path, to understand it, to become one with it, whether in the outer life they are married or not married. This is an affair of the soul with God. And all other considerations of life may continue. For it has naught to do with the flesh-and-blood consciousness but with the soul itself. And it is true that this path continues, whether or not the soul is with the physical body, even at inner levels in the retreats of the Brotherhood.

And so, my beloved, as the celebration of the ascension rings —as rings of light emanate from my heart through the heart of the messenger and your own throughout the earth this day—let these concentric forcefields of my own ascension, my own Electronic Presence, contain the message of love that the dove of your soul has found her nest on one of those rings of light, positioning herself there—and her heartbeat, one with my own, receiving the crystal flow of crystal waters.

I impart to you the desiring of my own soul prior to my ascension to be the fullness of that oneness with the universal Christ. I commend to you the Psalms as the expression of that longing.[18] And I come to you with the tender counsel of Saint John, that you might understand what you are experiencing when in the process of purging, when in the sense of aloneness, and feeling now the presence and now the absence of your Lord.

This path is one of the higher mountain. The air is rarefied and often thin. And in the absence of the Beloved you would faint for fear of loss of the perfect love of thy life. This is also a period of doubt and fear and questioning, not of God but of thine own soul and its capacity to be the perfect love of Christ—somewhat in this wise, wondering: "Will I be acceptable unto the Lord? Will he receive me? And when will he receive me?"

When you have these experiences, beloved, you must not equate them with the former grossness of doubt and fear or that of the world or of the fallen ones. But rather understand them as the sincere desire of the soul, that yet senses itself in the state of sin, to be purified and made white.

The nearer you approach to your Christ Self, the greater sense you have of an absence of purity until your very presence in the physical octave, even in the cities of life, makes you feel unworthy to even approach us at inner levels—preferring rather to but touch the hem of our garment, so aware are you of the difference between our ascended state and your own.

Blessed hearts, remember that we understand that you have volunteered to carry not only your personal karma but planetary karma and, therefore, to retain somewhat the garments of this octave for the very necessity of being the example of perfect love— perfect love that forgoes the ascension and the resurrection, to be crucified again and again that others might be caught up by your very heart's love of me.

A NEED WITHIN THE COMMUNITY

Your longing and your love of me is felt in my heart always. When there is a band, a spectrum in time and space where there dwell souls of light with such fervor, it is the sustaining grace of millions.

As you know, the orders of the Catholic Church have waned. There are not so many young who take the habit and become priests and nuns for the very love of Christ. And even now they are more concerned, engaging in politics for the sense of honor to the people.

But there is a need for those who recognize this walk. And thus, there is truly a need for degrees within the community, that those who are not quite so ready for the full purging may still consider themselves disciples and pursue a labor of the heart that will prepare the soul without trepidation to enter into these all-consuming fires so necessary prior even to the full illumination of thy crown.

THE CELEBRATION OF MY ASCENSION

I speak to you of love. And I am determined that in this year you shall know more love, if you will it so in Christ, than you have ever known in this life. It is the love of your God Presence and your Christ Self. It is your love of me and of my blessed Mother. It is your love of Saint Germain and our holy cause and of the little children and of the child of thy heart.

It is supremely your love of Christ as I AM in the hearts of the meek and the humble who are bowed down throughout the earth. For they long for me, yet have not received that teaching whereby the purging process might begin and the illumination might be won.

I ask for your love this day as the celebration of my ascension. I ask that you love me in those who have a threefold flame and a heart of gold who are not awakened, neither quickened, to the Beloved who is with them, hovering just above the temple ready to enter.

As you have known the longing for perfect love, understand that the Christ Self of these, my beloved, also has that longing to assume the soul unto itself. Therefore, let that perfect love be that sacred labor that brings to that Christ that I AM, wherever they are, the tear of compassion, the burning heart that desires their oneness with me as much as you desire your own. For experiencing your own desire, can you not then equate what is the desire of these souls, though they are covered over by centuries of indoctrination?

Some say Messiah has come. Some say he has not come. All are in a state of suspension, knowing not the truth of the Lord who will be unto them their righteousness and reprove the righteous and bring them unto sublime submission before the Word and the Lamb.

And then I ask for your love for the ascended masters, my cohorts of light, as they, too, long for perfect union with disciples upon earth. I ask you to comprehend the yearning for union twixt heaven and earth, Alpha and Omega—beginning with the smallest cycle of thy heartbeat, transcending the far-off worlds, and ending in the heartbeat of God.

All of life quivers—suspended, breathless—waiting for the consummate presence of the Lord.

Let your love be that love that enhances this union for every part of life. In this, then, fulfill my presence, fulfill my ascension on earth. In this, know me as I AM.

THE TENDER LOVE
BETWEEN THYSELF AND MYSELF

I speak to you in the softness of my speaking within your heart. I speak to you in the tenderness of the Beloved, that you might realize through all of the process of the purging that there is the most tender love between thyself and myself.

This knowing, this remembering each time you replay this dictation, will enable you to conquer that fear of the terror of the tyrant who is in fact thy own synthetic self—the synthetic self, the Antichrist that must be *bound* by you and you alone.

You will do so because I await thee, my love.

SEAL THESE SOULS UNTO THE PERFECT LOVE
OF THY SON JESUS

Messenger's Benediction:

In the light of the Blessed Virgin Mary, I seal you in the heart of Jesus Christ—in your very heart of hearts with your own beloved Holy Christ Self.

Beloved mighty I AM Presence, *seal* these souls unto the perfect love of thy Son Jesus!

In the name of the entire Spirit of the Great White Brotherhood, in the name of the Father and of the Son, of the Holy Spirit and the Mother, Amen.

May 28, 1981
Camelot
Los Angeles County, California
ECP

CHAPTER 3

I come, yes!—to transfer to you that light of Godhood. . . .
I come to seal you in the mighty I AM Presence of life!
I come to reveal to you the promise of ascended masters
stepping through the veil!

CHAPTER 3

SEEDS NOT WATERED OR PLANTED

My beloved, let us rehearse the familiar words: The flesh profiteth nothing, but the Spirit giveth life. Nevertheless, you are given to understand that Matter itself must be the instrument of the Spirit, and the crystal chalice is the bearer of the light.

Thus, I come to pour the light of the Spirit into the chalice that is yet fragile. Yet there is one that keepeth the chalice of thy heart, the chalice immutable that is the Holy Grail. The Christ Self of each one is the keeper of the Grail, the wine thereof. The Christ is the bread of life. I AM that manna which came down from heaven.[1]

Understand that which is meet for you to understand—that the bread of life itself cannot be assimilated except it first become the living Word. The wine that is poured must be assimilated. And the one born of the Spirit must come to earth to ratify the heavenly state midst those who have no access to the crystal chalice but are yet bearers of the fragile cup only.

How shall the fragile cup endure the pouring of the wine of the Spirit? It cannot. Therefore the priest or priestess partakes of the bread of life and of the wine and of the living water that descends from above. And the Grail then becomes the Word incarnate —and all come, holding out their fragile cups as the begging bowl of life.

THE LIGHT THAT IS GIVEN,
AND THE TESTING OF THE VESSEL

The bowl can contain only so much, and the trees grow only so tall, and the bounds of man's habitation allow only for light to be given and received increment by increment, lest the individual himself should dare to believe that he is become as the gods.

Sufficient unto the day is the light. For the light itself that is given is not intended of itself to be the incarnate Word, but to be the magnet that will draw to you the fullness of the Godhead mightily —for action in the hour of action, for the courage to be prime mover in the hour when movement is the call.

The light that is given is for the sustainment of your sharing in the gift of eternal life without your containing all of it in the imperfected state. Thus that which is given is an opening unto heaven, is a point of contact, is a sufficiency for thy life.

Always is the possibility that this light can become the crystal and the crystal itself multiply greater light. Always the option is given, but never is it given without the most intense initiation and soul testing—testing the levels of harmony, testing the levels of will to be purity in action, testing the levels of commitment, daring to determine to be the conqueror of life.

There are the lesser tests that are given only for the sake of those who yet bear the fragile cup. Then there are absolute tests that are for the testing of the vessel that is to contain the Spirit of the Great White Brotherhood. It is essential that you understand these levels of testing—for little by little, all must come to all. For it is never the Father's intent, though he established the bounds of habitation,[2] to ultimately limit the soul's soaring beyond those bounds when he has proven himself ready to move beyond with the angels in heaven and with the sons of God.

It sounds as though we speak again of the measuring rod, measuring in the outer court of the temple and within—measuring the Gentile evolution, measuring the sons of God, measuring the components of the capstone.[3]

How do you measure the levels of achievement in the classroom of school? By the testing of that which the individual is capable of demonstrating physically, on paper. What are you capable of precipitating?

The harvest, then, is the coming home of the results of the test given in the spring. All are graded, and it is very clear to each one —through each one's own Christ Self—what has been wishful or willful thinking and what is, in fact, in hand.

These are moments of rejoicing for the Daystar appearing![4] These are moments for the sealing of the harvest by the baptism of the sacred fire. These are the moments when the sons of God may be ordained as priests after the order of Melchizedek.[5]

COME INTO ALIGNMENT WITH THE WILL OF GOD

We come, then, to consider. We come, then, in the contemplation of the divine plan for your life. We come with the hosts of the LORD who are determined to burn back the barriers falsely set up by the fallen ones. We would establish the barriers of God consciousness and the opening wide of the City Foursquare[6] for newness of life and for these little ones to enter there.

Our gaze encompasses the earth. Our gaze is the filling of the stars. Our gaze is into the depths of the pool of the soul of selfhood.

My beloved, I am come into your midst vastly aware of the co-measurement of life. I am aware of the ongoing need of every chela of the sacred fire to come into alignment with the will of God. I am aware of souls of light descending. I am aware of offices within this community that need to be filled by hearts that have a joyous fervor for the will of God.

I am summoning my beloved for reinforcement—for service here at Camelot and at the Inner Retreat. I am calling those who understand the necessity of the capstone and of the fervent application of the light of Alpha and Omega. I ask you to apply your hearts and also to make application to our own messenger for service.

For there is a need for great expansion. And the geometry of the Word that is planned in the coming year is planned with you in mind, individually, and your service that can be given. It is therefore time to state anew what can manifest, what will be brought forth, and what will you bring as seed of light for the sowing.

We look, then, to the remnant of lightbearers worldwide for establishment of a greater concentration of light and a great, great effort to further the purposes of our Inner Retreat. We look for the keeping of the timetable for the mastery of space and for those who can understand the equation of Armageddon—those who understand that there is a defense needed in the physical plane, in time and space, at the Inner Retreat.

It is the hour and the call for some to go to be the firstfruits of the Virgin's seed. For it is my Mother's land and my motherland that we would restore. It is a place where those coming from all continents and nations might find a dedication of their nation's own dharma and preserve the integrity of those soul-groupings that must come together for the expansion/explosion of light unto a victory, until all may be perceived as one—one light and one banner.

For all the nations of the earth will one day uphold the banner of Maitreya. But first there is the calling. First there is the necessity of the planting of those flags of the nations here at Camelot as the sign of the trek of pilgrims of the nations coming on a spiritual pilgrimage—celebrating, two hundred years after the Declaration of Independence, a new declaration of liberty, a new thanksgiving. And now in the century of the five-hundred-year celebration of the discovery of this continent itself, there are those who have come for the discovery of the New World, those who have come for a new celebration of freedom. It is a replaying, in the spiritual spheres, of all that has taken place.

Let the pilgrims come. Let some realize that it is their dharma, in the manifestation of the Buddha of the nations, to remain with Padma Sambhava and the Mother on the mountain of the Inner Retreat.

It is necessary—and already the hour is late—for others to come and take up the flame of the day-to-day sacred labor of Camelot.

Let the heart then pulsate. Let the Son behind the sun now receive the reward of the pilgrims of the sun. Let there be new consideration and a review of life. For we would be in the hour of the Buddha's cycles—on time and in space—where the LORD God would have us to be.

There is a forcefield to be maintained in the state of Montana. There is a forcefield to be maintained of the ancient fires of the Yellowstone and of the Royal Teton Retreat.[7] There is a focus to be opened. There are ways to be charted. And therefore, let us consider, not only the necessities of the land and its economy but the spiritual mission itself for which some again must make the sacrifice that others might build and others might plant and others might tend the flocks and others might harvest!

LET THE CHALICE BE THE SYMBOL OF OUR STRIVING

Thus, beloved hearts, a new wave and a new light from Sirius descends in this day of Thanksgiving. Let the chalice be expanded! Let the permanent crystal chalice of the messenger expand. Let the fragile cups of devotees now be fired. And let them bring those cups to the feet of their own Christ Self, that they might find the strengthening of the chalice of being, the strengthening of the temple.

Let there be the chalice of our beloved Paul the Venetian.[8] Let it be manifest! Let it be revealed! Let it be unveiled to those eyes who have never seen before the magnificent chalice of our Paul that he has created for the New Age, for the Goddess of Liberty, for Saint Germain, and for devotees of the freedom flame.

Let the chalice be the symbol of our striving. And let us realize that the holding of this chalice—that it be not dashed from hand or lip—is the supreme mission of each individual lightbearer.

Think of hands raised, outreached, sustaining and upholding the chalice, that there might be a mighty outpouring from the very heart of Sanat Kumara in this year! Let us become one soul on earth, one heart, and one chalice. Shall we not all exchange the fragile chalice of the flesh that is without the Spirit for the permanent chalice of the Guru in our midst?

Let us come to understand the presence of the Brotherhood. Let us come to understand the true mystical body of God and the one consciousness of all.

Fear not, then, anything on earth or under the earth or under the sea. Fear not, but perceive how the pressing in of darkness receives a recompense of the pressing in of light—how there is an intensity, how there is acceleration, how the Adversary is bound, hand and foot, by the legions of our God!

Let us perceive, then, that the curtains of heaven open, one by one. And many a parting of the veil shall precede thine own fulfillment of the Law with the courage of life.

I AM thy own if you will have me. I AM the One Sent.[9] I AM the one whose vessel is provided. I AM the one. And I place my Electronic Presence here, that you might understand the stepping down of forcefields and your own dipping into the fires of the Holy of Holies.

I WOULD TAKE YOU TO NEW DIMENSIONS

I come to bless you with the light that is the blessed light of the heart of every son of God who has moved in our midst. I come to bring you all to the point of the movement of this caravan of light and the perception of where the sacred labor must be emphasized, where the true direction must be, where the effort must be placed. I come to give you a unique understanding born of a unique contact with your own fiery heart!

I come, yes!—to transfer to you that light of Godhood. I come to carry you far into the interior of your own God flame! I come to seal you in the mighty I AM Presence of life! I come to reveal to you the promise of ascended masters stepping through the veil!

I come to make known to you that this is indeed the hour of the Holy Grail if you can perceive yourself as worthy, oh, worthy of the cup—to hold it, to cherish it, and to drink all of it!

Tender hearts that are the tender vine—come! Come and be with me in this hour. For I would take the whole body of God upon earth into my heart. I would shepherd you to a new hillside and a new and holy calling. I would allow you to hear the hymns the angels sing and the preaching of the angel of the Everlasting Gospel.[10] I would take you to new dimensions where God has prepared the mansions of his love.

I would not leave you comfortless in this hour of cycles turning, nor in the hour of the persecution or of the affliction. I bring water for the watering of the seed and the plant of life and for the parched lips that pray the Our Father and give the decrees of freedom, hour upon hour.

I come for the recharging of your form and of your temple for that service that you would render when your hearts would faint—not for fear, but for the application of thy life to the duty at hand. I bring reinforcements. I bring angels of the sacred fire to take up the watch where the fallen ones have been and where they are no more.

I come to fill in. I plant new trees, evergreens, where the unfruitful plants have been removed. Where there is the barren fig tree, lo, I plant the living Tree of Life by the waters that flow. Lo, I release the waters that issue from the very heart of your mighty I AM Presence.

STRIVE AND STRIVE AGAIN FOR THE VICTORY

I say, there is a solution to planetary unrest. And the Lamb of God *is* with us! I say, there is a solution to world confusion. I say, there is a solution to the manipulation of the fallen ones! I say, there is a God-solution—and that God-solution is the light, the eternal light that I pour now into your hearts!

O my beloved ones, will you not receive me? For I AM both

the light and the outpouring of the light! I AM the light. I AM the light of the world, indeed, as long as I AM in the world.[11] And I have purposed that purpose of Almighty God to be in the world through your heart, through your own Christ consciousness that you diligently pursue.

You will not have it if you let go of it so easily, my son! You will not have it if you do not strive for it—even though it be a part of your causal body of light, even though it be the reality of thy Self at inner planes. There is a striving, there is a pulling on the cords of heaven that must be done and done daily, lest you lose that which is given for your calling in this life!

Yes, I am your Father. I have ever been your Father. For my Christic seed was sown and is sown in my embodiment as Joseph.[12] Therefore, you realize that I come as the Father of many sons upon earth and the specific son whose calling it is to realize the dharma.

Recognize that one cannot simply leave the great Tree of Life and all of its fruit waiting to be plucked and trust that anytime, any-where, some time and some day, the same opportunities will be there. These are momentous opportunities! These are momentous years! Do not resist the calling of the LORD—your own mighty I AM Presence. Do not set aside so lightly that which is the proffered gift.

After all, were you to stand in the place of the giver, as I stand this day, decide how long you would hold the outstretched hand of opportunity for an ungrateful, neglectful, or willfully ignorant generation. You would also decide, as a wise father, how long it is just to hold out the gift in hand and when it should be returned to the fiery core, that the individual learn a greater appreciation and the understanding of what it means to strive and strive again for the victory.

Though there be the favorite son, who is the Christ Self of all, the soul must not fancy itself in control of that son. Therefore, in the harvest of years, of lifetimes, of embodiments—which now comes to you as the most magnificent and golden opportunity you have ever seen in a million years or more—I say to you: *Flinch not, hesitate not, squander not thy light!*—but realize there are more important things to do than surfeiting in the same old habit patterns that are only indulged because of a certain familiarity and comfortability.

THE MOTHER WILL NOURISH

Therefore cometh the Mother and the Spirit of the Mother. Therefore come cosmic virgins to bring the flame of the Divine Mother in this weekend seminar,[13] that all might understand how the Mother will nourish, will bring forth, will provide, will be the raising of the ascension flame to reignite and resurrect the inner potential of life.

Blessed hearts, I must share with you something that is on my heart, and it is this: there are in some present this day kernels of light —as nuclei of potential, gifts of God and of the great causal body— which have been allowed to descend for the opening in this embodiment. These are sealed as seeds, not watered or planted or given to the sun.

These seeds rest in the chamber of the heart with thy Christ Self. And the seed is capable of bearing the fruit of initiation. The seed is capable of being the opening to the causal body of that which is necessary for you to earn the victory in this life and for you to give to the planetary body that without which it could not gain the victory.

On my heart, then, is the understanding that for some it is a matter of fear, for others postponement, for others hardness of heart or an absence of Self-worth. Whatever the reason of dalliance or merely the unknowing, these seeds of light that ought to begin their cycle of germination are not receiving the love, the intense love, that is the only way that the seed of life can be opened.

Therefore, I come to you with a recommendation that you apply yourself to your own Christ Self, giving the "Introit to the

Christ Flame,"[14] that you apply yourself deeply to the divine plan which you, as a co-creator with God, ordained and approved in the beginning. I recommend that you apply yourself to pray fervently at the feet of your own Christ Self that these opportunities, as seeds of life and of my very own heart, one with the Father, be not lost, be not cast aside, and that this incarnation of the Word of God in you—this which promises to be the final incarnation— be not lost, be not wasted, be not the setting-aside of this grandest and most glorious of opportunities of all previous incarnations.

Let us realize that each one is given all that he has need of to pursue the victory. All is contained. Some bear gifts indispensable to the entire community. Others are working on individual initiations first, to be prepared to take a greater responsibility and burden of light and karma.

Let those who have the greater light not be neglectful of holy office or the signs that are written in the sky and in the earth. Be not neglectful of the Word itself or the call of God. For, beloved hearts, if you think, after all, that you may determine the time and the hour and the space of the call, are you not placing yourself above God the Father? Is it really possible to say to life, "I will tend to you when I will"?

GOD HIMSELF WILL ORDER THY LIFE

To put oneself in the position of Father before one has become the Son is to interfere with the entire order of things and to seize a task that is mightier than one's capacity, and therefore to find oneself tumbling in confusion and chaos at the attempt to be the orderer of thine own life when God himself will order thy life when thou wilt come into submission to thine own inner being. After all, the surrender is not to something or someone outside of oneself! It is always the surrender to that which one already is— one is, perhaps, at the next octave or behind the next door.

Rejoice to look in the great mirror of life and to see the next image of thine own Christhood appear. Rejoice to be aware of that which is pure and perfect and powerful in true Selfhood. Rejoice to greet thyself in the embrace of the Father and the Son and, through that embrace, to become more of the One. Rejoice to know that thou art worthy of the call. And rejoice to know that the Father knows best the hour of the call.

I have taken the call. And I have made my own calling and election sure[15] by striving, by overcoming, by balancing my own karma, by dealing with the fallen ones, by retaining the sense of helplessness in God, that he might fill my vessel always. And so it is in heaven as on earth. The humility of the ascended masters, I think, would astonish some who ought to be emboldened by the Holy Spirit but instead are emboldened by a self-assurance not founded on the Rock of Christ within.

Well done, thou who art weary. Well done, thou who art filled with the living Spirit. You have gone forth, you have sown, you have returned. And you have something to show God and man for thy effort.

I speak to the Son of man in ye all. I speak to your hearts most precious. I speak to you the overcomers, my own co-workers in life: I love you. Oh, that you would understand my love and my presence and my nearness with you alway!

SPEAK WITH THE AUTHORITY OF MY NAME

Speak, then, to the Adversary. Challenge the liar in the way. *Bind!* the murderer of the most sacred love that we share. Speak with the authority of my name. I give it new to you, as I gave it to my disciples then. I affirm my name to you, as I affirmed it then, as the authority of your life to cast out serpents,[16] to exorcise the demons of the night.

I say to you who know me in the fullness of my ascended master light body and expanded, immortal cosmic consciousness: *Speak the name Jesus the Christ!* And in my name, in the name of

the I AM THAT I AM Sanat Kumara command life free and *bind!*
the entire conspiracy of the fallen race. It will come to pass. It shall
be. For I have ordained this authority upon *you* who are the living
Word!—you who are hearers and doers, you who dare daily to
drink of my blood and eat of my flesh.[17]

> Lo, I AM Alpha and Omega,
>   the beginning and the ending of cycles.
> *Lo, I AM Alpha and Omega,*
>   *the beginning and the ending of all cycles!*
> Lo, I AM in you.
> Lo, I AM displacing all that you and I have not ordained
>   in the beginning.
> I AM the binding of the false will of the oppressor
>   imposing itself in the place of thine own free will!
> Lo, I AM displacing that which is distasteful
>   unto the Holy Spirit!
> Lo, I AM come!—the purging fire and the cleansing light.
> Lo, I AM piercing the night!
> Lo, I AM going before the way of the Holy Spirit.
> Lo, I AM the Son of God in you, one with the Father.
> Lo, I take up my abode within you,
>   and I AM the transforming power of cosmos this day—
>   to raise up, to raise up, to raise up lightbearers!
> Lo, I AM the praise of the Lord within you.
> Lo, I AM that which exonerates each living soul
>   to be the fullness of God-freedom.
> Lo, I AM the forgiveness of sin.
> Lo, I AM the healing of the sick.
> Lo, I AM the presence of life that erases the imprinting
>   of the fallen ones and restores the cosmic memory of
>   the mind of God—of whom I AM THAT I AM.
> Lo, I AM the restoration of the mind of God within you!
> Lo, I AM the restoration of your soul to that perfect love!

Lo, I AM the restoration of that flow.

Lo, I AM the sealing of the temple door.

Lo, I AM come.

I AM the risen Christ.

I walk the earth as the risen Christ through my beloved.

Now let those who would be baptized come. And let those who would be witnesses be witnesses. And let all know that the baptism is indeed for the sealing of the soul and the chakras unto the original divine plan ordained.

Seize it, my love. Seize it, my child. Seize it, my son. For without it there can be only the canceling out of an identity in God that could have been, might have been forged and won!

I AM the Sun behind the sun!

I AM the reinforcement of the rod!

I AM the reinforcement of life.

I AM the will to be where thou art.

And I demand that the call of God receive the call

of the Son, that there might be the confirmation:

Thy kingdom come, O God, on earth as it is in heaven!

With El Morya I repeat: *Tempus fugit!* The hour is late. Let all who have the opportunity for divine Sonship come into that alignment and be known as witnesses unto me in all the earth.

I have spoken. I *charge* you! Do not forget my Word. Do not forget my seed. Do not forget my light within you. For you are a new person and newborn—*if you will accept it.*

November 26, 1981
Camelot
Los Angeles County, California
ECP

CHAPTER 4

Let there be light in the citadels of freedom
throughout the earth! . . . Let the mountain of adversity
be replaced by the mountain that is the Zion of each
one's I AM Presence. This is my Christmas message . . . .
Let it be the breath of hope to all who are
bowed down by the . . . fallen ones.

"GOD HAS PROVIDED THE RECOMPENSE"

The Authority of the Word of God Incarnate to Declare the Systems of the Nephilim Gods Null and Void

Deliverer of the Word, come forth! Thou who art the Cosmic Christ, *hear my plea!* I AM the living Son, Jesus Christ. I stand in the heart of the earth and in the heart of the Mother who is become my own.

Let there be light in the citadels of freedom throughout the earth!

O thou deliverer of the Word, unto the Most High God I appeal for the intercession of the mighty one of God, Sanat Kumara, not alone in Poland but in every nation where pacts, partitions, political treaties have resulted in the oppression, the repression, and the subjugation of peoples as slaves of a world totalitarian movement that is fed by both streams of East and West.

THE DECLARATION OF INTERNATIONAL INTERDEPENDENCE OF THE SONS AND DAUGHTERS OF GOD

I appeal, therefore, to heaven and to earth, to the Great White Brotherhood assembled here and in the octaves of light, for the speedy consideration of our Declaration of International Interdependence of the Sons and Daughters of God.[1]

Let delegates convene. And let the proposal of the Woman be verified, rarefied by her own seed and the seed of the Great God, Sanat Kumara.

When there is, then, the consensus of hearts and when the perfected document is prepared, I say: Let it be promulgated throughout the world and let the people be heard! Let their voices be counted. And let them know that this document is not written by mere mortal hands or human hearts, but that it is the statement of the World Saviour and the Saviouress who is come, that there is residing in the heart of earth not only the Saviour and the Lord of all, but the devotees of the Word who stand to defend that Word and who underscore the authority of the Word of God incarnate to abrogate and to declare null and void all systems, documents, treaties, legal agreements (national and international) of the Nephilim gods that exist and are bent to one purpose and one alone—and that is the continuous enslavement and murder of the children of the light!

Therefore I, Jesus Christ, declare the authority of my Word to be that of Lord Maitreya, deliverer of the Word as the Cosmic Christ, whose authority derives from the Lord of the World Gautama Buddha, whose authority derives from the Lord Sanat Kumara.[2]

This authority therefore I declare, vested in my servant and messenger, is set forth as the Word that will not be turned back and as the declaration of the voice of almighty freedom to all who would espouse it, all who will affirm it, all who will be the vessel and the outpouring of the vessel of light upon earth.

I declare, then, that this voice and the authority thereof is the voice of the Lamb and that this Proclamation of Christmas Day 1981 must be and is a part of the very foundation of the Everlasting Gospel of peace and freedom preached to all nations with the gathering of the sons of light with the Lamb on Mount Zion.[3]

Therefore is the hour come and is the coming of the Woman at hand. Therefore is the hour at hand of the gathering of the components of the LORD's mystical body with the Lamb.

Therefore with these signs know, O people of God, that the pouring-out of the vials,[4] that the judgment and the final conquest of the fallen ones by the Faithful and True and the armies of heaven[5] are at hand—that all these things should come to pass as the moving of cycles continuing again and again as all must be outplayed and outpictured individually, family by family, community by community, state by state.

THE EVENTUALITIES OF MY REVELATION TO JOHN ARE ONGOING

Understand the ongoing march of freedom and freedom's forces. Understand the meaning of the Word "which was in the beginning with God, which was with him, and without which was not any thing made that was made."[6]

Understand that "the Word was made flesh" and does dwell in the earth.[7] And though the Word was the Creator of the earth, yet his own received him not.[8] Understand that this incarnation of the eternal Logos is our celebration of the Christ Mass and of the outpouring light of winter solstice.

Understand that the eventualities of my revelation to John are ongoing in the lives of individuals. And though they appear to occur in different epochs, ages, centuries, and millennia, there is, however, the appointed hour and the appointed time of the march of the constellations and of the galaxies and of the worlds and of the turning of the Great Central Sun and all who are the mutual servants of this cosmic round—that there is indeed the great outbreath and the great inbreath and that indeed the Word comes down to earth this day as the living bread.

I AM the living bread. And my life is given for the life of all. And this is my Word and this is my desire: that this proclamation of freedom, backed by the authority of the Word incarnate and all the hierarchies of heaven, shall be the statement of Almighty God as the answer to the prayer of millions—so answered through the hearts of the devotees, so carried by the doves of the Holy Spirit, so carried by the shepherds who serve as world teachers—that the people of earth, the children of the light who espouse the integrity of the Great God flame, may know that the divine help is at hand, that the Comforter is with us ("God with us" as the Immanuel), and that the light will not forsake her own!

THE DETERMINATION TO STAND FOR FREEDOM

Therefore, God has provided the recompense. God has sent forth the sign, in answer to the prayer of the Mother's heart and the hearts of every son and daughter of God upon earth, that the beginning of the overturning of Babylon the great and the Great Whore and the false prophet and all that cometh out of the bottomless pit[9] is the mutual interdependence of the sons and daughters of God under the Almighty One whereby there is formed a diamond chain—links forged of the gold of hearts aflame with power, wisdom, and love—and that the forging of this union worldwide will provide the impetus to renew determination to the stand for freedom, to the parting of the veil, that the saints who stand on the line where Light meets Darkness and swallows it up will behold the parting of the curtain and see there the hosts of heaven, the armies encamped on the hillsides of the world, and the entire cosmic hierarchy ready to deliver planet Earth—ready to give birth to the Divine Manchild!

O living flame of cosmic freedom, I now set the light of my heart to the hearts of God's people worldwide! Let the believers in the Word and those who have originated out of the Word know that the sign of this declaration is indeed the sign when they may rise up with confidence, backed by the Faithful and True whose name is The Word of God, I AM THAT I AM.

Let this declaration ring the bell of the ancient memory of the Ancient of Days, that when the World Mother should come as prophesied and stand before the altar of God in the company of the saints to declare the freedom of all mankind—then should the age of the Divine Mother appear, then should Aquarius show forth her light, then should Saint Germain (my father and the father of the Holy Church[10]) appear to many, face-to-face across the earth. Then should the sign of the Woman clothed with the Sun[11] in the person of Lady Portia, Kuan Yin, Pallas Athena, Mother Mary, Nada, and all who serve with the Goddess of Liberty appear, then, at inner levels and face-to-face with the children of the light.

Therefore know, O world, that the LORD God Almighty, our Father who is in heaven and on earth, will not forever prolong the persecution of the lightbearer, nor procrastinate the judgment of the wicked, nor forever be silent in the face of the pleadings of the prayers of millions for justice. Nor will he forever hold his people in bondage to the chains of their own karmic condition.

But he will send the Saviour. And the Saviour will come in the Person of the Mother. And the Mother will appear over and over and over again by the purified, rarefied hearts of her devotees.

And her Word shall go forth! And her people shall rise up! And her place shall be secured! And the life everlasting shall be known! And the walk from the path of mortality to immortality will be as the ascent of Mount Shasta—up the pathway of light until, in the hour of the destination at the summit of that mountain, there shall be the God-realization of self-transcendence that

> Lo, I AM the heaven, I AM the earth
> And I AM fulfilled in the center of Almighty God
> Worlds without end!

Let the mountain of adversity be replaced by the mountain that is the Zion of each one's I AM Presence. And let the Grand Teton[12] portray to all the world the stepping through the veil, out of the etheric retreats, of the ascended masters unto the people of planet Earth.

Therefore, my beloved, this document, when it is sealed, when it is written, when it is published, and when it is signed by you by the authority of the flame of life that by the grace of God burns in the hearts of the people of earth—it shall be the notification served to all life that the hour of the Mother's judgment is come. And you shall behold the Blessed Virgin, right hand upraised in the name of my own God flame, therefore issuing the command of the dividing of the way of Light and of Darkness.

This is my Christmas message 1981. Let it be heard. Let it be sung. Let it be the breath of hope to all who are bowed down by the aggressors of the fallen ones.

In the name of the LORD God Almighty, in the name of the living Word, I, Jesus Christ, the issue of the only begotten Son of God, promise you that my Word "shall not return unto me void,"[13] that it shall return to me, by the order and the law of the Cosmic Christ by whose authority it is sent, to deliver this planet and this people into the hands of Almighty God.

I promise you that every call and every declaration God-ordained is now, will be, and shall forever manifest the recompense and the return—not alone in my name but in the sacred name of God, I AM THAT I AM, Sanat Kumara, and all who have passed through the initiation of the Lamb unto the ascension in the light.[14]

Let all who have fought the forces of light through the ages understand this Christmas proclamation as a warning and as a judgment in itself.

Hear! O world. The world is being aligned. For alignment I AM here! For alignment I AM come! And I *will live* to fulfill my destiny in this hour through this messenger!

I seal you by the authority of your own Christhood and the living God who sent you to support this noble cause!

Messenger's Invocation:

In the name of the light of God that never fails, we summon the souls of lightbearers the planet round. Enter now the cathedral of the heart! Procession here to the sanctuary of the Holy Grail!

Ascended hosts of light, sons and daughters of God who have sustained the holy cause of freedom worlds without end, all who are the components of the Holy Grail—O crystal chalice formed of hearts of all ages meeting at the nexus of the Now, come forth! Saints robed in white, the entire Spirit of the Great White Brotherhood, come forth in the great victory of the God flame!

Lo, I AM the action of the sacred fire. I AM the Great Central Sun Magnet of the Christ Child.

Lo, I AM THAT I AM. I AM calling forth the infinite light of Sanat Kumara for the acceleration of worlds, for the stepping up of heart flames of these lightbearers who hear and answer the call of the World Mother to be present with Maitreya, Gautama Buddha, and Sanat Kumara.

May the light of God that never fails now descend as the rain from heaven! And let every child of God's heart receive the baptism of the original fiat of the will of God. Lo, as Christ descended to that temple, let us also declare in entering these gates:

> *Lo, I AM come to do thy will, O God!*
> *Lo, I AM come to do thy will, O God!*
> *Lo, I AM come to do thy will, O God!*
> *Lo, I AM come to do thy will, O God!*

Let the will of God, as the sacred adventure of all of our incarnations, be consummated in this hour of the Christ Mass as we celebrate once again the incarnate Word. Lord Sanat Kumara, thou art where I AM the I AM THAT I AM. We celebrate in thy Personhood, lo, the incarnate Word. Gautama Buddha, Lord Maitreya, Lord Jesus Christ, even the Lion, the Calf, the Man, and the flying Eagle—lo, I AM THAT I AM where thou art, where I AM,

O God—in the heart of the chela who is the living God, in the heart of the Guru who is the living God!

> Lo, I AM the affirmation of the Word incarnate in this day
>   and in this hour of the victory!
> Lo, I AM THAT I AM.
> I stand on the earth and I stand in heaven!
> Lo, I AM the confirmation of the faith!
> Lo, I AM the victory of the Word!
> Lo, I AM the guardian action of the Church Universal
>   and Triumphant!

Saints of the Most High God, armies of the Faithful and True, come forth now for the deliverance of the captives and for the deliverance of the Word. We decree it in thy name, Lord and Saviour Jesus Christ, and all who are with thee as the members of the divine body of God in heaven and on earth.

In the name of the Father and of the Son and of the Holy Spirit, in the name of the Mother, Amen.

> In the beginning was the Word,
> And the Word was with God,
> And the Word was God.
> *Praise the Lord, I AM THAT I AM, Sanat Kumara!*
> The same was in the beginning with God.
> *Praise the Lord, I AM THAT I AM, Sanat Kumara!*
> All things were made by him;
> And without him was not any thing made that was made.
> *Praise the Lord, I AM THAT I AM, Sanat Kumara!*
> In him was life; and the life was the light of men.
> *Praise the Lord, I AM THAT I AM, Sanat Kumara!*
> And the light shineth in darkness;
> And the darkness comprehended it not.
> *Praise the Lord, I AM THAT I AM, Sanat Kumara!*

There was a man sent from God,
Whose name was John.
Praise the Lord, I AM THAT I AM, Sanat Kumara!
The same came for a witness,
To bear witness of the light,
That all men through him might believe.
Praise the Lord, I AM THAT I AM, Sanat Kumara!
He was not that light,
But was sent to bear witness of that light.
Praise the Lord, I AM THAT I AM, Sanat Kumara!
That was the true light,
Which lighteth every man that cometh into the world.
Praise the Lord, I AM THAT I AM, Sanat Kumara!

He was in the world,
And the world was made by him,
And the world knew him not.
Praise the Lord, I AM THAT I AM, Sanat Kumara!
He came unto his own,
And his own received him not.
Praise the Lord, I AM THAT I AM, Sanat Kumara!
But as many as received him,
To them gave he power to become the sons of God,
Even to them that believe on his name:
Praise the Lord, I AM THAT I AM, Sanat Kumara!
Which were born, not of blood,
Nor of the will of the flesh,
Nor of the will of man,
But of God.
Praise the Lord, I AM THAT I AM, Sanat Kumara!

And the Word was made flesh,
And dwelt among us,

(And we beheld his glory,
The glory as of the only begotten of the Father,)
Full of grace and truth.
Praise the Lord, I AM THAT I AM, Sanat Kumara!

John bare witness of him,
And cried, saying,
This was he of whom I spake,
He that cometh after me is preferred before me:
For he was before me.
Praise the Lord, I AM THAT I AM, Sanat Kumara!
And of his fulness have all we received,
And grace for grace.
Praise the Lord, I AM THAT I AM, Sanat Kumara!
For the law was given by Moses,
But grace and truth came by Jesus Christ.
Praise the Lord, I AM THAT I AM, Sanat Kumara!
No man hath seen God at any time;
The only begotten Son,
Which is in the bosom of the Father,
He hath declared him.[15]
Praise the Lord, I AM THAT I AM, Sanat Kumara!

December 25, 1981
Camelot
Los Angeles County, California
ECP

CHAPTER 5

Rejoice, O ye heavens and the earth!
For that power of Satan is bound, and that Fallen One
is judged and will no more go forth among the
inhabitants of this or any other world to tempt them
against the Person of the Lord Christ!

THE FINAL JUDGMENT OF SATAN

Messenger's Invocations:

In the name of the God-victorious one, let the light of the Word of God blaze forth from this altar in the very person of the Faithful and True. Come forth, O living Word. Lord Sanat Kumara, Ancient of Days, manifest the fullness of the sevenfold flame of the Holy Kumaras.

Beloved Gautama Buddha, amplify the sacred fire of Shamballa, amplify the mighty threefold flame! Lord Maitreya, Cosmic Christ, disperse the night! Disperse the darkness as misqualified energy! Let the blazing light of the Divine Mother come forth in this hour of the Kali Yuga!

I invoke the bursting of light from the Divine Woman. I call to beloved Alpha and Omega, our Father-Mother God. I call for the Cosmic Christ. I call for the wonder and the action of the sacred fire. Let the light of God blaze forth. Let the light of God blaze forth. Beloved Lord Jesus Christ, let the flames from your causal body burn brightly on this altar and in our hearts.

Beloved mighty I AM Presence of each one, we call forth the victory of God for every soul of light upon earth. We demand the binding of the fallen ones. We demand the binding of the dragon that gave power unto the beast. We demand the binding of the beast that was healed of his deadly wound. We demand the binding of the beast whose number is 666.

I demand the action of the sacred fire. Burn through, O living Word! Confound the fallen ones in their international and national conspiracy against the lightbearers! This call goes forth now for the immediate and instantaneous judgment of the international bankers and all members and agents of the Capitalist/Communist Conspiracy of the Nephilim gods against the children of the Most High.

I appeal to the manifestation of the LORD God Almighty for the saving of the earth, for intercession by Elohim on behalf of the Woman and her seed, on behalf of Church Universal and Triumphant, The Summit Lighthouse, Summit University, and Montessori International. I call forth intercession of the Four and Twenty Elders on behalf of every lightbearer, every child of God's heart upon earth who is striving to enter into union with the beloved Holy Christ Self.

I call to the beloved Holy Christ Selves of all sons of God upon earth, of every child of the light, of all who have come forth from the heart of Alpha and Omega. I call for the intensification of the mighty action of the light in this hour of the Christ Self, the one most holy and anointed of every child of God's heart.

Now be magnified, O Christed Ones! In the name of Alpha and Omega, I say, be magnified! And let every heart attuned to the Almighty know the Christ, know him as the Lord, both of heaven and of earth, the Lord of the individual manifestation of God upon earth.

Beloved fourteen ascended masters who govern the destiny of the I AM Race upon earth, we appeal to you to glorify God in our bodies, in our minds and souls. We call for the rescue of the children of the light. We call with all of the fervor of the mighty threefold flame burning within our hearts!

O living one of the sacred fire, beloved Christ Self of all, let us now so magnify the light of the Lord Jesus Christ, Lord Maitreya, and Lord Gautama that there is no longer any doubt or fear or ignorance of the Law on the part of the sons of light. Living Word of the sacred fire, come forth!

Almighty God, we beseech thee in the name of the I AM THAT I AM, let the glow of the fire of the threefold flame of Christ intensify and unite the sons and daughters of God upon earth in their international declaration of interdependence.

Mighty I AM Presence, let the New Day appear! Let the glory of the light shine! Let the wonder of God appear in heaven and on earth, as the Divine Mother does appear to her children everywhere upon Terra—for the union through the heart of Archangel Michael and the seven mighty archangels, for the mighty union of God with man, of the entire Spirit of the Great White Brotherhood and the chelas of the ascended masters! Let the union come swiftly for the holding of the light, O God! We decree it and we accept it done this hour in full power, Amen.

Beloved Jesus Christ, do not tarry but enter quickly. Come quickly, O Jesus Christ, into this temple, into the temple of the living God prepared by each of his Keepers of the Flame on earth.

Enter now, O beloved Jesus, and reign supreme forever, on earth as it is in heaven! Let thy kingdom come, O Christ, on earth as it is in heaven! Reign triumphant and supreme forevermore. Amen.

In the name of the I AM THAT I AM, I call forth the light of Alpha and Omega. In the name of Jesus Christ, thou who art a priest forever after the Order of Melchizedek, I invoke the Body and Blood of the living Christ. I call for the breaking of the bread. I call for the transfer of the wine. I call for the blessed Communion shared by the saints. I call for thy presence with us, O Lord.

Beloved Sanat Kumara, Gautama Buddha, Lord Maitreya, Lord Jesus Christ and all the hosts of heaven, come now into communion with us as we celebrate the presence and the victory of the Christ!

In the name of Jesus Christ, the LORD God Almighty deliver thee from all evil! Amen.

Jesus' Dictation:

O my Father, O my Father, deliver unto these, thine own, the fullest measure of my heart's light!

I AM come, beloved, here in the home of Mary and Martha and Lazarus, here to find hearts melded together in a mighty congregation of the righteous. So you have come, the assembling of the elect of God who have elected to do my will in Him.

I would be the Saviour of the lost sheep of the house of Israel.[1] I would be the Saviour of all life! And I do convey to my messenger that essence of salvation, that burning of the fiery heart, that presence of my Sacred Heart for ye all.

Blessed ones, thou who art the noble of the light ennobled by Christ in ye all, oh, rise in this moment of our oneness. For it is the hour when we worship together as of old, even the LORD God Almighty! And we offer praise and thanksgiving that the hour of his judgment is come, both in heaven and on earth.

Therefore, I announce to you that the Word has gone forth on Wednesday past, in the very triumph and the hour of the twenty-seventh, for the remanding to the Court of the Sacred Fire of the one you have known for so long as Satan.

Blessed hearts, some of you who are our disciples worldwide have known that many years ago, in answer to the call of our messengers when both were embodied together, Satan was bound and his power reduced.[2] Therefore, for the continuation of the flaunting of the law of the person of the messenger, of the person of the lightbearers, our Father sent forth the call to me to activate on that very evening the action of the call that would be for the judgment of that Fallen One.

Therefore, let it be known that the remanding of Satan to that court, where the Lord Sanat Kumara presides in the presence of the Four and Twenty Elders, has resulted in his final judgment. Therefore rejoice, O ye heavens and the earth! For that power of

Satan is bound, and that Fallen One is judged and will no more go forth among the inhabitants of this or any other world to tempt them against the Person of the Lord Christ!

Let us say together: *Alleluia! Alleluia! Alleluia!* For the LORD God omnipotent reigneth in his heaven and in his earth!

Some have noted the crystal clarity of the weather here in this area on the Friday of that victory, on the Saturday—on the very appearance of the dawn of a new era of expansion of the Christ in all. Blessed hearts, let us commune together as to the meaning and the ramifications of this cosmic event.

(Will you now be seated, blessed hearts.)

This event marks the second in the occurrence of the final judgment of the fallen ones by the work and the hand of our two witnesses, as the call has gone forth. You are aware of the judgment, the binding, and the second death of Lucifer.[3] Therefore, now be aware of the binding and the judgment and the second death of Satan.

Understand that the hour of the second death is following the trial at the court of the God Star. Thus, we have heard and we have borne our witness as to the influence not only of Satan but of the race of his seed called the Satans,* who have infiltrated every corner of this galaxy and beyond.

The seed of Satan has proliferated, blessed hearts, as you would not even conceive yourself in the most expansive imagination of your hearts. Therefore, even from that point—bound behind bars, lo, these many years—that Fallen One has had the focal point of a race of Satans who raised themselves up against the I AM Race so long, so very, very long ago.

Therefore, these who yet strut on earth and other planetary homes remain in that state of an accelerated dissolution and a deceleration. They have lost the impetus of the original seed and the one who held for them that comparable manifestation that my Sacred Heart holds for you.

*pronounced seh-tánz

This one, beloved hearts, has been the personal adversary of my lifestream and all who have come in the fullness of my joy. This occurrence, then, long anticipated and awaited by myself, will result in a new surge of power, wisdom, love, *healing*, transmutation, contact with my own through the blessed threefold flame of all hearts who are united with me!

CLEANING UP THE DEBRIS OF BABYLON THE GREAT THE MIGHTY WORK OF THE AGES

Blessed ones, though that seed is no more in its original manifestation, yet the stalking of the earth by those who are the copies of the original remains a point of alert to the faithful and a sign that, in the hour of their own dissolution, there is the ranting and the raving in those moments before the interior deterioration will manifest also in the final judgment that is become physical. Thus, all who were his seed and are his seed have also been judged at inner levels with him, for they are one and the same manifestation! But in the physical octave, there is yet the residual manifestation of these lifewaves.

And thus, I have come to you that you might understand how there is a gathering of the forces of these Antichrists and how there is the attempt, in the final hour just before their own disappearance from the screen of life, to move against the lightbearers and to take from them the imminence of the victory that does come in the hour of the sign of the marriage of the Lamb and the Lamb's wife.[4] Therefore understand that in the very hour of rejoicing, it is also the hour when the Judgment Call must go forth diligently to confirm on earth what has occurred in heaven.

You realize, beloved hearts, that in the casting out of the Fallen One, out of heaven to the earth, there was then the manifestation on earth (and continuing to the present hour) of the warring of the seed of Lucifer and Satan against the seed of the Woman. When there is the withdrawal of the point of the cause, you also know that the effect must come to naught. Nevertheless, there is a necessary cleaning up of the debris. And this, too, is the mighty work of the ages!

Thus, we summon you, O people of God, to understand that the city of Babylon and the person of the Great Whore represent the empire of the Satans in Church and in State—the ecclesiastical and the secular manifestation of that civilization of the fallen ones. Therefore, *in one hour is thy judgment come, O Babylon the great!*[5]

See how in one hour, beloved hearts, is the judgment of Satan come! And therefore, since we gathered last, even only a week ago —the earth has changed, the world has turned, the ramifications are vast! And therefore, you understand the why of the coming of Elohim.

They said that they would come for the turning of the worlds and they did. And by the saturation of the first cycle of the year with that light and the continuation of their work at inner levels, so the moment came when this shortening of the days and cycles for the elect,[6] for the judgment of that Fallen One, might appear!

Therefore, the hosts of the LORD give gratitude unto Elohim, unto their messengers, unto the disciples of the LORD God Almighty who came in answer to the call to be physically present to hold the balance for this conference—which, beloved hearts, was the most taxing upon our messengers of any that has ever come forth, inasmuch as the Light released was enormous and the pushing back of the Darkness and the consuming of it was also enormous! And therefore, the balancing of these pressures of Light and Darkness upon the heart of the messenger can well be understood by you.

And all of the faithful the world around (even those who know not that they are connected to the heart of the living Saviour) who have held the balance for the coming of Elohim may rejoice in their very personal and present and continuing participation in this judgment of that Fallen One and the ongoing judgment that must yet be invoked for those who yet abide in the physical and astral plane that were formerly connected with that one!

Therefore, blessed hearts, rejoice! Rejoice in understanding that though there is turmoil in the world, though there is turbulence, and though there is the sign of the fall of Babylon and that sign has even been heard this very day in the case of certain events taking place in the planetary body—so it is the hour when the LORD God says: Come out, my people! Come out, then, of Babylon the great![7] Come out, then, of the vibration and the plane and the physical forcefield of that civilization of Babylon!

FOR THE GATHERING OF THE SAINTS

Therefore, let there be the alert. And let it go forth as the second. And let the people of God be prepared to move, then, swiftly when called for the assembling at the Inner Retreat. And let their mercies go before them. Let their dedication go before them. Let their tithes go before them, that the place might be prepared, and that diligently, by those who are the first of the volunteers to prepare that place. For the gathering of the saints in the Holy City is come, and the gathering of the elect!

And let the call go forth! Let the teaching go forth! Let the decree go forth! For all these things must shortly come to pass. And, my beloved, as the cycles roll, you will discover how many manifestations may go on simultaneously.

Thus the moving and the movement to the Inner Retreat, thus the going forth stumping from state to state and the preaching and the publishing and the gathering of the lightbearers from every nation—all this is upon you. Therefore, make haste. Make haste to be delivered and to deliver thyself under the great canopy of thy mighty I AM Presence. Fulfill the Law in all points and come to the place of the heart.

Blessed ones, the fallen ones are depressed—for the communication has gone forth, and registered at the very level of the soul chakra, of this event. And they would prepare themselves, hoping against all hope that in their own judgment some merit might accrue to them for their human goodness. And I tell you, beloved hearts, it will take more than human goodness to save these ones! It takes godliness, righteousness, and the bending of the knee before the living Christ in heaven and on earth. It takes the adoration of Elohim. It takes the connection to the mighty I AM Presence and the swearing: Lo, I AM come to do thy will, O God!

Beloved hearts, they have sworn to do their *own* will, and that still remains the point of departure unto death and self-annihilation. For it is God himself that places his flame in the presence of the fallen ones. And because there is no God within them, therefore they disappear from the screen of both the Spirit and the Matter cosmos —for there is nothing in them of the body and blood of Christ, nothing in them of the Alpha and the Omega current! Therefore, all that remains is the burning of the flame, the all-consuming mighty flame of life, even the ascension flame and the white fire. Therefore, as it is written, Who shall stand in the day of his coming?[8]

RECEIVE THE MESSENGER OF THINE OWN GOD SELF, CHRIST SELF

Therefore stand and still stand and receive the messenger of thine own God Self, even thine own Christ Self! And endeavor to enter in and to stand with that Anointed One and therefore to be refined and purified, so that in standing thou shalt still stand in preparation when this own Christed One, thy very own, will draw thee up to stand in the hour of thine own judgment in the presence of thy mighty I AM Presence!

Clothed upon with the Christ, anointed of the only begotten Son of God, you will stand in the presence of the Father, in the presence of that mighty flame, in the presence of the Mother, and you will not be consumed but endowed with eternal life!

And thou shalt truly be born again—thou who wilt come, then, into the inner alignment of Lord Gautama, the Lord of the World, who is the Lord of the vibration of the planetary body who sounds the tone of the mighty threefold flame and its rising, and causes the flames of all who are of the light to rise also and to meet the required level of that pitch, of that frequency! And each and every day, the self-transcending nature of the flame makes that flame inaccessible, even to those who would ride upon the attainment of the sons of God.

> *They will not enter in! They shall not pass!*
> *They will not enter in! They shall not pass!*
> *They will not enter in! They shall not pass!*

Thus spake Elohim. So I speak in the name of Elohim I AM THAT I AM.

LET THE WORD BE CONFIRMED

Let it be, then, that by the authority of my Sacred Heart in the messenger—transferred to ye all, measure for measure, as your heart is able to receive it—you *will* cast out devils[9] from the earth! You will stand for the binding of the fallen ones! You will stand for the acceleration of their judgment! And therefore, what has been done by God in heaven will be done on earth by the ratification of the saints!

You who understand the Law, note well how it is you in earth who must confirm that which is in heaven, as was declared by Hermes: *As Above, so below! As Above, so below! As Above, so below!* Even my Father and my Mother now manifest in these hearts the understanding that they live to serve in confirmation of the Word!

> Let the Word be confirmed!
> Let the judgment be confirmed!
> Let the saints of God repeat it!

Therefore, once again together, my beloved, let us recite the Judgment Call that I gave to you. Please rise in the fullness of the resurrection flame of your own heart.*

---

*Posture for giving this decree: Stand. Raise your right hand, using the *abhaya mudra* (gesture of fearlessness, palm forward), and place your left hand to your heart—thumb and first two fingers touching the chakra pointing inward. Give this call at least once in every 24-hour cycle.

In the Name of the I AM THAT I AM,
I invoke the Electronic Presence of Jesus Christ:
They shall not pass!
They shall not pass!
They shall not pass!
By the authority of the cosmic cross of white fire
    it shall be:
That all that is directed against the Christ
    within me, within the holy innocents,
    within our beloved Messengers,
    within every son and daughter of God . . .
Is now turned back
    by the authority of Alpha and Omega,
    by the authority of my Lord and Saviour Jesus Christ,
    by the authority of Saint Germain!

I AM THAT I AM within the center of this temple
    and I declare in the fullness of
    the entire Spirit of the Great White Brotherhood:
That those who, then, practice the black arts
    against the children of the Light...
Are now bound by the hosts of the LORD,
Do now receive the judgment of the Lord Christ
    within me, within Jesus,
    and within every Ascended Master,
Do now receive, then, the full return—
    multiplied by the energy of the Cosmic Christ—
    of their nefarious deeds which they have practiced
    since the very incarnation of the Word!

Lo, I AM a Son of God!
Lo, I AM a Flame of God!
Lo, I stand upon the Rock of the living Word
And I declare with Jesus, the living Son of God:

They shall not pass!
They shall not pass!
They shall not pass!
Elohim. Elohim. Elohim.   [chant]

Let it be your mantra of light!
Let it be your God-determination!
Let it be the piercing of the night!
Let it be for the clearing of the highway of your return
    to the Inner Retreat!
Let it be for the clearing of the path for all souls of light
    to arrive there in cosmic dimension, in cosmic vibration!
Let the arrival be as the arrival of the heart
    and not merely of the physical form!
Let hearts rise to the point of the flame of Shamballa!
Let them rise to the level of the heart of Gautama!

Let Gautama Buddha be known. Let his Word be heard. Let his dictations be played, that all, in meditating upon his heart, might now bring themselves to the grand harmony of his great causal body.

I ANOINT THEE NOW UNTO THY OWN VICTORY, COME OUT FROM BABYLON THE GREAT

I AM in the fullness of the God flame. And I stand to deliver the fire of Sanat Kumara. Therefore, I desire that all who now hear my Word shall pass quickly to the front of this altar, that I might touch you and you might know that you are a part of the body worldwide who stand upon earth for this cosmic purpose—for the final judgment of the Satans and all enemies of the Woman clothed with the Sun and her seed—and stand for the victory in every hour of all those things that must come to pass shortly, and that you yourselves will stand for the protection of the continued physical incarnation of our Word in this messenger.

Come now, for I would receive you in this ritual of the oneness of the body of God, of the judgment within thyself of any and all things that are anti-Christ and would move against the fullness of your individual and personal victory.

Therefore, let the I AM THAT I AM descend! Let the LORD God Almighty, let Jehovah descend *now!* And let this people know that the LORD God omnipotent reigneth, that there is the call that goes forth: Come, my people! Come and stand forth and come out from Babylon the great, that her plagues may not befall thee!

Therefore, I anoint thee now unto thy own victory and the spiral of thy divine plan—for the beginning and the ending, for the finishing of thy work of God for this entire embodiment, for the light that is come unto thee!

Therefore, receive the fire. And let it be for the triumph of thyself over any and all seed of Satan implanted in the folds of thy garment in any incarnation whatsoever.

Be purged, then, of the vibration, the magnetism, and the lust of the fallen ones! If thou will, and only if thou wilt receive me, come forth now—only if thou wilt receive me in the name of the LORD God Almighty!

[Congregation comes, one by one, to the altar as the Master continues to speak.]

Out, I say, all demons of the Fallen One! Depart these temples! Release them now, beloved, into the flame. Release them by the authority of thine own Christed One.

Let all arrogance and rebellion disappear. Be purged, then, of the influence and recognize the power of human habit to sustain that which is already judged by the living God. Therefore I say, understand and recognize the opportunity of the hour to be purged by the determination of thine own heart to see that willfulness go!

It is the hour and the supreme moment of opportunity for a new integration with thine own Christ. Therefore, struggle no longer but accept thy deliverance! For it is in the acceptance of this judgment and of my Word that the power of God will come unto you—by the necessary faith, the very necessary faith that is required for there to be the confirmation in thy temple of all that has taken place at inner levels. This is the moment when you must recognize that only you can confirm the Word.

Realize, then, that this very dispensation may also pass you by when you are then, beloved hearts, not receptive or in that receptive mode. Consider the burden of accountability upon yourself, and that there is in this hour and this moment the peaking of your soul in that personal communion with your Christ Self, if you will receive it, and even with the Cosmic Christ.

Take care that your decisions are not in response, then, to the old momentums that have held power over you. *They have no power!* I declare it before you! But you *must* confirm it, you *must* accept it, you *must* recognize the power of God for the purging! . . .

I say then to every foul and unclean spirit that yet is housed in the fold of these garments: *Be* thou removed! *Go* hence! Be *bound* by the authority of my Sacred Heart! *Burn* through, O light! *Burn* through! And howl, ye fallen ones! Ye have no longer abode in my house and in my temple! . . .

Now seek me diligently, my own, and find the fullness of my Presence in thine own beloved Christ Self. . . .

Now I say, let all fear go hence. Be *gone* in the name of Almighty God! *Depart* from these temples! I AM *binding!* the power of fear and doubt and unbelief in the hearts of the living faithful.

I AM the manifest Presence. I radiate through your bodies the emanation of my Presence. I give you the fullness of my joy. I give you the electrifying power of my own I AM Presence! I give you the full power of my Electronic Presence! Let it radiate through! Let it dissolve every concept of error and all entities! Let there be the rolling of the light. And let there be the acceptance, O my soul! . . .

Now let there be the troubling of the waters in the astral plane. I send the light for the binding of all invaders of the temple of my people, worlds without end.

I AM the binding of the discarnates!

I AM the binding of the invaders of the temple!

I *command* you come out! Be *bound* by Elohim! Come out in the name of the Light, in the name of the point of Light in the very heart of cosmos! In the name of the Cosmic Christ, in the name of Alpha and Omega, come out of my people, possessors of their souls!

Bind now, O archangels of living fire: *Bind* the oppressing demons! *Bind* all demons of selfishness! *Burn* through and bind all demons of absence of vision! *Come out* in the name of the Cosmic Christ! I AM Jesus the Christ. I AM the sending of the power of the Holy Spirit unto you, worlds without end. *Come out* in the name of Elohim!

Let us, then, my beloved, chant the name of Elohim. For by that power are ye saved.

ELOHIM ELOHIM ELOHIM   [7 minutes chanting *ELOHIM*].

Live then free and freeborn by the authority of my Light within thee, by the authority of my own path of victory, by the authority of the mighty I AM Presence of all worlds and the Cosmic Christ.

Draw forth the liberating power of the Word of God. Draw it forth, as you draw forth the sacred breath moment by moment! Breathe in the light and breathe out all that is unclean.

So shall thy days be filled with the glory of God. So shalt thou triumph on earth, even as the LORD God Almighty and his hosts have triumphed in this hour. So may thy triumph be full! So may thy joy be pleasing unto the LORD! So shalt thou be found clothed upon and in thy right mind,[10] as the mind of Christ with thee always and always and always.

I AM with thee alway, even unto the end of the world[11] of the fallen ones, of the world created by the Satans—even unto the end of thine own karma and all that is anti-light that is no more within thee! Lo, I AM with thee alway, even unto the hour of thy resurrection from dead works unto the living life universal and triumphant! So I AM with thee alway, even unto the hour of the ascent of thy soul unto God!

Peace, beloved, and good cheer! The victory is won. Many victories are waiting for your winning!

Oh, go forth in the winning spirit! Go forth confident in thy God! Go forth and tread the earth as a mighty conqueror!

Go forth now—secure in thy faith, secure in the arm of the Mother, secure in the blessed angels and the entire Spirit of the Great White Brotherhood holding thee fast, holding thee fast, holding thee fast even when thou comest in the way of the tempter who is there to tempt thee and to see if thou knowest truly that *thou art the victor, that I AM the victor, that God is the victor!*

See that thou knowest it, even as thou knowest it in my presence! So know it, O my beloved, in the face of Babylon the great. And take care that in the hour of her fall thou art secure and safe in the heart of hearts of the Presence of the living Word, Amen.

February 1, 1982
Camelot
Los Angeles County, California
ECP

CHAPTER 6

The fullest union . . . comes in the hour of the ascension.
But you can claim all the light you can contain on earth
and be . . . the bride incarnate if you only will let go
of the sense of limitation.

BELIEVABILITY

A Message to the American Woman

Now, my dearest hearts of light, Our Lord has sent me to deliver to you his message of Good Friday. For I AM the one, Magda, who acclaimed him "Rabboni" in the hour of his emergence from the tomb.[1]

Jesus has likened me and my experience, known to all, as the archetype of the soul of America, the collective soul of Israel, and of the descent of the seed of light.

The necessity for the purging of this soul is upon us, my beloved. And therefore, Our Lord sent me in my final incarnation from Canada in the north through a long route whereupon I finally arrived, as you have, in the City of the Angels to preach his Word and to be the instrument of his most Holy Spirit in the miracles and the healings he performed.

My beloved, this era of my life that has passed, its very manifestation, was greatly opposed. People remember me as Aimee Semple McPherson. But, precious ones, those who saw me or believed in the works of God in my presence truly saw the One who sent me.[2]

I knew myself then and now as his bride,[3] as the soul merging with the inner light. And so, this victory of the feminine ray is a sign that God has ordained this nation as the place of the victory of the soul. And the one out of whom he cast seven devils[4] is the first to see him.

This, beloved, becomes a precious treasure for those who sense themselves as sinners, though God himself has not decreed it. For they have so, so idolized the person of Jesus that no taint or mar could touch him. Having made him "the God," they allowed me to remain the human, and therefore identifiable is their consciousness with my own.

People today consider that they may have walked the path I walked and still have an opportunity to attain the resurrection. Thus, you see, the open door of my heart becomes a more plausible, understandable way! And yet by contrast, whether the figure of Magda or the figure of Aimee—by comparison to him, in their sight, they consider the doctrine laughable that I should have attained the resurrection from this very city and have been received by my Lord in the ritual of the ascension.[5]

Thus, you realize that this messenger and you yourselves have been ridiculed for this teaching, since I have been cast in a somewhat suspected light—this accomplished by the detractors who feared not I, but the I AM THAT I AM which was with me.[6]

If you read concerning my life and the challenges we faced here, you will understand that in some way he sent me to be your forerunner so that you could see what the victory should be.

In those very days, some in America had the gift of the violet flame. Jesus gave me that gift by direct transfusion, you might say, so that it was in and assimilated by me without the prior understanding or knowledge of its use or affirmation.

It was indeed the violet light, as the akashic records will prove, that flowed from his heart through mine for the healing miracles that took place. Yet I was in the tradition of the Church, for these were the sheep that must be reached. And Jesus desired to use me, in the fullest sense of the word, before the hour of my own ascension, that he might bear witness of the truth of God's life in me and of the opportunity of all souls to ascend—especially from the level of imperfection, the level of mutability, shall we say, which orthodoxy does not permit to be ascribed to him.

BELIEVE IN THE POWER OF THE SPIRIT

Precious hearts, the message of Jesus this day is a message to the American woman and to the man who understands himself to be the manifestation of light. It is a message to the soul of all nations, and it does indeed concern itself with the very present possibility of transmutation and of forgiveness of sin when there is repentance.

It is a message of the Holy Spirit! It is a message of believability in the power of the Spirit to transcend the frail, the imperfect, the incomplete—and that to occur right where you are.

Let us not allow the false measuring rod of that mortal consciousness to enter this congregation whereby you take measure of yourself, in the outer sense, and of everyone else and you consider that because you are so many inches high on the Path, it will take you so many miles and so many years to arrive at the point where you could be the instrument of the Holy Spirit! It is almost the sense "Well, we are growing up now. We are children. And when we are all grown up, then we will be able to be like Jesus, then we will be able to be like Mary."

Dear hearts, believe in the Holy Spirit! Believe in the power of the Son of God to come down from the cross in this hour and to stand where you stand and to deliver the full fire of the body and the blood of his Presence for the healing of the whole world!

Understand, when you place a limitation on your capacity to deliver light, you are limiting God and his ability to use your temple. In reality you are saying, "I do not want to be God's instrument in this moment, and so I will hold the concept of myself as *not able.*"

WHEN YOUR ABEL OVERCOMES YOUR CAIN

Well, if you are not "able," then you must be Cain! And, you see, Cain killed Abel.[7] It is the Cain consciousness that kills the sense of ability within you! And to be carnally minded is death. You cannot be both. You must choose.

And, in fact, the human ability is not even sufficient. You must go beyond both and seek the Son of promise. Seek the one called Seth, the archetype of Christ. Seek the one whose coming marked the era of men beginning to call on the name of the LORD.[8] For this type, this Seth, is truly the manifest Word. In the presence of the Word, they could only call upon the name of that Word, I AM THAT I AM!

Thus, when the worst of the human self is overcome by the best of the human self, when your Abel overcomes your Cain, you must not rest there. For the best of your human self is still not the instrument of the LORD—but the transcendent Self that you really are, the one who is the Doer.

THE SOUL OF AMERICA
MUST BE PURGED BY THE LIGHT

I AM calling in Jesus' name for an order of the sons and daughters of God to go forth in political, religious, educational action. I AM calling for a most stupendous covering of North America with the true teachings of my Beloved concerning all social issues and crises!

To you to whom the Word is given and the great miracle of the Holy Spirit of the gift of knowledge and wisdom concerning these events, I speak. I speak to you, that you might understand what is the burden of the instrument, as the messenger, who must give you the keys and the understanding and the outline—and the necessity of preserving the instrument.

When you are fed the teachings, you must go forth with them. This concerns women's revolution, the turning around of the Woman, the casting out of seven devils. This is the cleansing of each of the seven chakras. The soul of America—individual by individual, man and woman—must be purged by the light.

Jesus has called me to walk with him with you, at your side. As you teach and preach and lecture and deliver this most stupendous light and message, I will be a witness at your side that the sinner can be saved—that the Saviour can come, cast out seven devils in that one, in one generation, and two thousand years later raise up that same one in the fullness of his power of healing and miracles!

Thus, you will be able to teach: If he did it unto Magda, he can do it unto you. And you yourself can become the transparency for the Bridegroom—you, the one who becomes the instrument of the Teacher on behalf of the one to whom you speak, self-conceived as sinner. None can deny the reality. None must deny it!

And I charge you to preach of my own reincarnation, as well as that of the messengers! Allow people to face the great dazzling reality of my Presence. Allow them to realize that a so-called modern woman, having passed through the decades of this century in Canada and in the United States, could actually be received in heaven and take the initiation of the ascension—that one who made mistakes, even in the final incarnation, can be forgiven and move on.

ON HUMAN HABIT

Dear hearts, in a state of illumination and hope, you believe. But sometimes the underlying condemnation, the planetary consciousness of death that resists life, convinces you that you cannot break that mold of human habit!

The messenger has lectured, at our request, on human habit.[9] Where are the releases? The teaching is not in your hands. It is not being studied. It is one of the most important documents on life that you could have.

I beg you—for I am in a position to beg you—to assist us in this publishing. For the answer to the questions of millions is not in the hands of the people but lies buried in the files, in transcripts, and in tape libraries.

Surely, you who love Christ and appreciate the agony, not alone of his mission but of all the saints, can give some portion of your life to this task, that others might drink of the cup that you drink. It is almost as though not another morsel of teaching could be given, for that which is given would surely rot if it is not soon assimilated and consumed.

It is spoken for the people today—not for a hundred years hence! And for the saving of the nations, it is needed. Civilization may be judged, but the nations can survive in the very midst of the judgment, *if the light be there.*

The light cannot come except the reason and the reasoning mind, fastened to false logic and to the lie, be cut free by the statement of truth and the logic of the Logos. Not by argument, not by loud voice or flourishing phrases or high-sounding words are the people convinced. The Holy Spirit power of conversion needs the matrix of truth. That is why my Beloved has said, "Ye shall know the truth, and the truth shall make you free."[10]

SPIRITUAL MARRIAGE IS THE TRUTH OF ALL REALITY

The doctrine that Mary Magdalene could be the wife of Jesus[11] is laughable to many. Therefore, I must bear testimony that my soul, my heart, and the Presence of God with me is indeed the twin flame of Jesus, and that every soul whom God has made is created out of the white-fire core of the Great Causal Body of Life. And the twain, holding the balance of Alpha and Omega and the Spirit and Matter spheres, have gone forth from the beginning to prove the victory of eternal life.

Thus, in the great drama of our association you realize that as Jesus forgave me my sin, he was forgiving the feminine portion of himself that I am. And as I acclaimed him "Rabboni," I was acclaiming the masculine portion of myself, which is indeed the

Spirit of the living God, as my Saviour, my Teacher, my life.

Thus, beloved, Jesus comes a little closer to the humanness of life, to the needs of each one's heart. And as he is closer to you as friend and brother, as you can understand him as my husband in the Spirit, you also may dare to conceive of yourself as the bride waiting for the marriage of the Christ. For in the fullness of the Cosmic Christ, he receives your soul unto himself as the bride of the Lamb, as it is taught.

What is proven by one may be proven by all. As you become the bride of him as he is the Guru of the Piscean age, you may also conceive that your soul could be wed to your I AM Presence and, through that Presence, to your own twin flame. And you may also dare to consider your twin flame as the Cosmic Christ at inner levels.

Thus, we exhibit the great archetype of beauty, of perfection of the Law. And the spiritual marriage is the truth of all reality, and there is no need to be concerned with the human affair or with conjecture. For the reality and the truth of eternal life is the rock upon which we stand.

GOD CAN USE ME—I MUST BE READY, PREPARED

Now, then, to free the world from this mortal coil, from this round of self-inflicted punishment intensified by the fallen ones through their condemnation—this is the task of the stumpers who go forth with the message of truth, contrasted by the message of the lie of the fallen ones and their activities.

In this octave, the emerald ray of truth, of the blessed teaching of the Word incarnate, actually is enhanced when it is juxtaposed by the wickedness, the lie, and the murderous intent of the fallen ones. And the need for that truth becomes all the greater when the individual accepts his responsibility to do something about it.

I am speaking to you today, in essence, in the garment that I wore in my final embodiment. For I desire you to know me and identify me with a person like yourself who had to move against evil forces and contend with the burden that comes upon the body through long years of service. I desire you to feel my vibration. There are many yet in embodiment who remember attending services that I held, not only in Los Angeles but as far away as Australia and around the world.

Thus, *believability* is our reason for coming: *Believability* that in this very hour, Jesus—the Bridegroom of your soul—may also use you personally to deliver the same thrust, the same light, the same Holy Spirit.

You may remember that he said, "You have not chosen me, but I have chosen you."[12] You may say to yourself, "But he has not yet chosen me." Perhaps he has, but you have not quite stood on your tippy-toes to identify with that person of you whom he has chosen, the Higher Self—not so much higher than the outer self, but the best of yourself as you now know yourself.

You know that in your highest moments of attunement and of speaking the Word and of imparting love to friends, you have felt something more than yourself depart from you, be released from you as a mighty flow of love. And you have stood back in wonder and watched how God has performed his miracle of love, animated the Word, and you have seen the light leap from your heart and sparkle in the eyes of one who formerly was crestfallen. Thus, for moments you have seen the work. Therefore, *Believability!*

There is a believableness that you can become as I was. There is the sense "God can use me and I must be ready. I must be prepared. I must run to the scripture and know every word. I must study the dictations and find out what lie is binding me to my former self—what almost subconscious or subliminal unfact, untruth is yet resting at some level of the mind, preventing me from being the best instrument."

If you think God has not chosen you, you must have hope and faith and say, "If he hasn't chosen me today, surely he will choose me tomorrow! I will be more ready tomorrow than I am today!" And you can look at your watch and say, "It is nine a.m.

I have a full day. I will work twenty-four hours and tomorrow at nine a.m. the Saviour may knock on the door and I will be ready!"

BE THE BRIDE INCARNATE, LET GO OF THE SENSE OF LIMITATION

Dear hearts, many of the saints have prepared many lifetimes in this state of the waiting bride. I myself thought of myself as the waiting bride all of my life. I thought somehow, in my outer mind, that I would only be the bride when he would come and receive me in the rapture and I would meet him in the air. Looking back, I realized that he entered my form and temple and accepted me as his bride. And therefore, I could represent him.

The fullest union, of course, comes in the hour of the ascension. But you can claim all the light you can contain on earth and be no longer the waiting bride but the bride incarnate if you only will let go of the sense of limitation.

How much I love each one of you who come to this holy city to be a part of the continuation of his Word. I know that all have come following our Mother, for she has followed the call of Jesus to be here these years, knowing well the jeopardy of this particular geography, yet tarrying here—tarrying until the call should come to come up higher, moving on to higher ground.

Does that have a familiar sound and ring: ". . . moving on to higher ground"?[13] You who are grounded on the rock know very well that when it comes to building the house, it cannot be built on sand but it must be built on the rock.

Therefore, there are reasons and purposes. And in this city is truly the calling of the Lord—and going forth from this city, as you have.[14] But the work is not finished yet. The work demands acceleration. It demands, blessed hearts, a determination of a greater magnet of light in your heart to consume the greater darkness that has also arrayed itself here, almost with a vengeance against my own mission!

And the remnant of those who follow in my church[15]—they have not received the wine in new bottles but they have poured that Spirit into old bottles and therefore they could not contain it. The bottles have broken. And you find that some among them do not know the difference between the spirits and the Holy Spirit. They do not understand the mystery of the Holy Spirit. And in their desiring and their ambition to have that Holy Spirit before His call, they have taken into themselves impostors, lying spirits, psychic entities, dangerous to the true path.

There is no room for me to enter in to my own church. There was no room for Jesus to be received in the synagogue[16] except by the little people.

Thus, you may know our grateful hearts that we may come here and not be mocked and ridiculed, that you have an appreciation of life, that you dare to equate yourselves with us and our mission—you dare to follow in our footsteps, not as idolaters but truly in the realization that there is a mission that you must take. And you can go hand-in-hand with your own twin flame in Spirit, trusting the hand of the Christ of your counterpart and removing the longing for the mere flesh-and-blood contact when that is not available, when your own Beloved is ascended.

SEEK THE SPIRIT FIRST AND LAST AND ALWAYS, WHAT IS GOD'S WILL

Let us spiritualize all aspects of our lives and let the Spirit make these aspects physical. He who is closest to God has a most abundant physical manifestation as testimony of that oneness.

Seek the Spirit first and last and always.

And for this moment of renunciation on the cross with Jesus, will you not now with me surrender all desire to serve him in a specific way—your own way? Will you feel yourselves released for this moment from projects and planning?

Let go and allow God to do what he wishes to do through you.

Do you have a checklist of things you desire to accomplish before you take your leave of this planet? Give it to me, dear. I would put it in his heart, in the sacred fire, and I would give back to you his plan.

Jesus desires to work through you. And according to the will of the Father, to which he is obedient, he would tell you, hour by hour every day, what is that will. You may have perfectly beautiful plans and projects akin and aligned with the divine will in certain portions, but perhaps their timing is out of sequence so that when you ought to be doing one thing you are caught doing another.

Be relieved of the burden of figuring out what to do, but cherish oneness with your mighty I AM Presence, with Jesus and Saint Germain and all of the saints, and know that you will be used in a much grander way than even you could conceive of.

This is an important exercise when you are in the very heart of hearts of the Lord Christ. When you let go within his heart, it allows his light to pour through you and sweep from you those well-meaning plans that simply are not appropriate.

It is not a question of goodness or badness, or rightness or wrongness. But there is one important thing to do in each hour and day, and you need to be free to do it. And when you have too many lists and too many projects, sometimes you don't have time to hear the Lord. You shut the windows of your cell in case another assignment comes and you say, "I already have so many assignments. I cannot receive another."

This is a great release. As you kneel before the cross on Good Friday and contemplate the one fastened to it, know the sense of relief. Know the sense of the relief of the initiation itself.

Father, into thy hands I commend my spirit.

Now let the spirit be slain on the cross, even though the suddenness causes the soul to cry out, "My God, my God, why hast thou forsaken me?"[17]

Release thyself and know that in the hour of thy crucifixion, not "thou" but "I"—the "I AM"—does perform the work of the saving of the world. Release the sense of self totally, even the sense of the God Self. And allow the God Self to hold the immaculate concept of yourself.

A MOMENT OF MEDITATION— SENSE YOURSELF IN THE FIERY HEART OF JESUS

There is a time for doing, for self-reliance and responsibility. There is a time to be strong and bold and determined and purposed in Christ. And there is time to be re-created in the white-fire core of eternal Being. There is a time to sense one's nothingness and even one's noninvolvement with all outer spheres and senses.

This is the hour of our Mother's entering in to the initiation of the five secret rays, according to the sign of the cosmic clock. This, the hour and the number of the seven, implies a completion. Actually, it is the beginning of the eighth ray. Going in, then, to the white-fire core of being, you have a sense of the sacred fire, even under that hierarchy called Leo—the fire of the heart burning.[18]

In this moment of meditation with me, sense yourself in the fiery heart of Jesus where John has bidden you for this class[19]— John, my beloved brother in light.

Now sense the garden of Jesus' heart as the fiery heart burning and the utter relief of knowing that God can consume all that hinders what he has intended for you to be.

Remain now in the fiery heart burning until the resurrection morn, until Sunday and then Sunday evening, when you will go back to the place of your service and out into the seven rays again.

O children of the heart of Jesus, children of the heart of the blessed Child Jesus, how good it is to be together in the flame, the pulsating flame of the heart.

I, JESUS, SPEAK TO YOU OUT OF THE HEART OF THE FLAME AND OUT OF THE HEART OF MAGDA

Hear the message of the Lamb and of the Lamb's Word and of the Lamb incarnate.

Receive my own as I have received you. Feel the power of my Presence—and discern who I AM, speaking to you now out of the heart of the flame and out of the heart of Magda.

I can also speak through her heart, that you might perceive the Mother nature of Christ. Truly, in the oneness that you feel and sense of this great love, you understand that the whole world is included in our love. Yet, for so many this visualization of our wholeness cannot be accepted because it does not agree with the orthodox view of my life.

Take me down from the cross where they have left me, an idol of their fancy and their false belief that suits their waywardness and their desire to be free of me!

"Begone!" they say. "We will not have you, Jesus, as you are. We will only have you as we create you, that we might be gods over you and lead the people in our image of you. Begone! Begone, Jesus and your messenger! We will not acknowledge her—in the last decades nor in these. We will not acknowledge anyone who does not come to fit the mold of our idol."

One and all, they have denied me. They accept me in no form except their own, and their own can only magnetize the false Christs and the false prophets and the discarnates that come. Therefore, they are deceived and the blind followers of the blind leaders who will their blindness, that they might not be required to enter in to the findingness, the true finding of my reality.

I speak to you from the cross, as I will speak to you in the morn of my resurrection. For I desire that you should hear my voice as in the hour of the crucifixion and that you should feel the love of my heart pulsing for you and know that my life then and now is given that you might live with me, here in the world and in the next, as I AM.

I AM the resurrection and the life!

I AM the deliverer unto you of eternal life!

And if you will believe upon that resurrection and that life imparted to you by Almighty God through this Christ, you shall not experience death—not in the final sense but only as transition out of the socket of mortality into the new day of a reality that has always been.

My beloved, whosoever liveth and believeth on the Principle of Life, as "I AM" and as you are, shall never die. Believest thou this?[20] [Audience replies, "Yes."]

Then go forth, following this conference. For I have a mighty work indeed for you to perform—that the Father and the Son would perform through you—and I with you, together with my Beloved, Magda.

Out of the flame of the heart I speak. Into the flame of your heart I come. For you have called. You have said, "Come quickly, Lord." Therefore, I come.

Unto you who will receive it, I seal you forever, one with my heart, that you might never be alone or know that aloneness that is the sense of absence or separation.

I receive you as my own. I receive you as one.

Always know that your purest heart of hearts—your heart of Christ, which is your real heart—is individually sealed in mine!

Accept it. Be my own. Be free! And go forth to deliver all of my children.

We are one.

April 9, 1982
Camelot
Los Angeles County, California
ECP

CHAPTER 7

*I AM the heart—the beating heart,
the plaintive heart—of the unborn child!
I AM the heart of everyone who dedicates
his light and his life for freedom!*

TRUTH IS TRUTH WHERE IT IS FOUND

*My Easter Message to Christians and All Who
Set Themselves in the Seat of Authority
in the Churches of the World*

Peace be unto you. For I AM come again in the same manner in which ye have seen me go into heaven. For the coming of the Son of man is indeed the descent of the pure Christ into your very temple. And there, I bear witness unto your soul of its potential for immortality as you move toward the goal of your personal resurrection, which cometh unto you, my beloved, in the name of the Father and of the Son and of the Holy Spirit.

Therefore, the communion of the saints ever has been in my heart, and I have drawn you there again. And in this garden of my heart, all things are come to pass—the Last Supper, the betrayal of one of my own, the trial and the judgment of the Sanhedrin and of those fallen angels cast down into the earth who have set themselves as the representatives of the Almighty One. Yet, they shall not prevail.

I address my Easter message in this year unto all who call themselves Christian and unto all who set themselves in the seat of authority in the churches throughout the world that purport to represent me.

First of all, I say to you that I AM the ascended master Jesus Christ. And I have the power in heaven and on earth to commune with my own by the Holy Spirit! And as I stand and as I live, you will not set yourselves between my own and the Father and the Son.

You will not stand at the pulpit, neither in the congregation of the righteous, with impurity and deny my resurrection or my ascension or my presence here!

You will not deny my delivery unto John on Patmos of the revelation that is for my saints in this hour!

You will not take from my own the invincible Christ-reality that the Father and the Son have placed in their hearts. And you will not stand between them and their God, even the mighty I AM Presence!

Therefore is the judgment come again upon the wolves in sheep's clothing who tear from my very heart, and from my very life essence, souls entering into the path of communion, of oneness, of direct discipleship with my heart unto the ascension.

And I speak to the hierarchy of Rome. I speak to the hierarchies of all who have set themselves to represent me!

Why do you warm yourselves on the fires of the soldiers and the politicians and the powers that be and the seed of the wicked?

Do you take your example from Peter? *Truth is truth where it is found! Error is error where it is found!* And therefore, the cowardice to side in with the side that is popular or in power does not merit the authority of my heart nor the dispensation of this age!

Therefore, you who hold concert with the powers of World Communism and socialism and those who are part of the money beast worldwide and the international bankers, who keep afloat the sinking ship of World Communism—*you* who call yourselves Christians, you are judged this day! I have no part with thee, for you do not represent me.

You who are the prelates of the Church, you who profess to sing unto my glory and do not lead the worldwide crusade against abortion, the LORD will hold you in derision! And when those Watchers are judged, those fallen ones, you will be judged with them, for you have not represented the Christ nor have you dared to be crucified with me.

Therefore, I look to the other sheep. I look to the individual soul of light. And this is my temple and this is my Church—where the living Christ can dwell in the purified temple where the soul dwells who has the courage to be and to walk in my footsteps and not to compromise for the sake of power, which compromise has descended, lo, these two thousand years in the distortion of my teaching and my doctrine!

Therefore, let the exposure come to pass! And let it be known that this image of myself that I have released through the artist Charles Sindelar is indeed the very same image that you will find on the Shroud of Turin, and it is unmistakable.

And therefore, you will know that I have appeared to many saints throughout the ages. And I have spoken through many messengers who have appeared to deliver, by the miracle of the Holy Spirit, the healing light, the gift of wisdom, and the teaching of the Way. And I have sealed unto this witness the understanding of each one's own God-reality, *and none shall tear it from my own!*

For those who are called of the Father will know me as I AM and will not have the power to distort me or my name or my image or my presence. For I AM yet the Good Shepherd and I stand with every disciple on earth who is true to the calling of the Son of God! And those who are yet weak I strengthen when they pray and when they acknowledge that universal Christ, not alone in me but as the divine image out of which they also were made.

Therefore, O Father, hear my plea! For I do send, now, the twelve legions of angels to go forth and save my own in every nation, those who have not been supported by courageous ones who should have long ago risen out of the Church and out of the governments of the nations!

If indeed those governments are upon the shoulder of the Christ,
then let the representatives go forth for the rescue! And let my own dare
to challenge now this power elite who have sat where Pilate has sat,
who have sat in the place of Caesar, who have sat in the place of the
Sanhedrin!

And they have judged my children. Therefore, let their judgment be upon their own head. For inasmuch as ye have done it unto the least of these my brethren, ye have done it unto me!

I AM the heart—the beating heart, the plaintive heart—of the unborn child! I AM the heart of everyone who dedicates his light and his life for freedom!

Therefore, you who stand in the way of the victory of my saints in Poland, know, therefore, that the power of the resurrection this day is the power for the binding of you who are not the elite of God, though you have made yourselves the elite of this world!

Therefore, you are the tares sown among the wheat. And these legions of angels come, and they are descending to earth from the very throne of the Father, from the very light that is the light of Alpha and Omega. And they go forth.

Therefore, let the captains and the kings and the princes and the mighty men tremble. For the hour of your judgment is come! And the slaying of the holy innocents and the shedding of their blood is upon you, even as the judgment has come for the crucifixion enacted by these fallen ones!

BE THE OPEN DOOR WHICH NO MAN CAN SHUT

Children of the light, I charge you then: As you have seen the betrayers of the body of God, both within and without the Church, therefore go forth and stand upon the Rock of the eternal Word that God has ordained unto thee also. By the Spirit of the LORD that is present with you in this moment, let there be the sealing of your heart with the heart of that Christ Self. For this is my body which is broken for you, and the presence of the LORD with you is thy salvation.

Therefore, let us walk, let us run, and let us not deny the inner truth that is the light which lighteth every man that cometh into the world. Therefore, you are the light of the world, for the light of God is within you!

Look not, then, to these fallen ones, these individuals of power who proclaim themselves the servants of the people and the deliverer of nations! For they come as the death rider, and they bring death and destruction in their wake, and plague and pestilence and famine!

Heart of hearts, hear my call and let the light of my heart released in this passion now *flow* to your own, *flow* to your very beating heart, that you might know yourself anointed of that light! And this is the meaning of the Christed One, anointed in this age to be the open door which no man can shut!

Therefore I say, try the spirits, whether they be of God, and prove the LORD himself. For he will pour out a blessing unto you, and he will deliver his Holy Spirit unto you. And you will go forth in my name to the nations, and you will be astonished by the Holy Spirit that will release through you the light of conversion by the power of the immaculate Truth!

Thus, blessed hearts, as my Word does not pass away, so, by the Holy Spirit and not of this messenger, my Word is recorded in the heart of each and every one who has placed himself in the camp of Antichrist. And my Word is placed in the heart of every one who is the true follower of God—even that God that is real, that is tangible, that the soul may see face-to-face by the LORD's Spirit.

YOUR CALLING TO WALK IN MY FOOTSTEPS

This is the healing light. Therefore, receive it unto yourselves and live not again as mere mortals! But live, O my souls of light, as the Immortal One in thee. For I AM the LORD thy God in the very midst of thee! I AM the burning and the smoking lamp! I AM in the threefold flame of your heart, and by this light is your victory fulfilled!

Therefore, recognize your calling to walk in my footsteps, regardless of the false pastors and the false prophets and the false Christs who come. Beloved hearts, beware the cunning of the serpents! Beware the cunning, for though they may not proclaim themselves so much in words that they are the saviour, they do proclaim it by their stance, by their political rallies, by their promises that they cannot keep.

Look for them, then, in all the branches of human endeavor. Look for them in the economy and in the banking houses. Look for them in industry. For these are the self-styled saviours of a materialistic civilization. And I tell you, in the name of God—it shall go down, it shall be judged, and that which is real shall endure!

Therefore, take care with the coming of the angels of the harvest as they reap, for one is taken and the other is left. And there is no place to go, save in the kingdom of God and in the Christ that is within you. There is the sealing of the light! There is the message of the Word! There is the thunder and the lightning of the resurrection!

And therefore is the judgment this day come upon those who have never, never, never released the true message of my appearing to my own! In each and every hand, they have denied the word of the saints. They have denied the appearances of my Blessed Mother, who comes also for their judgment, as they deny her again and again as the origin of life and as the source of the descent of my own Christhood.

BE THOU MADE WHOLE

Believe me when I say unto you that it is the Father that speaketh unto you through me and that your own communion is direct. And therefore, affirm God and take the gift of my own beloved Joseph whom you know as Saint Germain and recognize that the Holy Spirit will cleanse of all sin and balance all karma by that violet flame! And it is the fulfillment of the promise of miracles and healings by the Holy Spirit!

Therefore, I say unto you, daughter of Jerusalem, son of light: *Be thou made whole! Be thou made whole! Be thou made whole!*

I AM the presence of the sacred fire, and I AM the purging light! And therefore, in the name of Almighty God, I AM THAT I AM, and by the authority of Christ within you, I exorcise those dumb and foul demons, those unclean spirits that have bound you to past habits of your own forgetfulness of your divine identity and of the grace of God within you!

Burn through, O my angels of the living fire! Bind now all that would possess, all that would malign the true Christ image within my own!

And I AM the exorcism in this city and in this society of the power groups and the money beast supporting abortion, pornography, and child abuse! For I AM determined in you to rid this city and this nation and this earth of the desecration of the divine Woman and her seed, and the desecration of the body temple and the sacred life force, which is the gift of God of eternal life and of your own Victory in the ascension!

Therefore, beloved ones, affirm this, my release, in your own dynamic decrees, that the challenge may go forth and that the LORD GOD will stay the hand of his judgment! For surely, surely the crimes of the people against the living Word in the slaughter of the holy innocents, in the desecration of their bodies, must come upon the nation! And unless there be true shepherds to lead the people in the crusade against all manner of infamy and all manner of abuse of the Word of God, then, I say, those false shepherds and their blind followers will also receive the judgment that our God has promised unto the seed of the wicked!

THE INNER MEANING
OF THE SECOND COMING OF CHRIST

Understand and hear my cry, O ye people! For you who hear and you who listen know that where I stand, there is the Son of God, there is your direct intercession and your oneness in heaven and on earth. And there is no division in the body of God, and the saints are one!

And therefore, understand the inner meaning of the Second Coming of Christ when he does enter his temple and live through you, preparing for the hour of your own resurrection and the ascension when you truly do meet the fullness of the risen Christ in the air, which is in the plane of God's consciousness and mind, with his angels who serve!

Therefore, let the cleansing light, let the crystal ray pass through you, that those who are waiting for the Coming might understand that the waiting entails the summoning of the armies of the LORD for the binding of the oppressors of my people!

PLEAD THE CAUSE OF THE INNOCENT ONES

Do not remain silent, blessed hearts, but speak your witness! For Christ is on trial in this day and hour. *And who will plead the cause of the innocent ones who suffer at the hand of the abortionist or of the molester or of the murderer? Who will come forth and be crucified for them?* For I promise you, this crucifixion is not unto the death but unto eternal life!

I ask you not to die for me but to live for me in this body and in this temple, that I might live in you! I ask you to speak out and invoke the light of Archangel Michael to protect your manifestation of the Word and your challenge to the judges and the courts and the legislators and all those who allow the continuation of the abuse of life on earth!

Therefore, go into the marketplaces. Go into the highways and byways. But be the instrument of the Word. I anoint you who have the understanding of the responsibility to receive the anointing of my own crown and crown chakra, that two drops of the golden oil might be upon you by the hand of my angels, and therefore you might know that God has ordained your speaking of his Word. And then, when you speak it, you will know that you are truly in my presence and one with the Word that I AM! And you will know the healing light. And you will know the infilling of your being with the Holy Spirit!

Therefore, do not wait, but be the instrument of the Word! And behold how the devils will tremble and be cast down! And the earth *shall* be filled with the knowledge of the LORD and the LORD's presence with them, even as the waters cover the sea! And they shall not hurt nor despoil in all my holy mountain.

For the mountain of God is the higher consciousness of the saints. And the mountain of God is *Zion,* which is the *individual ion* of your mighty I AM Presence. And when you are in that mountain of light with your mighty I AM Presence, there is neither hurting nor despoiling of the image, of the presence, of the Church, or of the Word going forth! Preach it, then, to all nations. Publish it abroad. For I AM the release of my heart to my own.

This day, then, is the decree gone forth and is the dispensation given that those who do not speak truth from the pulpits are bypassed, are cut down! And they shall not prosper until they bend the knee and recognize the ever-living presence of the ascended master Jesus Christ and of every son of heaven with me who has partaken of this glory, having walked the same path that I walk.

You, then, who make an idol of me, *you* who worship an idol and refuse to allow my heart to be one with the heart of my own: *Begone then! Get thee hence!* For you will see even the crumbling of your temple, as there was not one stone left in the crumbling of the temple of Jerusalem!

So the Word went forth! And it does go forth! And let the innocent of heart live to know that where there is innocence and humility and the fearlessness to stand with me, lo, I AM there! I AM with you! And there I AM the expression, the temple of the Church Universal and Triumphant—which is the entire company of saints, as Above so below, and therefore cannot be confined anywhere and can only be in the heart of the pure in heart.

The pure in heart see God, know God, and live as I AM. And *you* see me as I AM, for I AM standing here and your soul does perceive and you are blessed!

Suffer the little children to come unto me, and forbid them not: for of such is the kingdom of heaven.

I take all children of the world into my heart, that they might be loved and comforted and protected in this hour of their betrayal and their crucifixion.

I will not leave thee, O my child. I will not leave thee until thy holy angels receive thee in heaven forevermore.

Lo, I AM with you unto the end of the world.

Messenger's Invocation Preceding the Dictation:

FATHER, RAISE OUR SOULS TO THE SACRED HEART

LORD God Almighty, in the name of thy Son Jesus Christ, we commune together with thee! And in thy Holy Spirit, draw us now, by thy love, into thy heart of hearts, into the resurrection fire infolding itself.

We summon thee, O angels of the Most High God, angels of the resurrection flame!

Father, in the name of the only begotten Son of God, raise now our souls to the point of the Sacred Heart. Let our sins be washed by the sacred essence of his life. Draw us now into the mystical body of the saints, as we fear not to proclaim him Christ crucified, Christ resurrected, Christ ascended unto eternal life, Christ the victor over death and hell for us, for all life!

O God, let the earth be filled with thy gladness! Let angels rejoice! Let the heart of Christ, his own God flame burning in the heart of each tiny babe, now sing the song of victory!

O Immaculate Heart of Mary the Mother, hear our cry! Let deliverance come to this nation and the nations and to this earth! And let it come, O God, Elohim, according to thy will as we commune with thee, as we would follow, in our discipleship, his very footprints on Golgotha, all the way to Bethany.

O LORD, come into us, come unto us as thou didst promise, as we would be thy loving and obedient sons. Therefore, the Father and the Son should dwell with us and in us. In the name Jesus Christ, we invoke this promise fulfilled.

Beloved I AM Presence, beloved Christ Self, descend now into these hearts for the baptism of the sacred fire, as we rejoice together that he *is* risen! Let us sing together our praise unto the Lord, the Ancient of Days, whose name is forevermore Sanat Kumara.

April 11, 1982
Camelot
Los Angeles County, California
ECP

CHAPTER 8

Stand and still stand in this hour, O my beloved.
For the messenger has called and I have answered.
And John the Baptist and I gather, to gather you
into our arms for the victory of the God flame.

CHAPTER 8

MY ALTAR CALL: THE ONE CHOICE

Messenger's Invocation:

THE CALL AND THE ANSWER

Beloved El Morya, beloved Elohim of God, send forth thy piercing light of the will of God into our hearts, into our souls, into our minds. I call for the realignment of the four lower bodies of all who have gathered for this service on behalf of life.

O God, let their selflessness now register, and let all self-centeredness be consumed and be replaced by the mighty centering of the I AM Presence within us. O beloved Christ of me and of thee, come forth in the oneness of the God flame.

In the name of Sanat Kumara, beloved El Morya, let the will of God and of the Darjeeling Council now penetrate this activity of the light. Hold the balance of the government and the economy. Stand forth in the midst of the temple of thy people.

In the name of John the Baptist and Jesus Christ, hurl now the mighty action of the sacred fire of the white-fire/blue-fire sun! We invoke the full power of the white-fire/blue-fire sun! We invoke the full power of the white-fire/blue-fire sun!

Let the mighty action of thy sacred fire, O living Word, carve our destiny unto the fulfillment of that sacred purpose of beloved Archangel Michael, that we might find ourselves and this activity and everyone who is a participant thereof—every elemental, angel deva, and chela of the sacred fire—in that Place Prepared.

I call for the opening of the way and the sealing of the door where evil dwells. I call for the staying action of the LORD God Almighty, that we might accomplish his purposes on earth as in heaven, that we might seal our Inner Retreat and draw up now the mighty action of the light in this forcefield, draw up now the sacred purpose of every soul who is a part of this mandala of light.

By the full power of the Angel Deva of the Jade Temple, come forth now, beloved El Morya! Manifest the diamond heart of that perfect will. Let the perfect will of God be now for the sealing of these hearts and souls.

I call unto the All-Seeing Eye of God: Penetrate through the third eye of each one. Activate the divine economy in America and in their lives.

Let there be a consuming now by the sacred fire, by the violet flame, by the will of God, of all activities of anti-light within these forcefields. Let them be stripped now of all accumulated dross. I demand a stripping action of each one's own beloved mighty I AM Presence and Christ Self! Let them be stripped and let them know, then, in the leanness of the flesh, the full abundance of the Holy Ghost.

O beloved Maha Chohan, descend into our waiting hearts! O beloved Maha Chohan, descend into our waiting hearts! Carve a highway unto our God. Carve a destiny in the wilderness. Bring forth the Divine Manchild unto our hearts.

Let the Divine One appear. We decree it now, O Lord and Saviour, Jesus Christ. Let the Son of righteousness arise with healing in his wings[1] within these hearts.

Let there be going forth, then, from this sanctuary this night a mighty people, fierce in defense of the Law, who have not lost their vision, who have not lost the eagle eye of the living Saviour, of the Lord Sanat Kumara.

And therefore, let them be as pillars of fire unto the temple of

God and therefore a magnetic electrode for the sustainment of this mighty cloud of infinite energy.[2] And let this cloud over America be the witness unto our God that we stand and still stand in the face of all dire prediction and prophesying of the false prophets against the victory of the God flame.

Draw us into the union. Draw the community of the light into the perfect divine economy of the abundant life. And let it be adjudicated by the full power of the Christ consciousness of each one. Let there be the oneness of God in us. Let our Christ Selves unite now. Let our hearts unite now at the point of love of the Ancient of Days.

Draw us into thy oneness, O living Word! Draw us into the fiery oneness of this cloud! Draw us into the oneness of the heart of Sanat Kumara, Gautama Buddha, Lord Maitreya, Lord Jesus Christ, Saint Germain, El Morya, beloved Lanello, and my own heart flame beating in consonance with the Word.

Jesus' Dictation:

Lo, I AM the action of the sacred fire of the living Christ incarnate, releasing unto these disciples of the Word the full power of the Godhead to accomplish their mission, their divine plan, and the victory of their ascension in the light.

Souls of light, accept it and be free as the gift of Almighty God unto you this night—by the hand of the Great White Brotherhood, by the hand of the messenger of the Great White Brotherhood, by my own hand of light. For I AM the living Word and I AM the manifestation of that One. And therefore the Elect One cometh. Hear ye him.

In the name of the Cosmic Mother, in the name of the Virgin, in the name of the twelve pillars in the temple of my God who are the mighty seven archangels, I speak to you out of the sacred fire of the living Word.

For I AM your Lord and Saviour, Jesus Christ. And I bear the mantle of the witness and I summon you to the calling of your heart's longing and to the fulfillment of that purpose. And therefore, I caution you for the binding of illusion, for the binding of maya, for the binding of all that would compromise your holy purpose.

Therefore, stand and still stand in this hour, O my beloved. For the messenger has called and I have answered. And John the Baptist and I gather, to gather you into our arms for the victory of the God flame.

Therefore, you are the elect. Therefore, you have been summoned. And therefore, you will determine to bring forth the victory of the golden age!

I AM the Lord of Life with you, and I demand the flow now of the infinite light of the violet flame pouring forth from this altar that yearns for the very footsteps of the messenger once again to deliver the Word. Therefore, we summon you for the elevation and the raising of your hearts to that point of light of the Heart of the Inner Retreat, to that point of the heart in the heart of Electric Peak and the Grand Teton.

WE QUICKEN AND WE ALIGN

Beloved hearts of light, we quicken and we align. And by our focalization within the four lower bodies of the messenger, we hold the balance and the transfer of light from the very physical proximity of the Inner Retreat.

I am speaking now of the cosmic interchange whereby that forcefield is established here. And you may come to Camelot and know that you are tasting of the stream of Life and of the water of Life and of the mountains and of the pine and of the very essence of the angel devas.

For these elementals and these souls of light who gather there in the etheric octave in commemoration of your word do desire to manifest here that magnet of light, that Great Central Sun action whereby you may fulfill cosmic purpose, whereby you may bring the Alpha to the Omega of the cosmic spiral of your destiny in this place and therefore find that, by the equalization of the balance of the figure-eight flow, even as you fulfill your destiny here by the power of the Inner Retreat, you then will be whisked away by the wind of the Holy Spirit to that Inner Retreat at the appointed hour.

KEEP THE FLAME ALWAYS

Heed, then, my word and be not frivolous, O dear hearts of light, but keep the flame always. For each and every one of you has been tested in the seeming absence of the messenger—which is no absence at all for those who do not fall or falter in the way but understand the true image of Christ in the heart and will not be moved by the sense of being apart, for they know:

My Redeemer liveth! *Yea,* my Redeemer liveth! And he is the Lord of lords and the Ancient of Days, the Holy One of God!

Therefore, understand this meaning of the mighty Word of a cosmic flow—yes, a cosmic flow for the sweeping of the earth and the cleansing of the nations that are angry. For they are angry against the Word. But the mighty V of the God flame of your own record for the fiery branding of the earth of the descent and the ascent of the sons of God, as Above, so below, is the winner in the race!

Let there no longer be disgrace in any soul. For the light is too great and the Word is made known. And the day is far spent and the hour to atone must be fulfilled, for the hour of the Second Coming shineth.

And I AM the glory of the LORD within you. I AM that Son of Righteousness—that Sun of Righteousness who comes with the healing of the I AM THAT I AM that was before the birth of John and of myself. Thus, the prophecy is fulfilled in you and multiplied again and again and again each time you choose to be the Word incarnate.

Let there be one choice, one incarnation, one fulfillment. Let there not be many choices; for you see, when you must have many choices, it is a sign that you have betrayed your own word of your first choice and therefore must choose again because you have strayed.

Therefore, I say: Let the one choice in this hour and this moment of your confession of your own Christ Self *be,* then, for the sustainment of victory, for the sustainment of the cloud of infinite energy, for the sustainment of the sacred fire of constancy in the face of all the world's vacillation!

CHOOSE THIS DAY TO BE THE LIVING CHRIST

By my Holy Spirit, I charge you to choose this day to be the living Christ. And I tell you, you will not survive unless you choose to be your own Real Self. And there is yet danger that you will stray from this—the greatest and the only choice to live.

Therefore, because of the danger of forgetfulness, of the loss of sensitivity to my vibration, of the loss of memory of all that is gone before, I summon you to this altar. For this is my altar call, as I AM Jesus Christ.

I summon you to kneel, then—not before me and not before this messenger, but before the great, dazzling God-reality of your own Christed One—and then to confess that he is LORD and to choose to be that one. And when you go forth from this altar, let it be in the full power of the conversion of my own Holy Spirit, that you will sustain that promise unto God, unto me, and, above all, unto yourself.

John and I will stand as witness. The twin flames of the messengers will stand as witness. God Almighty will witness unto you. May you be a true witness of the power of living truth *where you are.*

I have many things to tell you, if you are able to fast and pray and tarry in the temple while our messenger is physically in this area. Therefore, await my call and heed it. For I shall come again, day by day.

Now then, it is the hour of your appearing in the temple. So do it in God's name.

November 10, 1982
Camelot
Los Angeles County, California
ECP

CHAPTER 9

*Dear heart, God has many ways of revealing himself . . .
through you. Take care that you are aware when holiness is
within your temple. . . . Guard therefore that holiness that
belongs unto the LORD. It is his, and it is his gift to you.*

THE PATH OF THE AVATAR

O my beloved, once again we gather on the hillsides of the world to hear the Word of God and to live. For the Word of God is Life. And those who receive it as the cup of pure truth, those who drink it, so live by that fount of everlasting life who is the Word that I am, that I AM.

Oh, the instrumentation of the Word is mighty to contemplate, and its mystery begins with the morsel of bread and the Communion cup. Not the whole loaf, but the crumb is the beginning of that meshing of the light with the soul, with the heart, with the very breath of the devotee of God. Therefore, let us begin at the beginning.

Let us also realize that this Word is in the process of descending where you are. And the full loaf *will* come. One day, here or in the hereafter, you will know the meaning of the divine incarnation. For some do not attain to the Word incarnate until after the resurrection, and some not until the fullness of the ascension in the light.

Blessed hearts, the fullness of the Word dwelling bodily in me[1] is the great miracle of God that demonstrates a science that transcends all science. Therefore, I come! I come as the vessel, eternal in nature, suspended in time—as the lamp itself, even the smoking lamp of Abram.[2]

Dear heart, God has many ways of revealing himself, manifesting himself, and expressing himself through you. Take care that you are aware when holiness is within your temple, within your eye and heart, and guard therefore that holiness that belongs unto the LORD. And it is his, and it is his gift to you.

Do not profane, therefore, the first rays of the dawn of the Word descending upon you and go again and behave as other men, as the mass consciousness or the ways of the youth of this planet. Do not profane the light I have given you, children of my heart, for it is a costly price that you pay for the nonrecognition of holiness and all things holy that are within the temple of the chela of the will of God.

Lo, I come to do that will, O God![3] *Lo!* I AM come to do that will. And that will is ordinate for these, thy servant sons. Let them, then, appreciate this perception of thy will, as the willing of the heart that becomes, itself, a flame of fire that bursts and consumes all unlike itself—a fire that becomes a magnet and one day magnetizes the *whole loaf* of the body of God.

O earnest hearts and fervent hearts, I beseech you, walk in the footsteps that I have carved out for you that are so carefully recorded in a number of my incarnations.[4] And the others remain for you to tap—secrets of akasha. I have tried to make plain the path of the avatar experiencing all of the experiences of life—and in previous incarnations, encountering the fallen ones, being tempted for a season, the clouding of the mind momentarily, even the soiling of the garment with the sense of sin. And then the sorrow and the aloneness, longing for the light and the return of the exaltation of God in the temple.

For the very holiness that is the LORD's can become commonplace when one is spoon-fed upon it. And therefore, only the loss of that holiness by some digression from truth can tell the individual what truly is the pain and the anguish of separation from Maitreya, from our Father, from our Guru, from our Eden of light that is our causal-body paradise of perfection.[5]

Therefore, you see, the LORD GOD allows us to return to his heart by the experience of the distastefulness of sin, as ashes in the mouth, as bitterness of gall in the belly. Blessed ones, so the child longs for the true milk of the Word of the Mother.

WE SEND ILLUMINATION, THE CALL, THE VIOLET FLAME, AND OUR HOPE

Now in this hour of Christmas, we send forth illumination and a name! And the name is Saint Germain! And the name is the violet flame and the science of the Word to implement the sacred name. We send illumination by the sign of our chelas' pursuit of its disciplines. By dispensation of the violet flame thus far garnered in the storehouse of being, we send illumination and the call and the violet flame and our hope.

Our hope is very high in this hour for newness of birth and light to America and the nations. Our hope is high for the full radiance of the Sun to shine once again that the people of God might respond and enter into a spiral of protection, following the pathway of light, sealed then in the Word and the teaching, to come apart, to be sealed, to be healed, and to prepare for those changes that will come to pass one way or another.

I AM the alchemy in you of a surefooted advance on the Path. I speak to the serious ones who do not come merely because it is another Christmas and I will speak and the radiation will be high and "what better have we to do on Christmas Day?"

No, I come to those who are not yet sealed in the rote of my coming. For it is not rote, but only in the outer consciousness. It is the great ritual that I reenact for the reincarnation again and again of the Word with you and of the Christ born. And in its contemplation, those who are so attuned become more and more of Christ with each passing year. If it were not so, our Father would not have given to you the opportunity for life and cycles and growth and star-fire descending, charging the chakras of your being and all of the elements of nature and cosmos inbreathing.

Why, the very heart in your breast is in contact at this moment with the heart of God in the Great Central Sun. Why, you contact by that threefold flame every cosmic being in all elevations of consciousness! You are God—if only you will accept it and *act on it* and step and stand for a higher way of life.

CONSIDER ALL THESE THINGS

Let us then see what we can do to thread this eye of the needle that Mother has given you at my request. Let us see what you can do to follow now the life of Elisha.[6] Take it and study it in your Bibles this day. Know his life with Elijah and know his courage. For it was God's courage in that soul, and it was the response of the heart of Christ in me throughout all ages.

Recognize the virtues necessary. Recognize the filament. Recognize what must be present for your alchemy. Secure it. Multiply light. *Be,* then, one with the Christmas angels throughout this year! I have heard, and Mary hears, and we will come for the fulfillment of the blue radiance of the will of God so invoked.

Cherish hearts. Clasp hands. Value your friends of light—one together in this sanctuary and community of lightbearers the world around. Listen to the winds that blow from Darjeeling, and interpret their message. Consider the lilies of the field,[7] consider your soul, and multiply that consideration with a Mother's heart for all souls of light on earth. Consider the emptiness of the fruitless consciousness, and consider the abundant life.

Consider all these things and the mystical significance of your inner name. And then, my beloved, place yourself somewhere on this vast panorama of life and cosmos and say:

Here, O God, I have found thee!
I have found thee in the wind and the fire
And the crystal and the snow.
I have found thee then in the heart, in the smile of a friend.

Here, O God, in this point I AM!
And I stand and I will be
And I *will be* all that thou art here!
And when thou dost pass by, O LORD,
I will be here at my post
And I will *still* stand
And I will be here at the rising of the sun again and its setting.
All through the night and the day
I will hold my flame,
I will keep the watch,
I will keep the light in the lighthouse window.

Here I AM, O God!
You can count on me!
I will do my part with constancy,
I will keep my vow,
I will see that this ship of Maitreya arrives at that port
And I will be with you, my LORD,
The Saviour of the World.
I this day will be born, my LORD, with you.
I will claim the Bethlehem star
Of the Great White Brotherhood
As the star of my appearing,
Even the mighty I AM Presence and causal body
Multiplied by the avatars of the ages.
Lo! I AM that Christ descending in my temple, O LORD.
Lo, I AM THAT I AM.
Lo, I stand and I summon and by my love I magnetize
The full-orbed Presence of the Christ of me in form
And lo, my soul does stand and know
The meaning of the oneness of that Christ!

I AM THAT I AM.
I will plow the field.
I will sow the seed.

I will water and I will keep the watch for God
To give the increase of my sacred labor.
Hearken unto me, O God,
For I AM a son of God in Jesus' name
And I have come to set the captives free
In this hour of the Christmas and the winter solstice,
In this moment of the Sun behind the sun
One with thy heart, one with my heart.
I AM the living One.
I AM the One—not two, but One.
I AM the One,
And in the Law of the One
The I AM of me does reign supreme.

Hear me, O Maitreya!
I respond as the Son of God, as Jesus did!
I AM fearless in thy name to wrestle with the snake,
To bind it and to walk in the wake
Of the mighty ship of life.
O My Captain, hear my call
For I stand, and I stand upon the watch,
And I AM the keeper at the gate
Of my consciousness and heart.

I, Jesus, remind you to keep your vow, made at this altar this very year, to be the Christ.[8]

PURSUE THIS PATH WITH DILIGENCE AND ALACRITY, YOUR CHRISTHOOD IS EXPECTED, DEMANDED

Christed ones, I salute you!

Lazy and slothful ones, I *rebuke* you for your failure to apprehend my own message of victory! I rebuke you for your forgetfulness to entertain angels[9] and your Christ Self. And I *demand* that you pursue this Path with diligence and alacrity and joy and drive, and that you do not *cease* to be myself in action! These are the chelas of El Morya.

And God our Father has demanded this day that you now repay what you have taken in light by giving, multiplied by the squaring of that light, to earth's evolutions, what you have been given and what you have taken at the altar of God.

Our Father Alpha demands of you, my beloved, the just and exact payment in kind of all that you have so freely taken. There-fore, hear me! For I warn in his name that you must give as you have received, else pay the piper.

The years are hastening on. Soon two thousand years of Christmases will have been celebrated in my name. Heed, then, the Law. For in the conclusion of the cycle of this life, your Christ-hood is not only expected, it is demanded. And to fail to be that one, therefore, will result in untold setback and the discontinua-tion of assistance and intercession by the hosts of the LORD. You will then truly be on your own.

This is the message of Alpha. For this is not the first embodi-ment when you have had such care, such nourishing, such succor. Blessed hearts, God has prepared you. Now you must give answer.

Realize, then, that intercession is also the gift of God as rein-forcement of your vow. Now, all of the angels confirm your promise. But if you do not fulfill that promise, or take for granted the back-ing of the Great White Brotherhood, you will see that in the next two-thousand-year cycle you will not have the same assistance. Others who have not had it will receive it, but you to whom it has been given and you who have not borne fruit, you will then be required to carve out of the universe itself your own God-identity. And I can tell you, as I see it clearly—you will long for that inter-cession, and it will not be forthcoming.

The greatest mistake of the gift of Christmas is to take for granted the mightiest gift of God himself—even his Son, your own Christ Self.

BECOME THE CHRIST
AND GO AFTER THE LOST SHEEP

In the name of that One sent to you, I, Jesus, serve. And I serve until the hour of his appearing in you, which is an hour appointed for you to choose to accelerate, on time and ahead of time. And I serve until that hour of the fulfillment of my service. And then I move on to cosmic spheres.

Now become the Christ and go after the lost sheep. For when our caravan moves on, they must be with us also. Lose them not, for I did not lose your soul. For you are here, and you are with me.

Pay the price for your salvation. Save those lost only because they are yours to save and you have not been swift to save yourself so that you could find and save the rest of your mandala of light.

I seal you with the promise of my love. I seal you with the promise of the Law, ever outworking the divine formula of your being and ever demanding that you enter the cosmic dance of the yin and the yang—the giving and the receiving, the receiving and the giving.

In the peace of the Christmas dove, I commend you to the heart of the Holy Spirit.

December 25, 1982
Camelot
Los Angeles County, California
ECP

CHAPTER 10

Know that heaven—Alpha himself, the blessed Father—
desires to increase day by day your assimilation of
resurrection's fires. . . . Understand that the resurrection
flame is a flame of the awakening . . . that must come
to the heart of each one.

THE AWAKENING OF THE DWELLER-ON-THE-THRESHOLD

H*ail,* beloved of my heart! I am in the midst of the sanctuary of my own, and I abide in your heart under the shadow of the Almighty—even your mighty I AM Presence.

From the heart of the ages, from the heart of the Ancient of Days, I bring comfort and a sword. Be seated then, my own.

I come in anticipation of our celebration of the resurrection. I come beforehand to establish a pillar of that resurrection fire here upon this altar. Let no staff, then, cross this step or stand where the messenger stands until the fulfilling of the purpose of this flame on Easter Sunday.

Therefore, beloved, know that heaven—Alpha himself, the blessed Father—desires to increase day by day your assimilation of resurrection's fires. Understand, then, the meaning of the flame of the resurrection. Understand, then, the meaning of the penetration of the rainbow rays of God accelerating as a bubbling fountain, a life-giving force, an energizing force.

Understand that the resurrection flame is a flame of the awakening, awakening then that must come to the heart of each one. All that is in thee must be awakened, must be brought to the surface.[1]

God has sent me with this flame this day because ye are able to bear it, because Christ in you is awakened. Truth is awakened first. And as the messengers have held the balance against the day of the awakening of the carnal mind, so you have prospered and increased in love and in your witness of truth.

Now cometh the hour when resurrection's fires must also awaken in you that awareness of the sleeping serpent—on the one hand, the dweller-on-the-threshold, the anti-self; on the other hand, the life force, the sacred fire out of the base-of-the-spine chakra.

These are most powerful energies. The energy of eternal life ascending in the temple is the calling of the LORD and of the Mother. It demands obedience and submission unto all of the flowers of the chakras, for the life force makes permanent that which it contacts.

Therefore, the sleeping serpent of the dweller-on-the-threshold must first be awakened and bound in the name I AM THAT I AM by the soul who is clothed upon with his own Christ Self. With the binding, then, of this not-self and the accumulation of its works in the coil of the electronic belt,[2] there may then transpire the awakening of the sleeping serpent of the coiled Kundalini, the life force itself.

May I remind you that this is the path of the *ascended* masters and of the ascension. This is not the path of the false gurus of the East who create, out of sensation and a yoga that is not lawful, a sexual activity and attempt to raise that life force without the Holy Spirit but only by the stimulation of the chakras, stimulating the energy to rise when the attainment is not there.

You will discover, beloved hearts, that those who pursue this left-handed path then use that life force to endow the dweller-on-the-threshold with permanence. These are the dark ones, and their seeming power is the misuse of the ascension flame to give immortality to the human ego. This, beloved ones, is the means whereby those on the left-handed path, the black magicians themselves, do gain the ability to work their works.

DESIRE ABOVE ALL ELSE UNION WITH THAT CHRIST, THE ALCHEMICAL MARRIAGE

Understanding then the mystery, all the more, little ones, ought you to run unto the LORD to be hidden in the garments of the Christ,[3] to run to the beloved Christ Self and desire above all else union with that Christ, who will bring to you chastening and outer turmoil and persecution and direct knowledge with the hatred of this world. But that Christ will not awaken in you the Kundalini until you are sealed in the alchemical marriage of the Christ of your being.

I have preached to you before concerning your striving for this marriage. May it be so among you—those who consider marriage as the next step on the Path, those who are already married in the rites accorded by God for those children evolving on earth, and those who remain unwedded in the physical sense.

Let all reconsider, then, approaching the celebration of the resurrection this Easter, that we desire to dedicate our coming together to the alchemical marriage, to the resurrection of the soul unto the Christ Self worldwide in the body of God that all might escape the wiles of the dweller-on-the-threshold of their own being until they may stand forth in Christ a knight, a lady of the flame, wielding the two-edged sword to bind that fallen one, that anti-self.

EASTER RITUAL: PREPARING AND WEAVING THE DEATHLESS SOLAR BODY

This is the desire of my heart—that you shall at least participate in this ritual on the cycling of your own cosmic clock to celebrate that union at Easter. And forty days hence, in the hour of the celebration of my ascension, you may use that day and that fire of my ascension flame to *slay!* then, the not-self and to slay the carnal mind and to get that victory over the beast[4] that it may no longer tempt and pull you away from the very threshold of the bridal chamber of your LORD.[5]

Realize, then, that this ritual of entering in, of union, and of the slaying of the not-self is something that is repeated, even as you repeat the holy days of the year and celebrate again and again the birth of the Christ Child and each of the points of acceleration on my own path. Would to God there might be a true calendar of my life whereby you could enter in more fully to my footsteps in all of the thirty-three years.

Thus, understand that this particular ritual of Easter is most important. It is part of the divine plan of Serapis Bey that you might prepare and weave the deathless solar body.

Brides of Christ are ye, fully and fairly chosen. Now you must choose so to be. You must not wait with trepidation the day of the awakening of the dweller, but run to greet that enemy. Fully clothed upon with the armour of God, you will say:

> You have no power over me! You may not threaten or mar the face of my God within my soul. You may not taunt or tempt me with past or present or future, for I AM hid with Christ in God. I AM his bride. I AM accepted by the LORD.
>
> You have no power to destroy me! Therefore, be bound! by the LORD himself.
>
> Your day is done! You may no longer inhabit this temple.

And then, my beloved, you wield that mighty sword as God wields it through you. And in the name I AM THAT I AM, so there is the binding of that foe with these words:

> Be bound! you tempter of my soul. Be bound! you point of pride of the original fall of the fallen ones! You have no power, no reality, no worth. You occupy no time or space of my being.
>
> You have no power in my temple. You may no longer steal the light of my chakras. You may not steal the light of my heart flame or my I AM Presence.
>
> Be bound! then, O Serpent and his seed and all implants of the sinister force, for I AM THAT I AM!

I AM the Son of God this day, and I occupy this temple fully and wholly until the coming of the LORD, until the New Day, until all be fulfilled, and until this generation of the seed of Serpent pass away.

Burn through, O living Word of God!

By the power of Brahma, Vishnu, and Shiva, in the name Brahman: I AM THAT I AM and I stand and I cast out the dweller.

Let him be bound by the power of the LORD's host! Let him be consigned to the flame of the sacred fire of Alpha and Omega, that that one may not go out to tempt the innocent and the babes in Christ.

Blaze the power of Elohim!

Elohim of God—Elohim of God—Elohim of God

Descend now in answer to my call. As the mandate of the LORD—as Above, so below—occupy now.

Bind the fallen self! Bind the synthetic self! Be out then!

Bind the fallen one! For there is no more remnant or residue in my life of any, or any part of that one.

Lo, I AM, in Jesus' name, the victor over death and hell!

Lo, I AM, in Jesus' name, the victor over death and hell!

Lo, I AM THAT I AM in me—in the name of Jesus Christ—is here and now the victor over death and hell!

Lo! it is done.

This judgment, my beloved, you may recite with me by means of the electronic recording and therefore have the power of my mantle in the binding of that one.

THE SECRET OF THE WILES OF ALL FALLEN ONES

Remember, then, my fast in the wilderness.[6] The encounter with Satan was the encounter with the planetary dweller-on-the-threshold who was yet unbound until the hour of the two witnesses in this century.[7]

Realize this: that though he was bound and judged and had no power over me, his end could not come until other saints had also overcome his power and his abuse of that power of the Woman and the Manchild, his abuse of the power of the Kundalini fire. This is the secret of the wiles of all fallen ones. Know it well, for this knowledge will serve you in the day of your confrontation with the enemy and your victory.

Therefore, you may call for the judgment of all fallen ones who misuse the life force, the sacred fire, and the ascension flame to control and manipulate life and who offer individuals all of the kingdoms of this world, all of their black magic, all of their manipulation of others.

See to it, then, for the mighty threefold flame within you, your mighty Christ, your I AM Presence is able to subdue even the manipulation of this light of Alpha and Omega. And as Saint Germain, my brother and my father, has told you, they will pay fully for every misuse of the science of God and the alchemy of his Word. Therefore does he sound the warning in his "Studies in Alchemy" that the science may never, never be misused with impunity.

Beware, then, the magnetism of the aura of those fallen angels who walk by the power of the misuse of the base-of-the-spine chakra, who even claim to take dictations from *me* by this power and these distorted sexual practices.

Blessed ones of the light, in the mastery you gain in the divine order that I have taught this day, you will discover that there is no need for tantric yoga. For when you raise the Kundalini fire, it is not by the sexual practices but by the lodestone of your mighty I AM Presence, by Christ in your heart who is the magnet for the consummation of that fire in the crown of life. And this fire is for the deathless solar body, and it *is* the ascension flame.

GIVE YOUR CALLS!
THEY SHALL NOT PASS!

In the name of Serapis Bey, I charge you, then, to give your calls upon those individuals and movements this day that would sweep the lightbearers out of the path of the Great White Brotherhood in America and other nations by the popularity of these ancient practices of the dark ones!

They shall not pass!

They shall not *pass!*

They shall not pass over the threshold of the bride and the Bridegroom! They shall not enter the marriage chamber of Christ and his beloved!

They shall not pass!

But the saints of God who follow the Lamb whithersoever he goeth, who follow the Christ by the fixing of the star of the attention upon the Bridegroom—the one hundred and forty and four thousand who move to the Mount Zion,[8] the place of the I AM Presence—they shall overcome, they shall inherit, they shall have the light of the Mother flame rising within them. They shall seal it in the third eye.

They, therefore, shall be called virgins—not of the flesh but of the Spirit. For the virgin within them is the virgin light *sealed* in the third eye! And therefore, they are not defiled by the Great Whore but are carried up, and their sin remaineth not but is consumed by the violet flame! And therefore, they are purified and made white—not of their own righteousness but of the Righteousness of the LORD who dwelleth in them.

See ye to it, my beloved, for it is the hour when the dark ones seek to manipulate even the ascension process. They would gain eternal life by mixing their seed, the seed of the godless, with the lightbearers. Take care, then, that you understand my word: What fellowship hath light with darkness?[9]

Realize that you may not partake either of the flesh, either of the synthetic image of the Cain civilization, lest you be caught in a long, long spiral of karma—a similar one that you now are ending by the power of the Great Divine Director given unto you for the arresting of the spirals of death and hell.

Have you forgotten that call of the Great Divine Director who has *empowered* you to arrest the spirals of unreality?[10] I bid you listen to that release this day that you might understand how to wield the mighty two-edged sword.

Therefore, take care that you do not, through sympathy, enter in anew into those associations that we have freed you from in these hours of your path. But move upward and receive, then, the joy of the resurrection flame. For this flame shall be unto you the quickening of light, the quickening of all momentums of God's goodness, God's attainment within you, until your strength is one with the strength of Christ.

And when you feel it and when you know it, then watch and pray—for the next awakening will be of the dweller. And thus, beforehand begin to pronounce the judgment I have given you this day that he might be significantly reduced even before he is awakened. Thus, there are strategies of light, you see, even as there are strategies in darkness.

WHEN YOU HAVE THAT VICTORY OVER THE BEAST

And finally, when you have gotten that victory over the beast, the awakening will be of the ascension flame rising within you. And then you will know the meaning of the conquering ones— not the pride of those who condemn and condemn and condemn our messengers and our disciples worldwide. They know not the heart of our servant. They know not the heart of the chela.

I know your hearts, beloved. I know your hearts. Fear not, for I know your love. But only be concerned that that which sets itself against thy heart from beneath be taken and bound and cast into the fire by your conscious will, by your conscious devotion, before it put upon you any further burden.

Why do you suppose, blessed ones, there is the failing of men's hearts for fear?[11] It is because the heart becomes burdened by the toxic waste, if you will, the substance misqualified in the caldron of the electronic belt, and it rises against the heart chakra and the physical heart. And instead of pouring forth the balm of Gilead in Christ through that heart, instead of discovering the divine nectar of the crown by the union of the life force of Alpha and Omega, instead of the violet flame, these individuals go after heart surgery, heart transplants—as though they could create a heart of life and of God.

What a pity, so much striving to discover the mechanical means to ascend, blessed ones—almost uncomprehensible! Yet more's the pity, this is all they have to hope for—the mechanical manipulation of life—hoping against all hope, indeed, that by material science alone they shall discover the fount of youth, they shall meet the mighty youth Sanat Kumara[12] or somehow know the state of grace. And how they suffer in their striving for their physical perfection!

All of this for what? What god do they serve? Surely not my Father and your Father, not my God and your God, beloved. Surely not the dharma of the Buddha. Surely not my way.

What god do they serve? Why, beloved, they serve the god they have made out of the dweller-on-the-threshold—enthroned and enshrined—the stony-faced god, the condemner of all people. You see, they stole the light of the Mother Goddess and endowed the dweller with life, and thus they attempt to perpetuate that dweller.

Many in the world today long ago took the left-handed path, long ago enshrined that fallen one, you see. Their choices are long past. They do not stand where you stand at this portal of opportunity. They are old, old souls. This is why they are called laggards. This is why they have lived so long in other worlds and systems.

They laugh at the innocence and the simplicity of the children of light, for they have long ago done away with any desire for religion or God. It has availed them nothing, as they have offered nothing unto him.

Thus, you see, some have sustained the not-self. By usurping that ascension flame, by usurping the Mother light of Lemuria that burned upon the altars there, they have discovered even how to tap the magnetism, the life force at the center of the earth and in the heart of a living cell. And this they gather, and this they imbibe, and this they take in for the feeding of the beast.

Now you understand why it is the Day of Vengeance,[13] why judgment is at hand. Those who have clearly set themselves in the seat of the scornful dweller, they—*they* now know their time is come, because my little ones and my brothers and sisters have chosen to become one with me, with my Christ and your Christ, with my mighty I AM Presence and your mighty I AM Presence.

THE CALL OF THE JUDGMENT IS POWERFUL IN YOU, YOU HAVE THE POWER OF CHRIST

You wonder why they could so perpetuate themselves so long, so steal the light of the Virgin so long. Well, beloved, it is because the sons of God must descend to their level for that judgment. It is because the children of the light must also have the opportunity to choose to live as Christ, to choose to slay the dweller, to choose to raise the life force.

When all these right choices are made and you have overcome, then you stand, *then* you stand—then, you see, you stand. And the call of the judgment is *powerful* in you! For you have the power of heaven, your mighty I AM Presence, and of the Father. And you have the power of the earth, the sacred fire of the Kundalini, your Mother. And you have the power of Christ, as Alpha and Omega are one in your heart, because your soul has chosen to be with that heart and to merge with my own.

Thus, the cycles for the fulfillment of this generation cannot be fulfilled till all these things be fulfilled in you.[14] Now you understand at least another facet of the mystery of the diamond-shining mind of God and of how and why and wherefore you walk this earth and you are witnesses to these conditions.

When you look at planetary evil, when you look into the very teeth of the Watchers and the serpents who parade before you daily on the television screen, you must surely come to the place of the mature son of God who must say:

In my heart I know what I must do in order to rid the planet of the Evil One. I know that I must conquer where I am and not delay and not tarry! I know that I must overcome in God! And I know that he awaits my coming, that he might speak the Word through me of judgment that will be finis—the end!—the final end of the doctrines of the wicked.

A PERPETUAL AND INESCAPABLE REMINDER

Beloved hearts, if you would know the truth, I would tell you that evil still stalks the world so that the good people who desire to follow me will have a perpetual and inescapable reminder that they have not yet slain their own carnal mind! And they have contented themselves to remain at the halfway point, satisfied to feed the beast and thereby tame it rather than starve it and slay it.

Many have made the choice to feed the beast, satisfy it with creature comforts and various addictions of the various chakras. But, beloved, choose not the way of all flesh[15]—and know that your victory is an individual and planetary victory, and that the planetary dweller is reduced by the power and the magnitude of your overcoming of the energy veil within yourself. And ultimately everyone upon earth, if he would ascend, must slay the enemy within and the world consciousness of sin.

I have taught you, then, what is within your power to receive and to understand. Now, lest you be weary of so much light and exposure,

I take my leave to the higher octaves of the New Jerusalem. I go to prepare a place for you at the Inner Retreat. And I AM with you always, even unto the end of your own self-created unreality.

For then, you see, we will be more than companions, we will be one—I AM THAT I AM.

BLESSING OF THE LOVE OFFERING

Beloved mighty I AM Presence, by the light of Alpha and Omega within us, by the light of the Cosmic Christ, by our own Christ Self, multiply this our offering. Let it be upon the altar of God as a testimony of our victory as alchemists in Spirit and in Matter.

God, we are grateful for thy gift of Selfhood. And we are grateful to give this gift of our hearts. Receive it now.

Dear God, may all your dreams come true through these blessed chelas of El Morya.

In the name of the Father, the Son, the Holy Spirit, and the Mother, Amen.

March 13, 1983
Camelot
Los Angeles County, California
ECP

CHAPTER 11

*We are in search of the remnant—the true white-fire core
of the seed of Sanat Kumara, the seed of Abraham . . .
ancient souls . . . and the new lightbearers as well
as those Gentiles who qualify as the bearers of
the seed of Christ—new vessels.*

CHAPTER 11

THE GLORIFICATION OF THE SON OF GOD

Scriptural Reading:

THE CONSPIRACY TO KILL PAUL

And as we tarried there many days, there came down from Judaea a certain prophet, named Agabus.

And when he was come unto us, he took Paul's girdle, and bound his own hands and feet, and said, Thus saith the Holy Ghost, So shall the Jews at Jerusalem bind the man that owneth this girdle, and shall deliver him into the hands of the Gentiles.

And when we heard these things, both we, and they of that place, besought him not to go up to Jerusalem.

Then Paul answered, What mean ye to weep and to break mine heart? for I am ready not to be bound only, but also to die at Jerusalem for the name of the Lord Jesus.

And when he would not be persuaded, we ceased, saying, The will of the LORD be done. . . .

And when the seven days were almost ended, the Jews which were of Asia, when they saw him in the temple, stirred up all the people, and laid hands on him,

Crying out, Men of Israel, help: This is the man, that teacheth all men every where against the people, and the law, and this place: and further brought Greeks also into the temple, and hath polluted this holy place.

(For they had seen before with him in the city Trophimus an Ephesian, whom they supposed that Paul had brought into the temple.)

And all the city was moved, and the people ran together: and they took Paul, and drew him out of the temple: and forthwith the doors were shut.

And as they went about to kill him, tidings came unto the chief captain of the band, that all Jerusalem was in an uproar: who immediately took soldiers and centurions, and ran down unto them: and when they saw the chief captain and the soldiers, they left beating of Paul.

Then the chief captain came near, and took him, and commanded him to be bound with two chains; and demanded who he was, and what he had done.

And some cried one thing, some another, among the multitude: and when he could not know the certainty for the tumult, he commanded him to be carried into the castle.

And when he came upon the stairs, so it was, that he was borne of the soldiers for the violence of the people. For the multitude of the people followed after, crying, Away with him.

And as Paul was to be led into the castle, he said unto the chief captain, May I speak unto thee? Who said, Canst thou speak Greek?

Art not thou that Egyptian, which before these days madest an uproar, and leddest out into the wilderness four thousand men that were murderers?

But Paul said, I am a man which am a Jew of Tarsus, a city in Cilicia, a citizen of no mean city: and, I beseech thee, suffer me to speak unto the people.

And when he had given him licence, Paul stood on the stairs, and beckoned with the hand unto the people. And when there was made a great silence, he spake unto them in the Hebrew tongue, saying,

Men, brethren, and fathers, hear ye my defence which I make now unto you. (And when they heard that he spake in the Hebrew tongue to them, they kept the more silence, and he saith:)

I am verily a man which am a Jew, born in Tarsus, a city in Cilicia, yet brought up in this city at the feet of Gamaliel, and taught according to the perfect manner of the law of the fathers, and was zealous toward God, as ye all are this day.

And I persecuted this way unto the death, binding and delivering into prisons both men and women.

As also the high priest doth bear me witness, and all the estate of the elders: from whom also I received letters unto the brethren, and went to Damascus, to bring them which were there bound unto Jerusalem, for to be punished.

And it came to pass, that, as I made my journey, and was come nigh unto Damascus about noon, suddenly there shone from heaven a great light round about me.

And I fell unto the ground, and heard a voice saying unto me, Saul, Saul, why persecutest thou me?

And I answered, Who art thou, LORD? And he said unto me, I am Jesus of Nazareth, whom thou persecutest.

And they that were with me saw indeed the light, and were afraid; but they heard not the voice of him that spake to me.

And I said, What shall I do, LORD? And the LORD said unto me, Arise, and go into Damascus; and there it shall be told thee of all things which are appointed for thee to do.

And when I could not see for the glory of that light, being led by the hand of them that were with me, I came into Damascus.

And one Ananias, a devout man according to the law, having a good report of all the Jews which dwelt there, came unto me, and stood, and said unto me, Brother Saul, receive thy sight. And the same hour I looked up upon him.

And he said, The God of our fathers hath chosen thee,

that thou shouldest know his will, and see that Just One, and shouldest hear the voice of his mouth. For thou shalt be his witness unto all men of what thou hast seen and heard.

And now why tarriest thou? arise, and be baptized, and wash away thy sins, calling on the name of the LORD.

And it came to pass, that, when I was come again to Jerusalem, even while I prayed in the temple, I was in a trance; and saw him saying unto me, Make haste, and get thee quickly out of Jerusalem: for they will not receive thy testimony concerning me.

And I said, LORD, they know that I imprisoned and beat in every synagogue them that believed on thee: and when the blood of thy martyr Stephen was shed, I also was standing by, and consenting unto his death, and kept the raiment of them that slew him.

And he said unto me, Depart: for I will send thee far hence unto the Gentiles.

And they gave him audience unto this word, and then lifted up their voices, and said, Away with such a fellow from the earth: for it is not fit that he should live.

And as they cried out, and cast off their clothes, and threw dust into the air, the chief captain commanded him to be brought into the castle, and bade that he should be examined by scourging; that he might know wherefore they cried so against him.

And as they bound him with thongs, Paul said unto the centurion that stood by, Is it lawful for you to scourge a man that is a Roman, and uncondemned?

When the centurion heard that, he went and told the chief captain, saying, Take heed what thou doest: for this man is a Roman.

Then the chief captain came, and said unto him, Tell me, art thou a Roman? He said, Yea. And the chief captain answered, With a great sum obtained I this freedom. And Paul said, But I was free born.

Then straightway they departed from him which should have examined him: and the chief captain also was afraid, after he knew that he was a Roman, and because he had bound him.

On the morrow, because he would have known the certainty wherefore he was accused of the Jews, he loosed him from his bands, and commanded the chief priests and all their council to appear, and brought Paul down, and set him before them.

And Paul, earnestly beholding the council, said, Men and brethren, I have lived in all good conscience before God until this day.

And the high priest Ananias commanded them that stood by him to smite him on the mouth.

Then said Paul unto him, God shall smite thee, thou whited wall: for sittest thou to judge me after the law, and commandest me to be smitten contrary to the law?

And they that stood by said, Revilest thou God's high priest?

Then said Paul, I wist not, brethren, that he was the high priest: for it is written, Thou shalt not speak evil of the ruler of thy people.

But when Paul perceived that the one part were Sadducees, and the other Pharisees, he cried out in the council, Men and brethren, I am a Pharisee, the son of a Pharisee: of the hope and resurrection of the dead I am called in question.

And when he had so said, there arose a dissension between the Pharisees and the Sadducees: and the multitude was divided. For the Sadducees say that there is no resurrection, neither angel, nor spirit: but the Pharisees confess both.

And there arose a great cry: and the scribes that were of the Pharisees' part arose, and strove, saying, We find no evil in this man: but if a spirit or an angel hath spoken to him, let us not fight against God.

And when there arose a great dissension, the chief

captain, fearing lest Paul should have been pulled in pieces of them, commanded the soldiers to go down, and to take him by force from among them, and to bring him into the castle.

And the night following the LORD stood by him, and said, Be of good cheer, Paul: for as thou hast testified of me in Jerusalem, so must thou bear witness also at Rome.

And when it was day, certain of the Jews banded together, and bound themselves under a curse, saying that they would neither eat nor drink till they had killed Paul.

And they were more than forty which had made this conspiracy. And they came to the chief priests and elders, and said, We have bound ourselves under a great curse, that we will eat nothing until we have slain Paul.

Now therefore ye with the council signify to the chief captain that he bring him down unto you to morrow, as though ye would inquire something more perfectly concerning him: and we, or ever he come near, are ready to kill him.

And when Paul's sister's son heard of their lying in wait, he went and entered into the castle, and told Paul.

Then Paul called one of the centurions unto him, and said, Bring this young man unto the chief captain: for he hath a certain thing to tell him.

So he took him, and brought him to the chief captain, and said, Paul the prisoner called me unto him, and prayed me to bring this young man unto thee, who hath something to say unto thee.

Then the chief captain took him by the hand, and went with him aside privately, and asked him, What is that thou hast to tell me?

And he said, The Jews have agreed to desire thee that thou wouldest bring down Paul to morrow into the council, as though they would inquire somewhat of him more perfectly.

But do not thou yield unto them: for there lie in wait for him of them more than forty men, which have bound themselves with an oath, that they will neither eat nor drink till they have killed him: and now are they ready, looking for a promise from thee.

So the chief captain then let the young man depart, and charged him, See thou tell no man that thou hast shewed these things to me.

And he called unto him two centurions, saying, Make ready two hundred soldiers to go to Caesarea, and horsemen threescore and ten, and spearmen two hundred, at the third hour of the night; and provide them beasts, that they may set Paul on, and bring him safe unto Felix the governor.

And he wrote a letter after this manner:

Claudius Lysias unto the most excellent governor Felix sendeth greeting.

This man was taken of the Jews, and should have been killed of them: then came I with an army, and rescued him, having understood that he was a Roman.

And when I would have known the cause wherefore they accused him, I brought him forth into their council: whom I perceived to be accused of questions of their law, but to have nothing laid to his charge worthy of death or of bonds.

And when it was told me how that the Jews laid wait for the man, I sent straightway to thee, and gave commandment to his accusers also to say before thee what they had against him. Farewell.

Then the soldiers, as it was commanded them, took Paul, and brought him by night to Antipatris.

On the morrow they left the horsemen to go with him, and returned to the castle: who, when they came to Caesarea, and delivered the epistle to the governor, presented Paul also before him.

And when the governor had read the letter, he asked of what province he was. And when he understood that he was of Cilicia; I will hear thee, said he, when thine accusers are also come. And he commanded him to be kept in Herod's judgment hall.

Acts 21:10–14, 27–40; 22; 23

Jesus' Dictation:

THE GLORIFICATION OF THE SON OF GOD

Hail, O infinite light!
Hail to the sons of God!
Hail to the Keeper of the Flame!

I AM Christus. I AM your brother Jesus ascended, and I AM come in this hour of the glorification of the Son of God that you might learn of me the initiation of the Lamb in the cycle of Aries, in the cycle of the spring and the spring equinox.

Truly, the Lamb who is slain from the foundation of the world does stand in the margent of the earth at the point of the rising of the sun, there to send forth the mighty light rays from out the Great Central Sun, from the heart of Alpha and Omega, anchored then in the hearts of those who receive him now.

I come in the fullness of my ascended master consciousness two thousand years hence and almost two thousand years since the initiation of Saul of Tarsus in the way of the Lamb in this cycle. I desire that you should understand that the blessings given before my ascension to the apostles were therefore by the nexus of the then attainment of my lifestream, and the initiation given unto Saul was by the full power of the ascended Presence.

MY SECOND COMING,
ONE WITH EVERY LIGHTBEARER ON EARTH

In this hour I come, having multiplied that Christhood, lo, throughout the Piscean dispensation. Therefore, in the hour that the Father has sent me to return in a mighty and glorious Second Coming, I AM this day, as announced to you last evening, now one with every lightbearer on earth, everyone in whom there burns a threefold flame. I AM there in the fullness of my Electronic Presence, multiplied by the light of the bearer as I multiply that light and soul freedom.

This, then, is the glory of this Eastertide: that I AM come in the fullness of a working relationship with certain souls who have been quickened to the Path and others who have not, yet in whom there burns no guile but purity and love—no leaning or penchant toward error or calumny but only the path of truth.

Wherever the walk is, there I AM with those hearts whose fire burns with a love for the ruby ray and will accept the consequences of wearing, even with an archangel, that mantle of the ruby ray. Here I AM, therefore, O people of God! And I have had set before you this afternoon the mighty light of record—a portion, therefore, of the experiences of Paul, whom I named following his conversion.

Understand that this divine encounter with my ascended master Presence is what is in store for those who now receive me by this dispensation of my Second Coming in the Electronic Presence, which means in the full magnitude of my auric emanation as the individual is able to bear it and therefore somewhat stepped down until they themselves can mount to the point of their personal Christ Self and also receive the fullness of my attainment.

Understand the greatness of the Father, who gives to the Son the magnificent opportunity of bearing the burdens of his own and the multiplication of the whole loaf of my consciousness to every living soul on earth in whom there burns the threefold flame, that threefold flame held and intensified as a devotion to truth—thus, not merely threefold flames in embryo or embryonic consciousness, but a threefold flame that has been tried on and worked, identified with, and that has become the guiding light and the lamp unto the soul. Day by day, therefore, I trust that as those who are yet infants, who develop that flame, may also receive my Presence when a certain quickening does take place.

Let me make clear then, beloved hearts, that this opportunity is one that I have come surely to fulfill and surely to enhance and with that Holy Spirit to make known to you, by the very example of Paul himself, what is the experience that can be anticipated by those who truly have received the engrafted Word,[1] who have received my personal Presence unto themselves as Paul did, who, despite the warning of the Holy Spirit and my own, determined to go and preach to the Jews in Jerusalem, contrary to the counsel even of my flame and my Presence.

Thus, beloved, you understand a free will that was exercised by Paul, who insisted in taking my name before those, the very ones and seed who had already moved against me and been instrumental in the acceleration of my own initiation of the crucifixion. These, howbeit, were Asian Jews and they came against Paul with a mighty vehemence and, as you have heard the record, determined by a vow and a pact that they ought to murder him.

REGARDING YOUR OWN MESSENGER

Beloved ones, I tell you this day that the murderous intent is also abroad regarding your own messenger. And yet this murderous intent takes the form of the determination to destroy this Church, this organization, and to destroy the reputation, the character, and the image. But if it were possible, they would push their anger all the way and also complete their vow of the death pact against the light incarnate.

Therefore does the heart of the messenger leap to rejoice—as did the heart of Paul—to bear my name, to witness of me, to carry a light so bright that it is an offense unto those who pursue the way of the Satans[2] and the desecration of the Mother chakra and of all of the chakras by their incessant carnal hatred and their incessant chatter, heaping gossip upon gossip that has no origin in fact but only the fancy of their minds and the fantasy that they desire to place upon the image of the one I have sent to you—not only to *preach* to you but to *ordain* you and to raise you up that you might know the meaning of the Lamb and the coming of that Lamb and that you might partake of that Lamb of Aries and realize that Sanat Kumara *is* in our midst, and the dividing of the way is so that the lightbearers may be exalted. For we cannot lift up the ones who are not of the light.

Therefore, by one means or another, they must effect their own exit. For they are no part of the light or of the dispensation, nor can they receive what beloved Saul received from my heart.

Learn well of me, therefore. For I, the ascended master Jesus Christ, did exercise my authority and my right to contact the un-ascended Saul—true, a Pharisee and a Roman and a Jew, a persecutor of me and of Christians, who stood by even at the death of Stephen by stoning.[3]

Therefore, realize that the acts of the individual are not the final conclusion as to the quality of the soul. For there were other Pharisees and Sadducees in those days who outwardly kept perfectly the Law but inwardly were ravening wolves[4] and had not the quality of heart to be initiated.

THE QUALITY OF HEART IS THE FOUNDATION

Understand, therefore, that no matter what the accusation of physical acts that are charged against the messengers, we have chosen *because* we have chosen, and the quality of heart is the foundation of the instrument.

Therefore, see to it also, in thy preparation for our calling, that you bring therefore a live coal, a lively coal of fire and fervor for the truth as you understand it. For this was the quality of heart of Saul of Tarsus—believing what he had been taught, even a false teaching regarding Jesus Christ, my own name and my life and mission.

Therefore, he persecuted my followers and, in them, persecuted my Presence. For I was in them, and my light was an offense to those who therefore enlisted Saul in their ways of exterminating, imprisoning, persecuting, and torturing Christians.

Blessed hearts, realize, then, that the fervent heart when hitched to the wrong star may be unhitched and redirected and therefore scale the heights of mastery, leaving behind those who seek to perfect themselves by the Law without the Spirit, who engage in rituals without love, and who are mechanistic in their judgments, very eager to point the gnarled and bony finger against any light-bearer for a single sin that they do think does soil the garment.

Well, sin may or may not soil the garment. But the Holy Spirit is able. And that Holy Spirit in me did raise up Saul, and therefore he received upon himself that substance of his karma that created the state of blindness. And my instrument again, Ananias, therefore did pronounce that he should see by that Holy Spirit—and he did see.

And Saul therefore became Paul and went forth as a chief apostle, one that I would send to the Gentiles. And yet he, being a Jew, determined to preach to the Jews, not realizing how infamous and how wicked was the core of their hatred and their rage against the living Christ. Thus, I came. Though he did not take my advice, so he loved me and I comforted him and gave to him protection, even through the Romans.

And you see, therefore, that God is no respecter of persons, and we of the ascended hosts may raise up friends of light where you know not. And I tell you, in these very months, total strangers of this Church and of this organization and of these messengers have come forward to stand for them in such nobility and honor and truth and defense as to make almost the angels weep; whereby contrast those who, having been with them so long time, should pick apart the hairs and determine that they are not worthy any longer to bear the flame of the World Teachers.

Thus, one is taken and another is left. And the great sword of living truth will cleave asunder the Real from the unreal even within your own members, within your heart and soul and consciousness, dividing the way between truth and error and showing you, if you will be God-taught, what is truly the way to become my apostle in deed.

Thus, Paul spake to them, believing surely that because he was a Pharisee and a Jew of some standing, having great knowledge, having been taught by Gamaliel . . . (blessed ones, Paul was no new-comer, nor was he without the proper station in life or training or background) and therefore he was determined that his own people should hear him and be convinced and be converted.

THE HEART OF THE ONE NEWLY COME INTO THE PATH OF CHRIST

And so it is with the heart of the one newly come into the path of Christ. There is always the desiring to take up one's family, one's own, one's relatives, one's community and karmic group and say, "See, I am one of you! I have seen a great light of God. I have received this blessing, I have been converted, I know the Lord Jesus Christ!"

And they would not hear it, as they stopped their ears in the presence of my preaching through Saint Stephen. For I did preach through him, by the power of the Holy Spirit, his final words spoken, which remain for all time a testimony of the Word.

And they stopped their ears. They could not bear to hear it! They could not bear the sacred fire or the release of light because their hearts were evil. And immediately they took up stones against that Saint Stephen, and he gave up the ghost—but not before seeing my very face, the face of the Son of God in heaven. And I received him to myself.

Understand, therefore, that in my heart of love I understand your need to bring the greatest light to those who are familiar. And I understand sometimes what is a fallacy of thought—that because individuals are like you in background or in race or in karmic group or in a similar economic or educational situation, that they will, by the very fact of outer circumstance or perhaps bloodline, receive the mightiest teaching of all ages, which is: Christ *in you*, the hope of glory! These are my words to Paul, and these are the words he pronounced again and again.[5]

Therefore, not heeding the warning, he was almost murdered by those Asian Jews, who determined (they were so highly offended by the light) Imagine! that they would neither eat nor drink until they had murdered him. And therefore protected, the Romans sent an army to deliver him therefore to Felix where he would appear, and also to Agrippa, and finally take his case before Caesar himself before he could be delivered.

Such a tumult was made by the chief priests, the very same tumult they made against me. But I was then the ascended master, and therefore I placed my Presence over him. And it was the will of God and of my heart that he should be spared and go forth, having seen through the utter crassness and the materialism and the blasphemy of the Jews—that he might leave behind those who had chosen not to receive the Christ in me or him and go on to the Gentiles who had not the descent of Sanat Kumara, yet in whom there burned an innocence, a hope, a certain faith whereby the field of consciousness was fallow and could receive the spark of Christhood.

This is the meaning of the tremendous promise of Almighty God that those who would believe in my name, even through my disciples and apostles, that these should also become sons of God.[6] And did I not say that God could "of these stones raise up sons of Abraham"?[7]

IT MATTERS THAT THE HEART IS INCLINED TOWARD THE INFINITE

Understand the mystery of Almighty God once and for all. It is not the physical temple you wear, it is what is inside! What is inside is the mystery of the kingdom of God, beloved hearts, and it matters not what evolution or what source or where that body temple originated in all of the experimentation of these systems of planetary bodies. It matters that the heart is inclined toward the Infinite.

And you will find that the blackest of souls may dwell in immaculate-appearing bodies, moving in the right circles. And you know these are the Watchers or their offspring, the giants or the demons themselves incarnate.

And therefore, there cannot be a flesh-and-blood lineage of any kind but only the infinite bequest of the Almighty of the lawful inheritance of the sons of God who take up their abode where least expected so that the proud may be humbled, so the rich may be embarrassed, so the poor may find the treasure of heaven and therefore shun the things of this world.

Therefore, I AM Jesus. I come to you in this body, and I would come to the world in your own body as well. I must give you, then, more than I can tell, but this I may say: that the presence of my being with you is the first step—but the quickening, the initiation, must come by an inner accord and an agreement that you understand first and foremost that Christ who comes to you to initiate you by the sacred fire of the Lamb of God must cause to have delivered to you a certain portion of your karma that must be transmuted within you ere you can move upon that life of service.

And therefore, by prior decision, you must know you are willing to bear—whether it be adversity, whether a physical burden, whether a hardship, whether grief, whether suffering loss here or there. You will understand that the coming into alignment of your soul with God must be an adjustment.

You have seen the adjustments that have been necessary this year in the nature kingdom for bringing into alignment certain discordant and karmic conditions in Southern California; you have seen the suffering of the people in Northern California and other areas of the nation and the world. And you have not always understood why, nor have the people who have cried out to God.

And yet they themselves have desired at inner levels of their souls' evolution to go farther and higher in the light. And therefore, they have agreed to that adversity and that burden while others themselves, refusing to bend the knee, have had the mountain fall on them, as the Rock itself, even the stone, must grind them to powder[8] lest their inordinate pride carry them off in some other area of destruction against the holy innocents.

Therefore, whether by judgment of Almighty God to the non-surrendering self or by the delivery of a burden of great love, of personal and planetary karma, some have borne a little more inconvenience and indeed suffered loss for the sake of the total evolutionary chain of this planetary home. For the lightbearers also learn from the judgment of the souls of the wicked. And the wicked also learn, and they are somewhat contained—though not for very long. And the lightbearers themselves understand the path of karma *even though* their preachers will not preach it unto them.

So I preach it unto you, beloved, that you may understand that no matter what the current fad in doctrine in this or that century, the inexorable laws of Almighty God move on. And his mercy is with the lightbearer, and his judgment is there to curtail the Fallen One until all balance be brought into manifestation.

WRITE A LETTER OF YOUR SOUL TO YOUR CHRIST SELF

Therefore, I ask you not, in this hour of this Easter Sunday, to make a fervent call to me as you would now, caught up as you are in the rapture of my love. But I ask you to write down a letter of your soul to your own Christ Self when you are alone with your thoughts and with your meditation and to surely set forth in writing what it is you are willing to bear in order to be my instrument.

And the reason I request this of you, beloved, is so that you will keep this letter in your Bible. Insert it in the Book of Acts so that you will read the life of Paul. And you will also have that life delivered to you—preaching therefore on these Sundays, as I shall, showing you step-by-step the way of overcoming and that you might be thoroughly acquainted with the path ahead.

Thus, it has come to pass often in previous dispensations that I have given my offer unto souls of light, and in a moment of great desiring and devotion, they have offered everything. And when I have given the initiation to them, they have utterly forgotten by the weight of their own personal karma that they even volunteered to go through an experience of hardship in order to balance that karma, in order to come to the place of being a part of the mission of the apostle Paul.

Therefore, not desiring to place you in the jeopardy of the law of your own being and the law of your own word and the attendant problems of the forgetfulness of the outer mind, I desire that you should write your letter. I desire that you should keep it in your Bible as a sacred thing and review it from time to time, and also study the life of Paul and other saints and the martyrs and understand what truly is the meaning of the bearing of my light on earth.

For this initiation, when it comes, cannot be turned back, cannot be taken from you. Once you receive it, you must move on with it. And I would not have you fail in the course of your discipleship for the point of Christhood that is truly the culmination of your life's work on earth.

Therefore, my beloved hearts, I desire you to consider not only the initial burden of bearing to oneself some record of the past with which the Holy Spirit will not endure, but also to recognize day by day that as the light increases, as the light intensifies, there are many who will be offended—those who are of this world, those who exist to preserve the status quo of materialism, those who are called Jews who originally had a dispensation long, long ago even in other systems of worlds.

And they were given the light of the threefold flame, and instead of using it to glorify the Son of God, they used it to enhance the development of the intellect, to enhance their position of material control and scientific learning and the manipulation of genes and the creation of life and all manner of advancements that they then did bring with them to this planet, which were outpictured on the continent of Atlantis and even in previous ages not available in the records of outer history.

And therefore, these individuals became laggard evolutions. A laggard is not one who merely lags behind his evolution, beloved hearts. A laggard is one who takes the light of the threefold flame and inverts it to the perpetuation of matter rather than exalt it and thereby exalt the Son of God within himself. It is the utter denial of the living Christ no matter what that Christ is called, no matter what the religion.

It is not so much a problem of Christian and Jew; it is a problem of the individuals in every race and nation and religion who turn their back upon the initiation of the Son of God and desire the light without the sacrifice. And these are they who prefer to perpetuate this Cain civilization and this darkness. And therefore they become enraged when one soul of light breaks loose from the grip-hold of the toils and the toiler and does therefore receive the mighty light of the Holy Ghost that does sever the tie and the bondage.

It does set the captives free! It does break the chains of the prisoner and loose him and let him go! And no matter what crime one may have committed, in the hour of that freedom one *is* free, one is on the Path. And because of the quality of heart and the fire of the heart, though that one may err or stray, there is always the lovingness of the ascended masters to draw that one back to the Path and take that heart into a higher dimension of understanding.

DILIGENCE ON THE PATH

This you must realize, beloved hearts, for some fear lest they should make one single mistake and be cast out of God's kingdom forever. Beloved ones, this is the preaching of Satan, it is not the preaching of my heart. And therefore, there is no need for rigidity, but only diligence on the Path. For diligence is never rigidity, but it is a love so great that with all your might and heart you seek to serve always to the best of your understanding and to be God-taught and corrected when that understanding proves to be not the fullest.

But therefore, you may go on to a new chamber of the mind of God and find there a higher definition of selfhood, a higher manifestation, and leave behind the old man.[9] And therefore that old man and his garment is cast into the fire. And I know it, and the Father knows it, and the angels know it, and the brothers and sisters in Christ know it.

But the fallen ones will hang on to the old image, and they will hold it up and they will say, "See what this individual did in 1913? They will never escape that sin—no, never—and forevermore be damned!" And they will go to every past embodiment, and they will go back and finger through the decades and attempt to place their hands upon what they think is or was your identity.

And never, never, never do these individuals ever take accountability for their own sin, much less the forgiveness of that sin that was given to them while they made an attempt to follow the path of discipleship, but in fact never did because the mercy of God was not in their hearts. Therefore, they could not forgive themselves any more than they can forgive anyone else on the Path, beloved hearts.

And so, you see, by nonforgiveness and nonmercy there is a nonhumility. There is actually the reservation in the heart that says, "I do not need Christ. I do not need his forgiveness. I can climb the ladder by my own personal and human excellence." Therefore, there have been among you those who are humanists to the core, who desire human reward for human achievement, and the human consciousness is exalted.

And therefore, they move against the light. They bring their suits against the Mother because they desire the reward in the human octave. And by desiring that reward, they lose entirely anything of good that might accrue to their karmic record whereby they could have some opportunity in the very day of judgment to balance their infamy against the light, which is no new infamy but has been carried on for aeons.

Thus, the opportunity of the Mother flame is a final opportunity of teaching and the Path ere the judgment come. And they are self-judged. And nothing I might do or say—with all the power and the glory God has given unto me as the Saviour of the world— there is nothing I can do with the unfruitful heart even as there is nothing I can do with the tree that bears not fruit, but it must be withered and it must be cast into the fire.[10]

Realize then, that the fruit of the consciousness of Christ is mercy, is forgiveness, is transmutation. For change is the order of the Path, and all disciples are moving onward in leaving behind the old order. And when they leave it behind, that old man and that old order ceases to exist. And no one can dredge it up and say, "This is *really* what you are, this is *really* what he is! He is not what he pretends to be, for *we know*."

And these individuals say, "we know," because they themselves have the computerized mind of the laggard races—gathering data against the lightbearers, but only human data. For they have never, never in all eternity penetrated the secret chamber of the heart, nor have they ever observed the souls of the beloved in union with the living Christ in the presence of the Father dwelling in the temple, in that secret chamber where no man can enter except the soul himself drawn by God, drawing himself by love and pursuing a oneness with all fervor and innocence, purity and honor.

I therefore point out to you that these fallen ones, who would drive their armies against the light and against The Faithful and True, did descend on the apostle Paul. They moved against him. They formed their mobs. They hid in secret, they lay in wait as they did for my own soul as David.[11] As Saul's henchmen sought to kill me, to surround my house and lie in wait, so they did for Paul. So they will do for you. And therefore, this also must be considered as you write this letter to the Christ of your heart and to my own Presence.

TRY ON THE SHOES OF THE APOSTLE

Not being familiar with all of these situations, you cannot deliberate on them if you do not know fully not only what are the physical consequences, but what are the forces of hell that come as a weight of the astral plane upon you to hold you down and to be there night and day so that your entire effort of your life must be to *praise* God, to preach his Word, and to release the light of the Word through you by the Holy Ghost. And that Holy Ghost is a consuming fire that consumes the very hatred that is projected against your own skin, against your own life, your effort, and the very eyes that burn with the coals of living fire.

Realize then that the continual pushing back of world hatred becomes the way of the apostle who would move among men and nations. Therefore I would suggest that you try on the shoes of the apostle before you come to me asking for the initiation of the Lamb, that you walk in the shoes of Paul or even walk in the footsteps of the messengers you know today, and understand what is this life to be lived week in and week out, year in and year out— understanding that I, too, had no place to lay my head but went here and there because, you see, I was constantly moving to separate myself from those who lay in wait for me, even unto the hour of my crucifixion.

Thus, the very initiation itself was a relief—to finalize and have actualized the presence of my Christhood and it sacrificed for the world and given freely as the life essence of my being, that I might move in the earth as one who is untouchable, not as the lowest caste of the planet but as the highest caste.

For you see, those who are resurrected in glory are the "untouchables," and they cannot be touched by the fallen ones. And therefore, you will come to understand why the sons of God eventually take the ascension in the light. For they bear so much of world hatred—and then, not because they weary of bearing the burden, but because they know in the ascended master light body they may walk the earth midst their disciples and do more for them and protect them than remaining in the physical octave with so much concentration of hatred against the one self, and therefore against the followers of that self.

MY ELECTRONIC PRESENCE OVER YOU

Realize, therefore, that I AM here in my Electronic Presence over you to now create the situation whereby though I AM ascended, I AM yet on earth. In one sense, the clock has advanced two thousand years and the new momentum of my lifestream of attainment of these years is in the earth. And in another sense, the clock has moved backward to the hours before my ascension.

For the Presence I place with you, as I have said, is the Presence that you can bear, and it was what the apostles could bear, also. Those who could not even recognize me in the resurrected state could, of course, not receive the full glory of the ascended master Presence that I was able eventually to convey fully to Paul.

Therefore, it was John who carried the flame of my ascension, and the others were able to carry a certain essence up to the point of the resurrection. And thus, you see, each one would bear testimony by the level of his own witness. And this is why some of the witnesses differ, even those who might be a part of the original band.

Now understand that my placing of a Presence with you is so that you may have me with you and also that I may retain the frequency of the ascension flame. This has, therefore, a twofold consequence. For having the power of the Presence, the Electronic Presence of my own flame with you, you receive a multiplication of your actions, of your service. You can go farther and contact more people, and I am there to assist you in sustaining the attempted setbacks or the moves against you.

On the other hand, the power of my Presence will draw an increased level of persecution, especially if you come under the initiation of the Lamb and desire the increase. It can be magnified tenfold. Thus realize that the advantage of accelerated chelaship and initiation unto the ascension must be weighed and balanced with the increment's light and what it will produce as an alchemy in the world today, in the world thought, in the mass consciousness vis-à-vis your lifestream.

Now therefore, I have taken this hour of the celebration of the resurrection to speak to you concerning those things that have been upon my heart, beloved, for hundreds of years as I have walked by your side, as you have pursued the path of the Christian mysteries or been called by me in areas of service even through the last thousand years and beyond.

THE OVERLAPPING OF THE PISCEAN AND AQUARIAN DISPENSATIONS

And as you have made progress, and as I have spoken with my Father, and as I have spoken with Maitreya regarding this hoped-for and longed-for dispensation that I might bring to you, their counsel has been that it could only come in the hour of the overlapping—the overlapping of the Piscean and Aquarian dispensations whereby the power of that blessed father Saint Joseph, as Saint Germain, might also be combined with my own.

And the dispensations and opportunities of the Aquarian age, being for that soul freedom and an opening of the way that could never have been opened in Pisces, would also be upon those disciples. And it was also necessary that upon you, my disciples, there might be the maximum attainment that you could achieve without my physical presence yet with my guidance and love and spirit with you in these centuries.

Therefore both have come to pass. You have moved forward on the path of discipleship. You have encountered Saint Germain.

You have used the violet flame; you have indeed transmuted considerable karma, even before the divine encounter with me (and this the beloved Paul did not have when he was Saul). And so, you see, the violet flame in itself can cushion a good portion of this initiation. And this also, this fact, I would have you realize in understanding what is the possibility for us—you and I as two in one and three in one for the Holy Spirit with us, and the fullness of the Father in me, can achieve one by one upon earth.

I also tell you that the additional blessing of my Presence is that it does take some pressure off the messenger herself, who is not in any way scheduled to take her leave of you and has no concern whatsoever or consideration to be moved by the hatred of the fallen ones and the betrayers but stands staunch in the earth to deliver the Word and to finish a mighty mission.

And therefore, you can understand that when I myself am duplicated many times over, there are many more targets. And therefore, by the division itself, each and every one who does accelerate into my ascended master Presence will not necessarily have the full impact of Paul the apostle or others who have stood alone in past centuries without the additional dispensation of Saint Germain.

YOU HAVE TIES TO WONDERFUL PEOPLE ON EARTH AND IN HEAVEN

Now I have desired to make plain to you, out of the love of my heart, the various facets of cosmic law that pertain to each individual's homeward path. And the path back Home, beloved hearts, does entail many considerations. And you all have ties not only to wonderful people on earth but, I might say, to wonderful people in heaven—even ascended masters you have known and perhaps served or even done a favor for in past lives.

You have many more friends of light and cohorts than you realize, and so I have called this the *Conclave of the Friends of Christ* that you might realize that my friends are many in heaven. And therefore, when I espouse you as my friend here and now, you will increase therefore your circle of influence in the courts of heaven by the increase of my own friendship. For I have many among the ascended masters who will "go to bat," as they say, for any disciple for whom I request a favor.

These favors are not the favoritism of a decadent system, but rather a favor that comes under the heading of the grace of God whereby a lifestream has truly earned a grace—by a kindness, by a love, by a stand for truth, by an honor of heart, by taking a more difficult way, by self-effacement in allowing another to take the prize or the crown when perhaps it was not due.

Therefore, you see, the friends of freedom, friends of Saint Germain, and the friends of Christ are many. And we look forward to a wide-open dispensation and opportunity because of my descent. And all of my friends above and below will also *seize* upon this opportunity to increase light on the earth!

For with the coming of my Presence is also the coming of the judgment. For it is ever my purpose in the world that the Light should bind the Darkness and those who willfully ensoul it, that the children of the light might be free to express that which is within.

Now, my beloved, in a great love of my heart for Paul, I surely give to you the tenderness, the closeness, the intimacy of our walk together. If you will study the existing records of Paul diligently, you will come to understand just how personal is the interaction. Paul's sense of me was the sense of a friend almost physical who walked at his side.

He was ready to live or to die for me because I was so real to him—more real even than anything in this world. Yet I did not desire he should die, but *live*—and live to be the heart's instrument of my own flame to those who would receive me, no matter what their background or karma.

A CONTINUING MISSION—SEARCH FOR THE REMNANT OF THE CHRISTED ONES

Thus, my beloved, I have a continuing mission to do this. And those who are called the Gentiles, supposedly those who have not a threefold flame or very little soul substance, are the ones to whom the light must be passed even in this age. Thus we are in search of the remnant[12]—the true white-fire core of the seed of Sanat Kumara, the *seed* of Abraham who have never sacrificed their light or threefold flame to material pursuits, to greed or its Moloch or to any of the other gods of the Canaanites.

We are in search of the remnant of the Christed ones, those ancient souls sponsored by Enoch, sponsored by Adam, sponsored by Seth and, ultimately, Noah. We are in search of these who must make their ascension at the conclusion of the coming dispensation, and we are in search of those new evolutions, the new light-bearers as well as those Gentiles who qualify as the bearers of the seed of Christ—new vessels.

Thus, see what is the mighty dispensation of the LORD. I repeat: Judge not, lest ye be judged. For whatsoever ye mete, it shall be meted unto you—measure for measure.[13] And this is the Law. For a judgment is a pronouncement concerning an individual. And when the pronouncement is made, immediately it must manifest upon oneself. I speak of that judgment that is the critical analysis and the attempt to define of what sort an individual is.

The true judgments of God are delivered by the Christ Self in the nonpossessive sense, remanding to him and to the Lords of Karma that judgment. Yet in the final hour of the Last Supper and in the final hours of my presence on earth, I did make the promise, "Whose soever sins ye retain, they are retained; whose soever sins ye remit, they are remitted."[14]

This is the power of the Holy Ghost when that initiation of the Holy Ghost is come upon you and the Christ in you is still the one who determines either the retention or the remitting of those sins.

Realize then that always it is God within the individual who responds and makes the determination according to the level of initiation.

By the Sacred Heart, therefore, I AM the judge. I manifest my judgments true and holy and clear and just within my messenger as I so choose. And I render judgments through your own Christ Self by your giving of the Word and the call. And some of these are not even known to you, for it is Christ in you and not the outer mind that must make the determination. And the outer mind may not be ready for the full understanding. Yet, I AM within you! I AM the Lord Christ and I AM forevermore the manifestation of the Father, of the Son, of the Holy Spirit, and of the Mother.

For I AM THAT I AM. I AM that Word! I AM that incarnation of the I AM Presence! I AM that ascended master light! And I do enter your temple in this hour, in the name of your own Christ Self. And I come to tarry there until the fullness of your joy be made known, until the *fullness* of your joy be made known unto me—until your joy be full and I may release to you that which Almighty God can and shall ordain according to your free will, and only your free will, united in Christ.

Therefore, in the hour that you ask, it will be your Christ Self, it will be my own Presence deliberating with your soul, and we will give you answer as to what part of your demand for initiation shall be met. For in the final analysis, it is the judgment of Christ in you, the eternal Christ that is the only hope of your glory through the sacred path of initiation.

This is my message that is the promise of the resurrection to those who can hear and understand and know the meaning of hearts one, congruous in harmony as in heaven and on earth.

THE BAPTISM OF MY FLAME AND HEART

I now prepare to baptize you. I desire to perform this, that you might know the baptism of my flame and heart to each little one and to each one who so chooses. Therefore, the touch, the gentlest of touch is all that is required, and your names may be read by our scribe. And thus, the name pronounced, given unto the angels, kept of record, will show that I have touched you this day and dedicated you to the will of God.

And therefore, if you would be baptized and receive the certificate of baptism, know that it is a baptism for eternity. It may not be increased or redone. And if you have been baptized by the messengers before, you have received my blessing, I can assure you, and you cannot lose it. For it is sealed by God in a secret place of a certain chakra of your life.

The baptism is the sacrament, it is the blessing of the consecration of your life to the will of God that is your inner blueprint, given to you and agreed upon by you by your free will in the beginning. Baptism, therefore, does draw you into alignment and even gives some token of a rearrangement of karma for a better manifestation of that which is within.

The light may be received and make you feel uncomfortable for a while, but this is only the adjustment of the chakras that are truly changed and charged by this increment of fire promised of God and given in the beginning and in the ending of the journey of life. According to the divine plan, may this be the victorious incarnation of your soul unto the Victory of the ascension in the light.

I AM Jesus. Make no mistake, for it is not only possible but actual that I may speak to my own at will through those whom I appoint as messengers from century to century. It is actual and physical that I may, through the Holy Ghost, reach my beloved as tangibly and, yea, more so from the ascended state as I did on the Galilean hillsides.

Yes, beloved, the Father has not cut off my communication with my own. And therefore take care against entering the sin of the gainsaying of Core.[15] For those who denied the mantle of Moses as the Messenger of God are the same ones who have denied my own mantle as Jesus, the mantle I placed upon Paul, and the mantle that I have placed upon this and every other representative of my heart.

There are those who will not admit that the Christ Self of every man can speak, can work and perform. And I AM here to say that your Christ Self is *ordained* to speak to you of salvation— to reprove, chasten, love, correct, exalt, and uplift. And your soul has a right to that communion and that communication, even as you have a right to hear me through one whom I raise up and train and seal against the hordes of night.

For I tell you, no true messenger of my heart could stand in the earth against the hordes of death except the dispensation of the entire Spirit of the Great White Brotherhood be upon him. Understand and know, therefore, that God does pay the price, the Brotherhood does pay the price, I pay the price, and the messenger pays the price to stand and still stand—to uphold *what?* To uphold the very principle of the Word and of communication that, by right, heaven may descend to earth at any moment and raise up a single soul in glory, that God may descend, that the Holy Spirit may be with you.

And you are not cut off or forsaken! You are not bereft! And there is *no* wall between heaven and earth except the wall you make, except the wall of the scribes and the Pharisees and their false doctrine and their cutting off of my message and my lifestream and my ongoingness.

I AM here to testify of *me*. For I *will* testify of me that you may know that I AM in the earth and that *I go to El Salvador this day to bind those who move against my hearts of light!* And I ask you to go with me in your finer bodies to overthrow the hordes of the planetary body determined to move against this nation through Central America. Will you come now? [Audience responds, "Yes!"]

Armies of heaven and Christian soldiers, we go! And we place our light bodies there, our ascended master light bodies! For you now have my own, and I wear your physical forms. And I AM there, and we will roll them back and rout them out. But I must have the perpetual praise and Word and the dynamic decree, for my angels may only obey the mandates of the daily call. Therefore in the call itself is the salvation of this planet.

My beloved, come and be baptized. For I would also sanctify you to the mission in the heart of the ruby ray. I bleed for thee— which is to say, I release my heart's essence, that you also might be comforted and drink of me while I AM drinking thee.

FROM THE MESSENGER'S HEART
AT THE SUNRISE EASTER MORN SERVICE

Alleluia, He is risen! Alleluia, He is risen!
Alleluia, Christ is risen this day!

Beloved Father in heaven, LORD God Almighty, in the name I AM THAT I AM, we invoke here the mighty angels of the resurrection and the full power of the resurrection flame.

Lord Jesus Christ, come into our midst. Show yourself to us in this hour in the great victory of the flame. O eternal life, O thou victor over death and hell, now prepare the way for our union through the Sacred Heart with the purest light of the resurrection.

O saints of the Most High God, O universal light rejoice with us, for in Christ's glory is the kindling light of our own victory this day!

Therefore, we sing to God. We sing to the Almighty! We sing to the Lord Jesus Christ, the mighty archangels, and his saints!

O Holy Spirit, in the name of the Father and the Son, let us commune with the body of God worldwide and worlds without end, that the oneness of our hearts' love might celebrate with him the eternal victory for our earth over death and hell and war and strife and division among the brethren.

Let us rejoice in the mighty liberating power of the sacred fire of the Holy Spirit! Let us visualize the earth filled with the Holy Ghost as the violet flame frees all because of the victory of Jesus.

In the name of the Father, the Son, the Holy Spirit, and the Mother, Amen.

. . . Ought not Christ to have suffered these things and to enter into his glory? Is it not wonderful to discover our risen Lord and to know that we can follow him in the very same footsteps all the way Home?

Is it not a source of great rejoicing, this resurrection morn, to understand that even as he prophesied to his own that persecution would follow those who followed him, that he moved with boldness and joy, with love and obedience, to drink that wondrous cup that we might live?

This courageous heart, this living Saviour, the Son of man, also our brother and our friend (for he made us so in the final hours of his mission), shows us that we must do these things also.

Today we see world persecution in every nation of those who are the lightbearers. In every religion and in every walk of life, we find that there are the hearts who bear the flame as Christed ones, those who serve the light of the Mother, of the Buddha out of the East, of Lord Krishna, those who serve the Almighty One, bearing that light in the darkness of the world. These are the ones whom we comfort during this Passion Week. For they are one with him, not only in the sorrow but in the great joy of drinking the cup— all of it.

Therefore, blessed hearts, we pray as he prayed for strength for all time to come to his own who would believe in that light, that Word which came into the world, the true light which lighteth every man, every woman, every child. This is the great kindling light of Easter. Hallelujah! The mighty light of God in our hearts *is* the very personal Presence of Jesus.

Even so, Lord Jesus Christ, come quickly into my temple! And in so coming, Lord, let me know all of thee. Let me understand

and walk with thee. And also rebuke me, Lord, if I might be reticent also to suffer with thee all these things and thereby know thee in the fullness of thy glory. So we would also know that path.

We pray now, O God, for those who suffer in Poland, in Afghanistan. We pray for those who suffer in Central America, who meet the adversary face-to-face as the movements of world tyranny move against the light of the heart. For this is not a political struggle, it is the struggle of the Darkness against the Light.

Therefore, Lord Jesus Christ and thou Faithful and True and beloved Maitreya, lead us, then, in the victory of the light by the power of the Word with us. For we know the oneness of our hearts. And our prayer united in the communion of saints everywhere is truly the deliverance of those in our own nation who suffer under the yoke of an economic burden—those who are hungry, those who are not fed, those who are sick, those who need to know thy glory.

O Christ, come into thy temple! Come into the mosques and the synagogues. We welcome you into all places and especially into the hearts of the mighty souls of the ages who are following the thread of thy heart back to the Almighty Father. Though they know not the source of that thread, O God, illumine them, open their eyes. For even as the disciples did not know thee, therefore have mercy upon those who do not know thee as thou art.

O beloved Jesus, we thank you with our heart's deepest gratitude for showing us the way to run with haste to meet the risen Saviour, to run with haste to meet our own deliverance. By the love in our hearts, therefore, we pray:

Transmute world hatred, and world condemnation of the Christ. Let there be a cessation of strife, brother with brother, in Northern Ireland! Let there be the flame of peace in Belfast! Let there be the flame of peace in every city and nation. Let there be the unification of nations.

Let the people of the Middle East this day, in the very land where thou wast and art victorious, know thee as the true Messiah—

as the Coming One who is able to deliver all people, all nations from the darkness of sin to the victory of eternal life.

Our prayer, O God, is that you might move us onward in the path of discipleship, that by thy light and thy Presence with us we might glorify thee also as God has glorified thee.

In the name of the Father, the Son, the Holy Spirit, and the Mother, Jesus our Lord, *seal* the unborn! *Seal* the sweet children of God's heart coming to earth. Protect them from every danger and deliver to us, therefore, the Manchild as the Christed One in the heart of every newborn babe.

O Lord, break thou the bread of life with us, for we desire to drink of thy blood and eat of thy flesh. For thy body is meat and thy blood is light. And with this essence, the power of thy presence of Alpha and Omega, we are strengthened for our own walk and discipleship.

O Lord, we pray. We pray we might be worthy to be joint heirs with thee as it is taught to us by thy apostle Paul. Make us one, O Lord, as thou art one in us—the Father and the Son dwelling with us.

Now break this bread. Bless the wine, bless the bread. Charge it with thy substance, even thy resurrected Body and thy resurrected Blood.

This we do in memory of thee, O Lord, knowing that it is by the transfer of thy light that Christ is kindled in us, and we may walk the earth as instruments of thy light.

In the name of the Holy Communion of the Father, the Son, the Holy Spirit, and the Mother with us, Amen.

. . . Lord God Almighty, in thy name I AM THAT I AM, in the name of Jesus Christ, send thy mighty archangels to the Middle East in this hour and let the flame of the Prince of Peace bind, then, all strife and war!

Let there be peace among the Jews, the Muslims, the Christians, the Palestinians. Let *peace* come now to the Middle East by the power of Elohim, by the power of Jesus Christ, by the power of Alpha and Omega.

We call forth the hosts of heaven and the mighty armies of the Faithful and True to bind, now, every foe of peace, all war and the engines of war, and all strife!

Blaze forth the mighty flame of the victory of Christ this day! And by the heart's love of all the people of the whole world, let there be the descent of the Holy Spirit and the divine consciousness of the Almighty One to raise up these peoples that they might live in love and harmony and equality and with a homeland for everyone—and that the justice of Almighty God might reign. This is our prayer, Lord Jesus, in this Easter morn.

Blessed Mother, we call for thy intercession. Let there be the healing of that strife, that this hallowed land might serve all peoples as the place of the pilgrimage to the highest understanding of God.

In the name I AM THAT I AM, we call and, beloved Jesus, we accept thy promise—whatsoever we call unto the Father in thy name, so he will give it unto us. Let the fervor of our hearts be the fire that also is multiplied by thine own. And let the mighty alchemy of the Holy Spirit melt the elements of hatred, human pride and division, self-righteousness and all of these.

Let the power of the Holy Ghost melt now and dissolve and consume all records of centuries of strife and opposition. O by thy flame, O God, we accept it done this hour in Jesus' name.

In the name of the Father, the Son, the Holy Spirit, and the Mother, Amen.

April 3, 1983
Camelot
Los Angeles County, California
ECP

CHAPTER 12

*And the whole earth is bathed in my love and
my heart and my wisdom. And the Holy Ghost will come.
And you shall survive. You shall see the New Day!
You shall go to the place prepared.
You shall have your individual victory!*

CHAPTER 12

THE SECOND ADVENT: "THE DAY OF VENGEANCE OF OUR GOD"

O Lord, Our Lord, how excellent is thy name I AM THAT I AM in all the earth![1] I AM the Son of God this day. I AM Jesus the Beloved, and I have descended to you in my ascended master light body in the same manner as I have ascended into heaven. And I have shown the messenger my descent out of this heaven in this hour, descending into your midst that you might know that the prophecy of the two men in white unto those who gathered in the hour of my ascension is fulfilled this day, May 8, 1983—that you might know that this same Jesus which is taken up from you shall so come in like manner as you have seen him go.[2]

The descent is an extraordinary light to an extraordinary woman, as you understand the meaning of *person* and as you understand the meaning of *woman* itself. You who have the mystical awareness of the office of Messenger, only you can understand by the Holy Spirit the anointing of the one and then the anointing of the many, and the cherishment by God of those whom he does raise up to be the instruments of his Word.

Therefore, this is the hour and the Day of the LORD's Vengeance.[3] It is the very point of the designation of the mantle and the authority of the mantle of the judgment itself, in the earth as in the heaven, upon the messenger.

You realize that I have delivered to you the Judgment Call and means for the implementation of the judgment by your own Christ Self.[4] There has been, therefore, the building toward this moment as the path of Christhood has moved on, not only in the messenger but in your own souls of light. The hour and the day must come, therefore, when one also as the physical embodiment of that Christ becomes the authority of that judgment. For if I judge, my judgment is true. For the one who judges is the Word.[5]

Therefore the mantle is on the Son of man—the fusing of the person with the Son of God. And the mystical understanding of this union in the one before you enables you to understand the coming day of my own appearing and my own descent into your own living temple.

You must know the example. You must feel by the LORD's spirit and my own the confirmation of holy offices in the earth so that I may anoint you. I anoint the one, that I may anoint the many, that the many might prove themselves. For the believing of the Christ in me is the confirmation of the first Advent as I lived.

Thus I come in the Second Advent with clouds of glory, with hosts of the LORD, and with light. And that Second Advent is as the appearing of the sign of the descent of the entire chain of the Christed One—of Sanat Kumara, Gautama Buddha, Lord Maitreya, and myself therefore embodying this Word in the messenger for a holy purpose.

Therefore this day is this scripture fulfilled in your ear![6] And I have called her to witness unto this scripture on this holy hill that is consecrated to my ascension, that I might also descend here as I ascended from Bethany's Hill. And I have called you, each and every one, to bear witness: "Yet in my flesh shall I see God." For it was the word of Job,[7] and it has been the word of my own heart as David,[8] and it has been the word in the heart of every son of God who determined that in his flesh all would be overcome and the light would shine and the light would be there for the fulfillment of the promise.

If it cannot be fulfilled in the one, then it cannot be fulfilled in the many. And the very moment it is fulfilled in the one is the open door of the initiation of Christhood and of the vast ages that roll.

Therefore, will you also cast the messenger over the brow of the hill[9] or will you enter in to the consummate love of my own ascended master Presence? For I AM here in the Second Advent. Truly I, Jesus, stand in your midst and I also touch with you now that Christ Self. And the preparation of my Electronic Presence with you has been for this completion of the cycle that shall be then sealed this Thursday, marking the celebration of my own victory of the ascension.

I ask you to rise in honor of the One Sent and of my coming. For truly, beloved hearts, the world of Christendom has desired to know the day and the hour of the coming of myself.

I have ever been with my own. But there is a moment in the turning of cycles of that Advent, and this hour is the hour when I have descended precisely in like manner as I ascended. And through the dispensation of my Presence with you, beloved, therefore all may come to understand this meaning. And all may understand that progressively each one shall receive the revelation of that Second Advent until they shall actually see in the golden age the ascended masters walking and talking with the saints of God on earth.

THE COMING OF MESSIAH

And therefore, understand that there comes into the vision of each and every person the coming of Messiah. It is something that the heart knows. And groups of people who evolve together may acclaim that coming decades or centuries hence, or on the morrow or the next year.

But, beloved ones, I desire to have recorded in these very hills of the Motherland that my descent is in the West, on this day and date. And you may move forward—for I come to the Jews as Messiah, I come as the Second Advent to Christians, and I come also in the spirit of Maitreya, as he is one and I AM one, to deliver not only the mandates of the judgment but the full teaching unto the ascension in this age.

Beloved, won't you be seated in the presence of your own Christ Self.

There have been those over the centuries to whom I have appeared. And therefore, there is a mighty spiral of the Second Advent, and it is the Advent when I, Jesus, come into the temple of the One Sent and raise up fully the Presence of that Christ to perform the work that I have ordained. Thus individually you must know the same path. And this Presence comes in this very hour, as the Day of the LORD's Vengeance has turned the cycles of planetary karma at the point of the Piscean dispensation.

Understand that the coming, the mighty descent of my Presence here, is for the action of the sacred fire to *consume* this very world karma! And I tell you, without my pressing-in into the very flesh and blood of the messenger, into your very hearts, which are come sacred by your Christ Self, there would not be the meeting of the planetary momentums of death. For the records of death and hell carried out by the murderer of the lightbearers on every continent represent a force of malevolence that has to do with the fallen ones and their judgment in this hour.

Therefore, I desire to make known to you the publication of this book. [The messenger holds up *Forbidden Mysteries of Enoch: The Untold Story of Men and Angels*.[10]] And I, Jesus, bless this book and seal it. I seal it with my heart, and I proclaim it as the focus of this Day of the LORD's Vengeance. It is timed precisely with my descent, the descent of that ascension fire into the earth, as on no other occasion. For it is the ascension fire of the Son of God that does challenge the Watchers, the godless, and the fallen ones.

Therefore, I say, cherish it! For as the hands of the messenger are placed upon it, so my hands are upon it in this hour—and on every copy, so is the blessing duplicated throughout all editions and reprintings. And you will recognize this to be the focus of the Day of the LORD's Vengeance and the fulfillment of the prophecy of our Father Enoch in every way. And you will understand me coming as the Elect One in the person of this messenger and in the person of every one of you as you also are raised up, as you joyously balance your karma and pursue the path of the 100-percent balancing of that karma.

The words of Lord Maitreya: "Understand that as Jesus Christ came for the judgment of Satan, so yet he allowed himself to be the instrument of their judgment [the judgment of Satan and his seed] by the crucifixion. This same Jesus that I AM, this one to whom I refer as myself in incarnation, this same Jesus in your midst, therefore does focus in you the understanding that in each succeeding two-thousand-year dispensation the coming of Christ is for the new manifestation of the Cosmic Christ."

UNDERSTAND YOUR OWN PATH AS THE PATH OF THE MESSENGER

The Day of the LORD's Vengeance, then, has come! And you may understand your own path as the path of the messenger. Whereas I came into incarnation in my final embodiment almost karma-free, retaining a few percent for the remaining of my life on earth—these messengers have come, as it was spoken in the Book of Revelation, "clothed upon with sackcloth,"[11] clothed upon with a full portion of their karma, not yet even having balanced 51 percent.

And this has been for a purpose. For the bearing of the burden of one's own karma and of world karma simultaneously has been demonstrated to you by both messengers that you might understand the Path and not consider that it is far from you, that you may also balance that karma (the 51 percent) and then move on to the attainment of the avatar as the incarnation of God through the reaching of the full 100 percent.

I point out to you, then, that as I spent forty days in the wilderness fasting and praying and met the temptation of Satan,[12] so it was given to the messenger Mark to ascend February 26, 1973; and for, therefore, this messenger as the Mother to be in the wilderness, tempted seven years of the seed of Satan.

And many representatives have come into this organization, and without, as the seed of Satan. And the descent into hell after the very crucifixion in the hour of the ascension of Mark therefore lasted seven years and a certain portion thereafter. Thus with the coming of Easter in 1980, you see the turning of the cycle of the eighth ray, the balance of Alpha and Omega, and the return and the resurrection of the Mother.

You will understand, therefore, that in these seven years there has passed before her the darkest of the very darkness of death and hell, and the direct confrontation of the war of Armageddon and the fallen ones of other galaxies who had actually journeyed to this planetary body for the tempting of the Woman—taking embodiment here, coming to this very activity with the message in their teeth: "I have come to destroy you." These have come one by one to transgress the light of the seven chakras of the Mother.

You will understand, therefore, from her experience—by trial and error, by passing through veils and veils of illusion, by coming in contact with the mind of the Evil One and the machinations of that mind, by the analysis of the ways of darkness—how step-by-step she was required to put upon herself the mantle of that garment.

Realize, then, that the "suddenness" of the descent of the mantle is *not* sudden, that your Christhood is not a miraculous suddenness of a new person in your body, but it is the activation of the mind of God with you, passing through the darkness of the very dark ones, living in and amongst them, understanding them twenty-four hours a day, writing down the strategies of darkness, and making the right choices—sometimes the wrong choices, but always moving toward a greater and greater circle of the awareness of the victory of the Son of God.

This path you must understand. Many have thought to go into the wilderness and fast forty days, to take upon themselves the confrontation with the false hierarchy. And *many* have lost their minds in so doing! They have been put upon by demons and discarnates through an unbalanced path of fasting. They have not understood that the forty days represents also the forty years in the wilderness—which could have been the forty years for your own Elizabeth had it not been for Saint Germain and that in the last days, the days should be shortened for the elect.[13]

Because they were shortened for her, they may be shortened for *you.* And instead of the world's criticism, you ought to have compassion, and understand the Path that has been walked and the burden that has been borne—an untold burden that I dare not unveil to you fully in this hour, but which one day I will recount as my own dictation through her heart. For all should understand and know what is the confrontation with Evil.

THE SIGN OF MY COMING MARKED BY THE COMING OF A COMET

And therefore, I tell you that the sign of my coming in this hour has also been marked by the sign of the coming of that comet that is close to the earth and closest in this very week.[14] The origin of that comet is a distant galaxy, and out of that distant galaxy came the very Evil One who should be the tempter of her soul. And the fallen ones of that galaxy and other galaxies, who have also sent the seed of Serpent to the earth to tempt all of the light-bearers, have arrayed themselves against the coming of the light in the messenger and in you all—as their opposition to my descent has been grave indeed, as they have attempted to muster all that they could find to move against the Woman, to tear down the image of Christ in her, and to desecrate the face of the Mother.

They will not tear the veil from the Cosmic Virgin, nor will they take the veil of your own soul's purity from you! For in the path of discipleship we have sealed, as the ascended masters, your right to become the Christ, your right to pass through trial and error in preparation of your lifestream, your right to balance your karma, your right to wrestle with the fallen ones and even to make decisions at times (which you have later regretted) to become entangled with them. But all of these experiences, beloved, have shown you the way of darkness as you have understood the psychology of the Evil One that you must then judge, for whom you must cast out the dweller-on-the-threshold.

This earth is a schoolroom. And it is a final schoolroom also for the Mother and for her seed. Therefore, the importance is not the mistake; the importance is the victory! And I proclaim that victory in the messenger as possible unto you all. And I adjure you to consider this entire life—no matter what the darkness you have been into—as the opportunity for you to see the face of the synthetic self and of the Evil One and to choose to live after the path of Christ.

Therefore, I, Jesus, in the person of my messenger bestow upon you the forgiveness of sin that you might be free from condemnation, that you might be free from the accuser of the brethren[15] who will tell you, as that one would tell the Mother, "You can never rise! You may never rise again, for the power of our word and the word of blasphemy that *we will make true* is the word that will destroy you!"

They have no power, beloved ones, unless some give them power. But I, Jesus, have chosen to withdraw that power from them and therefore to bestow upon you the opportunity to accelerate, to see that many of you are approaching also the balance of

51 percent of your karma, that you must hold on to what you have received and what you have gained, that you must understand also in the midst of all of this that the sign of my coming is the sign of the Advent.

And the sign of the comet is the sign of the opposition to that coming. For this comet has borne a great darkness of the fallen ones of that galaxy who have sought to send into the earth and transfer through it to the astral plane, to the individuals of darkness, a *new impetus* and a new momentum of the darkness of the Liar and his lie and the Murderer and the murderous intent.

Thus by fire and by ice, the fallen ones attempt to hurl their momentum of Antichrist as a final attempt to tear down the messengers of the Great White Brotherhood and every single one of you who is ordained to be apostle after the calling of my heart, even on the path of beloved Paul.

I, Jesus, am here this quarter of Summit University, and this is why I have come. I have come because it is the hour of the Second Advent when all the world must rejoice that because I am descended, so the Second Advent is the coming of The Lord Our Righteousness within you!

May you recognize that the Day of the LORD's Vengeance has not yet passed and that the judgment of the Watchers and the fallen ones is upon you. Therefore, study well the teachings of Enoch, give the Enoch Rosary,[16] and realize that your calls will confirm the Second Advent in you one by one. And the more you embody your Christ Self, the more you will realize that every word of prophecy that is given is confirmed not only by God but by God in manifestation.

Therefore, I say to you that I have planted my feet in this earth as the sign of the ascension flame. And on the hillsides of all the world I have also impressed my footprints as in the hour of my ascension, that the earth might be quickened with the Rose of Sharon,[17] that the earth might be renewed, that you might rejoice, and that you might keep the vigil and realize that this is the hour when the Woman fully redeems—from the point of Eve to the point of Mary to the point of the Woman clothed with the Sun. The redemption is of the soul—the souls of Alpha and Omega who rise up to greet the dawn of the Sun of Righteousness who is come to you with healing in his wings.[18]

WELCOME TO THE PATH OF CHRISTHOOD

I AM Jesus. I bid you welcome to the path of Christhood once again. I point out to you that you need not fear the descent into hell. For the one before you has gone there in my name, has returned, and stands with the victory of God as the mantle upon her.

You therefore may understand that there are some things that you need not go through alone because the messenger has gone through them. And through the direct confrontation of the seed of the Watchers there has been once again the dispensation of the Christ that comes in each two-thousand-year period—that a part of the mantle of the Great White Brotherhood therefore is yours to claim, and that the attainment of the one can become the attainment of the many to prove.

Therefore, I say to you, you need no longer be entangled with Antichrist or the fallen ones! You need no longer be unequally yoked together[19] with those who are not of the light. You need not be overcome with the evil of death and hell. But by manifesting the community of the Holy Spirit and the science of the spoken Word, you will see how it is the dynamic decree, the Word of our Brotherhood, and the action of the Faithful and True that conquers death and hell and completes the fulfillment of all of the prophecies in Revelation.

I have set forth these prophecies for your own victory, to show you the path that is ahead for the binding of the beast of blasphemy and the casting of the fallen ones into the lake of fire.[20] The final judgment is nigh, even day by day. One by one as they pass from the screen of life, the fallen ones are taken up. And day by day the lightbearers are being born!

Will you hold the balance, beloved? For this is the hour of the trembling of elemental life and of the earth changes. Will you hold the balance while I, Jesus, now wash the feet of planet Earth?

And the whole earth is bathed in my love and my heart and my wisdom. And the Holy Ghost will come.[21] And you shall survive. You shall see the New Day! You shall go to the place prepared. You shall have your individual victory! For I desire to see you return Home with 100 percent of your karma balanced, as it was told by Lanello some years ago.[22] [Read Isaiah 61:3–62:12, which prophecy this paragraph specifically recalls and fulfills.]

I desire to see you understand that the Path is possible because one has passed over and is yet with you. And because you balance the fullness of karma and are fearless to face now these fallen ones, even the interplanetary and intergalactic mind of Evil, you therefore may set the record in the earth for millions to follow. Thus, earth shall become indeed Freedom's Star.[23]

Blessed ones, the Mother truly is come for the proving of Light's victory over the Darkness. May your compassion unto her be returned to you tenfold by the law of God himself, who extends to you mercy and forgiveness even as you give it out. Thus as you love yourself and forgive your soul, you will find yourself carried up by the wings of the Sun of Righteousness—your Christ Self with my Presence, and by the authority of the mantle that is upon her for the victory.

Watch and pray, for it is a new order and a new day. And as you walk down the mountain, I walk with you as I walked with my disciples and the other seventy and the multitudes. For I walk down the mountain in the presence of my own—and we are one. And the Father and the Son have come this day to you, dear hearts, to take up their abode in your temple.[24]

I seal you with the sign of the Holy Spirit. I seal you with the sign of the Mother. I seal you with the sign of the Father and the Son. And I ask now that Holy Communion be served in my name, and that you receive it as my Body and as my Blood.

May 8, 1983
Camelot
Los Angeles County, California
ECP

CHAPTER 13

*I desire to see you with the understanding of Self as Christ,
as Anointed One—as one who must discover the formula
of being and win consciously in this fight to defeat
death and hell one by one within the self.*

THE LORD'S REBUKE
OF THE BETRAYER OF THE WORD

Peace be unto you!

As the Father hath sent me, even so send I you![1]

I AM the mediator of your Christhood.

I AM one in the flesh with the messenger

And I AM one in the Christ of the disciples

Who are daily drinking my blood and eating my flesh

And becoming the fullness of my heart's light.

I have delivered to you the momentum of my victorious cycle by the Holy Spirit, that you might understand, by one closer to you than I in the physical octave, the real demands and the considerations of this path. I desire to see you with the understanding of Self as Christ, as Anointed One—as one who must discover the formula of being and win consciously in this fight to defeat death and hell one by one within the self.

I have come, therefore, for the sealing of the mighty action of my flame. I have come for the sealing of the Second Advent and the Day of the Lord's Vengeance and your own consummate love of your own Christ Self. I have come for the sealing of the mantle of the Mother and for the binding of the betrayer of her light.

Christ/Antichrist juxtaposed . . . until the Christ consciousness swallows up all unlike itself and the whirling sphere of the

Great Causal Body of cosmos does therefore contain the light that has gone forth, does extract by the sacred fire the misuse of the light in the ill-gotten fruit of the Fallen One.

Therefore, it is *seized* then from the seed of Serpent! The light they have taken from the Mother, from the Great White Brotherhood, from the Central Sun in all of their aeons of evolution is now taken from every cell and atom. And it does return to the heart of God by the open door of the sacred heart of the One Sent.

I AM that One. I AM THAT I AM where I AM. I AM the reinforcement of the pillar of fire of Sanat Kumara! By the Holy Ghost, I reinforce the light of Gautama and Maitreya, as the path of the ruby ray and the path of the rose cross is sealed in the heart chakra, sealed in the heart chakra—*sealed,* then, in the heart chakra!

By your understanding of the mystery of the Word incarnate, you understand that all things are one where you are, where I AM —where the individed Word is, where the messenger of the Word is, where your Holy Christ Self is. Thus, the Law of the One is truly the understanding of the mystical oneness of our hearts. It is the mystery of the Second Advent that I would seal in your hearts in this hour. I would that you would understand the true meaning of oneness—the oneness of Christ in this body, this body of the whole community worldwide of the Holy Ghost.

I would that you would understand the oneness of the I AM THAT I AM, even the Great I AM individualized as the Presence where you are. I would that you would understand the curve of space and all points of light meeting in the One by the convergence into the very center of life.

Understand the oneness and the unity of consciousness, yet the maintenance of individualization. Understand it, yet transcend the understanding. For the mystery of God demands climbing heights of a new wonder, a new miracle, and a new presence, beloved.

Therefore, realize that this fire that I release on this occasion is truly that the *non*believer, the *un*believer, and the *dis*believer is judged and bound and cast out! For I will not have feeding upon my light or the light of the heart of my own those individuals who send back the muddied stream of their disbelief.

I say, *expand* the center of the heart! *Expand* your heart chakra that you might contain the affirmation and the confirmation of my Word present with you. For the responsibility is upon you for the belief itself. And to believe, you must contain that portion ordained by God of The Lord Our Righteousness of your own Beloved. And to contain it, you must love that one—and that love is carried out as the fulfilling of that Word, hour by hour.

Look upon the mystery of life in the sons of God of all ages. You will see them about their Father's business,[2] thoroughly engaged in the bearing of fruit as the Tree of Life.

THE REBUKE OF THE FALLEN ONES

I AM therefore that Jesus who is come and come again. And I AM that One Sent for the rebuke of the betrayer of the Word. Therefore, I stand and *I rebuke the betrayer of the Word of the Great White Brotherhood!* I rebuke the fallen ones who carry their threat unto the death of the lightbearers of this planet!

I rebuke the betrayer of the living flame of the messengers, and I say: You have *no* power, your day is *done!* And as you have denied me before men, so I deny you before my Father![3] I deny you before the LORD God Almighty. I deny your name and the soul-identity that I have healed again and again and again as my duty to the Most High God.

And I bring forth the judgment of that soul and the canceling out of the record of life itself unto the betrayer of the Word incarnate within the messengers. And therefore, you will *see* come to pass that my Word shall be fulfilled! And heaven and earth may pass away, but the Word of the judgment of the Son of God within the messenger and within the disciples shall be carried out![4]

And therefore, as I have said, so I say it again: *Depart* from me, ye *despisers* of the Word!⁵ And let the *despisers* of the Word, by their own unbelief, receive the damnation of the Son of man and the Son of God and the I AM THAT I AM.

For I AM standing here as physical as you have ever seen me. And my physical atoms are the physical atoms of this body that I use, that you might understand that heaven and earth are one. And this Second Advent is the inauguration of the ascended masters bearing in and being a part of the believers in the Word of the I AM and in their own mighty I AM Presence and in the conviction of their Christ Self.

They *cannot*, no, they cannot in all eternity deny the presence of the One Sent. And therefore, you will see the annihilation of selfhood by many until these things be fulfilled in this generation of the judgment of the seed of the wicked.⁶

And you will understand that individuals by their own condemnation have condemned the LORD God where they stand. And by their public issue and their proclamation and their defense of the lie, so they themselves are judged by Truth.

I AM the Lord Christ, and henceforth you shall see me, and henceforth you shall say, "Blessed is he that cometh in the name of the LORD!"⁷ And those who bless not the coming of the Son of man in the One Sent and in every messenger of the Christ Self within shall realize that they themselves are self-judged. And there is no return. There is no return to life or eternal life unto those who are the betrayers of the Word.

And you will see the sign of my judgment as you have never seen before the sign of the Son of man in the earth.⁸ And you will know it—from the very center of the earth to the very center of the God Star—that I, Jesus, have come, that I have pronounced in the earth this day the rolling back of the hordes of night and of their mouthpiece. And you will understand what is meant by the Day of the LORD's Vengeance.

Count not, therefore, the cycles of time and space. For the LORD's coming is not known by any[9] but by the Father and the Son, and the Father *in* the Son, and the Father and the Son in the soul of light!

And therefore, each individual will give testimony of the binding of the dweller-on-the-threshold of the false-hierarchy impostor of his own office. And each one will give testimony in his own life of the binding of the dweller-on-the-threshold of the beast whose name is Blasphemy,[10] of the Antichrist,[11] and of the accuser of the brethren which accused them before our God day and night.[12]

THE FILLING OF THE EARTH
WITH THE GLORY OF THE LORD

See then how Christ in you is the hope of glory[13] and the binding of that beast! *See* then how I have pronounced the Word in this hour of the Christ Self of every son of God on earth. And it shall come to pass. And you will see it, and you will note that the new day of the filling of the earth with the glory of the LORD is nigh. And you will live to see a great glory upon earth—even as you will pass through that travail that leads to the peace of God in your heart forever and forever.

Though you have not understood, yet I have spoken. Though you *have* understood, yet I speak to your heart. And I proclaim the coming to the earth now of ascended masters who have graduated not only from other systems of worlds but other galaxies—and they gather for the reinforcement of the Faithful and True and the armies of heaven.[14] For they are now summarily encamped on the hillsides of the world, and there is an inner preparation of these armies of light.

And you will understand the coming of the army of light and the Faithful and True as never before. You will understand the coming of the Son of man. And you will realize that there is a moment of the gathering, which is in this hour, and the formation of the ranks of the spiritual army and the counterpart in the earth. And there is a moment for the marching of the armies around the world itself for the victory of the light as never before.

Therefore, all is in preparation. And one beholds the Son of man as that Faithful and True and as that Word, seated upon the white horse. And one finds oneself a part of that great army of heaven. And one *sees* the sign of the coming into the very earth body of the fulfillment of the age and of all prophecy and of Maitreya himself and the consummate word of love dissolving all that is anti-love.

And one will see the glory of God. One will behold it! And one will understand the tribes of the earth that mourn,[15] for the light is not in them. Yet these tribes may yet believe and be saved,[16] having had preached to them the word of the Everlasting Gospel.[17]

Yet you will understand how the captains and the kings and the mighty men of old are bound and cast down, and how they themselves become that momentum of energy that becomes the feast of light to the sons of God who sup with him.[18]

KNOW THAT YOUR VICTORY IS NIGH

Therefore, understand the meaning of transmutation. Understand the *meaning* of transmutation! Understand the coming of the violet flame to the earth body and the erasing of the old records of fear and doubt and death and destruction—and the bringing forth, therefore, from the earth of the new bud and the new plant and the original green blueprint of life that is the eternal matrix of the emerald fire within the soul.

And as there is the clearing of the old record, so the new soul is born, and hope is born—and the light of God does not fail. The light of God does *not* fail!

The light of God *does not fail!*

The light of *God* never fails! The light of *God* never fails!

The light of God never fails, and the beloved mighty I AM Presence is that One!

And therefore, the name shall be known, and it is the name of light. And the name shall be heard and the Word shall be heard and the prophecy shall go forth and the teaching shall go forth!

And I, Jesus, will see to it that everyone upon earth to whom I have given that teaching shall receive it, shall know it, shall walk the Path, and shall ascend with me into a higher glory as the earth is received in the light. And those who ascend will ascend, and those who do not will meet their own self-judgment as I have stated.

I AM Jesus of the cosmos, having long graduated from Nazareth. And I AM the prophet that is received in the whole country of God,[19] worlds without end. And I stand as that prophet of the sacred fire. I stand as that prophet declaring the Word and the fulfillment of the mission of the witnesses and the fulfillment of your ascension in the light.

Each and every one of you who have committed to that end, so receive then the blessing of my hand and of my heart. And *know* that your victory is nigh! And *know* that it is indeed a new dispensation, and the Fallen One is bound and cast out. And you will see it, and you will know it in yourself. And you will see how God does triumph in your life, in your body. And you will see how you will know God as you have never known him before!

THOSE THINGS MUST PASS SWIFTLY, THAT THE NEW DAY MIGHT APPEAR

Beloved ones, I stand because it is a momentous occasion for the two witnesses—to find, therefore, that the condemnation of the accuser of the brethren and of the mouthpiece of the beast of blasphemy is now bound by the very contempt of the LORD God himself for the infamy against the light.

And you will realize the fullness of my message as the cycles pass. And you will come to understand perfectly your own sacred labor and the path of your ascension and the path that leads to the very Heart of the Inner Retreat.

I send forth the call in the name of Saint Germain for the fulfillment now and the sealing of the obligations on that land, that you might receive the impetus of the God of Freedom to the earth in that moment that is so ordained by the mystery of the Word. Let, therefore, the bringing of the tithes into the storehouse[20] come forth, let it be manifest, and let us move on in the great victory of the Central Sun! For those things which come upon the earth[21] must pass swiftly, that the New Day might appear and that the light of the Son of God might be fulfilled.

I AM the proclaiming of the word of your ascension. I AM the release of the dispensation for it. I AM the energizing of your chakras for a new thrust of a cosmic purpose. If you seize it, if you do not squander it, if you take seriously the opportunity at hand, if you become strong in the LORD and in my Word, if you understand the true presence of Christ incarnate with you—you will go forth, you will conquer, and you will see how this earth will come into that golden age, as Saint Germain has said.

I stand for the fulfillment of the prophecy of the Woman and her seed. I stand for the fulfillment of the prophecy of the Cosmic Virgin and each and every one of her sons and daughters upon earth. I, Jesus, am come with the miracle light of the Father that I would deliver to your heart in this moment. [Pause]

Receive ye the Holy Ghost for the confirmation of the Word where you are! And know that the Holy Ghost I send forth as a breath of sacred fire is also for the judgment of the unbeliever in the mystery of the Word with him and with Our God and with the saints of heaven and with the messenger and with the chelas of the sacred fire itself.

I say, therefore: Angels of the sacred fire, angels of my band, angels of the dispensation of Pisces, *bind* then across the earth this night—*bind* then the state of unbelief and cast out the dweller-on-the-threshold! For I, Jesus, choose now to accelerate the Dark Cycle in Pisces by the binding of those things of doubt and fear and by the increase of the light of my own God-mastery in my own upon this planetary body.

Therefore, *bind* then those who perpetrate the lie and the deception of their doubt and fear and their own anxiety and their own revenge and their own desire to gain a net gain against the victory of the Word!

Bind then the entire momentum of the infamy of the fallen ones, and replace it now with a flame of God-mastery, which therefore in itself (as the Holy Spirit of my causal body) does judge those who persist in pitting themselves against the great logic of the Word, who persist in their unbelief.

Beloved ones, the testimony of my life and that of ascended masters throughout cosmos and that of Almighty God before everyone in embodiment is so abundant, so redundant, so miraculous, so entirely full of the light of the Spirit that there is no one upon this planetary body who has any further excuse to doubt the living Word and the living Presence of God.

And therefore, I, Jesus, bring the judgment of doubt and unbelief in this hour, and I *cast* it out as the poison of the seed of Serpent and as a nasty indulgence of those who ought to be fulfilling cosmic purpose!

I cast it out this night, and I cast it out on the morrow. And on the third day, I say, those who retain it shall be bound and judged themselves as though they themselves were the dweller itself. For those who align themselves with the planetary momentum of fear and doubt and nonbelief in my own Christhood now have been served notice by my own Father, by the LORD God Almighty, that the prophecy of the damnation unto those who do not believe in that Christ[22] is upon them.

And that prophecy of damnation must come to pass, and it must come to pass in the concluding shadows of the Piscean age, preparatory to the manifestation of the full-orbed manifestation of the light of Aquarius through the heart of beloved Saint Germain.

THE TRUE LIGHTBEARERS RISE

Understand the meaning of my Word! *Understand* that these things are coming to pass and these prophecies are not forever moved into the future, but they *are* at hand. And this *is* the Day of the LORD's Vengeance, this *is* the day of the tribulation![23] And this *is* the day of the falling from the heaven of those hierarchies that have occupied their positions too long. And therefore, they are bound and they are cast down! And those who have misrepresented the hierarchy in the office of the Son and the stellar bodies now find themselves removed and the true lightbearers rise.

Why, even in this community of the Holy Spirit, you find yourselves rising into positions of your own Christhood—because of the wickedness of the fallen ones (and its presence) no longer here. Therefore, they are removed. And the sons of light can fly! And the children of the light can swim! And they can move and sing and dance and play in the springtime of Pallas Athena and of the beloved Amaryllis and of the beloved Amerissis and all of those souls of light who are the ladies of heaven who have committed this year to bring the light of the Woman and the Mother into interaction in society and in education and in every facet of human living.[24]

I say to you all and I address you now as Christed ones and as the anointed of my heart: *Hear* me, then! *Hear* me and confirm my Word! Confirm my Word of this judgment in this hour and cast out the dweller yourself of that doubt and fear and the record of sin. For doubt is indeed one of the gravest of sins in all of cosmos and life and being. For nothing may manifest where doubt is.

Doubt is the slayer of the Lamb from the foundation of the world,[25] and it will slay your soul and your mind and your heart and your own Christhood. Therefore, I say to you: *Believe* in me, *believe* in Christ, *believe* in the One Sent! *Believe* in your beloved Christ Self and mighty I AM Presence. *Believe* in the LORD God Almighty and the company and the communion of saints.

Believe then in the absolute manifestation of the interaction, as Above, so below—by the heart, by the very living heart, by the heart flame and the heart's magnet of the One Sent.

And the One Sent *is* your beloved Christ Self. And the One Sent *is* the messenger. And the One Sent *is* my own flame. And the One Sent *is* the ascended masters of the Great White Brotherhood!

So be it. For I have spoken this evening, the entire evening, of my message. And now you have the opportunity of the acceleration of it and the acceleration of the Holy Ghost and the descent of that Holy Ghost by the power of the mantle of my ascension flame.

Therefore, I AM sealing you in the new manifestation of the Electronic Presence of my being with you. I AM sealing the dispensations which began nine months ago in preparation for this hour. I AM sealing you in an inner light and an inner mystery which you know not of but which your soul shall know this night in meditation with your own Christ Self.

Therefore, believe and be saved. Believe in the power of Christ in you to transform the world, and believe not the Liar with his lie. For I AM the true witness of our witnesses. I AM the true witness of our apostles, our messengers, our chelas, and the disciples. And I AM the witness of the true and living God, the Great I AM and the Great Mediator where each one stands. And I AM the fulfillment of the promise and I AM the fulfillment of the mission.

THIS MISSION SHALL BE FULFILLED

And I say to you: By the authority of my own name, by the authority of the name of God, I, Jesus Christ, promise you—as I stand and as I live—that this mission shall be fulfilled, that the witnesses shall return, and that the spreading abroad of the teachings of the ascended masters, as the waters cover the sea,[26] shall come to pass.

And if you endure tribulation,[27] you will see, then, the Second Advent in your life and you will understand the meaning of the binding of the Fallen One and the casting out of darkness in the Day of the LORD's Vengeance.

This is the Day of the LORD's Vengeance, and I AM the one with the avenging sword. I AM wielding that sword and I AM *thrusting* upon the fallen ones the entire momentum of their murder of the prophets! For the blood of the prophets is required of them this day,[28] and a full accountability in this hour. So it shall be.

And so, as it has been declared, they shall be cast into outer darkness and their names no longer written in the Book of Life.[29] For they never shall be anymore! For they have elevated the Serpent, and the Serpent himself is judged. And there is no more identity to those fallen ones. And they stand judged and consumed at the Court of the Sacred Fire upon Sirius this night!

Therefore, O world, be delivered. Therefore, *O world*, be delivered! Therefore, O world, be delivered! And let the travail of the Woman and her seed bring forth the manifestation of the Manchild[30] universally upon planet Earth, beginning with the very heart of those who are the ascending ones.

I AM Jesus Christ, and as I live—and as I live in this temple— so you will *see* the Son of man! You will *see* the glory of God! You will *see* the judgment! And you will *see your own ascension in the light!*

I AM the sealing of that hour. As you confirm it and live it, so it shall be. And *none* can stop it, *none* can delay it, none can stay the hand of the Almighty nor say unto him, "What doest thou?" For I, Jesus, am the messenger of the Almighty, and I bring you the sign and the hour of victory!

———————————

Messenger's Interlude:

Let us meditate on our vow, "I *will* walk with God," as we listen to Joe Feeney sing that song from the heart of our beloved Mark. Let us repeat the mantra:

> I *will* walk with God!
> I *will* walk with God!
> I *will* walk with God!

I *will* take his hand!

"I *will* take his hand!"
"I *will* take his hand!"
"I *will* take his hand!"

I *will* believe in the Son Jesus Christ!

"I *will* believe in the Son Jesus Christ!"
"I *will* believe in the Son Jesus Christ!"
"I *will* believe in the Son Jesus Christ!"

I *will* believe in the One Sent!
I *will* believe in the One Sent!

"I *will* believe in the One Sent!"
"I *will* believe in the One Sent!"
"I *will* believe in the One Sent!"

Even the messenger of his anointing!

"Even the messenger of his anointing!"
"Even the messenger of his anointing!"
"Even the messenger of his anointing!"

Even my beloved Christ Self!

"Even my beloved Christ Self!"
"Even my beloved Christ Self!"
"Even my beloved Christ Self!"

LORD God Almighty, I submit to thy law of love!

"LORD God Almighty, I submit to thy law of love!"
"LORD God Almighty, I submit to thy law of love!"
"LORD God Almighty, I submit to thy law of love!"
"LORD God Almighty, I submit to thy law of love!"

And to the Law of the One!

"And to the Law of the One!"
"And to the Law of the One!"
"And to the Law of the One!"

I'll Walk with God

I'll walk with God from this day on
His helping hand I'll lean upon
This is my prayer, my humble plea
May the Lord be ever with me.

There is no death, though eyes grow dim
There is no fear when I'm near to him.
I'll lean on him forever
And he'll forsake me never.

> He will not fail me
> As long as my faith is strong
> Whatever road I may walk along.

I'll walk with God, I'll take his hand
I'll talk with God, he'll understand
I'll pray to him, each day to him
And he'll hear the words that I say.
His hand will guide my throne and rod
And I'll never walk alone
While I walk with God!*

JESUS AT THE ALTAR OF THE MOST HIGH GOD IN THE GREAT CENTRAL SUN

I, Jesus, standing before the altar of the Most High God in the Great Central Sun, raise my right hand and deliver to the Almighty and to his people the full-gathered momentum of my ascension flame, multiplied by the two-thousand-year dispensation of my ascension, on this day and date in this year of Our Lord, 1983—that momentum of power for the judgment, then, of the betrayer of the Great White Brotherhood, that betrayer as an office held by many fallen ones throughout the galaxies.

---

*words by Paul Francis Webster; music by Nicholas Brodszky

Both the betrayer and the office receive the judgment now—the betrayer of the witnesses, of the messengers, of the avatars, of their apostles and disciples, of the prophets and the holy ones of all centuries and planetary bodies and galaxies.

I, Jesus, take now the full-gathered momentum of the portion of my lifestream as the ascension current, and I deliver it by my right hand. For the Father has appointed the judgment unto the Son.[31]

By my right hand, I deliver that judgment now upon the office and the person of the betrayer of the Great White Brotherhood and its representatives on earth and in heaven—namely, this messenger Elizabeth Clare Prophet; namely, the messenger Mark L. Prophet and all messengers from the very foundation of the systems of worlds who have gone forth and been sent as a part of the angelic evolution of the Most High God to rescue the children of the light from the betrayer and from the momentum of the betrayal held in that office.

Therefore, it is the judgment of Almighty God in my heart that they shall no longer pass the threshold of the living Word of truth. They shall be bound, they shall be cast out, and they shall be *judged!*

In the name of the cosmic cross of white fire, which I now place at the very feet of every son of God, I likewise pronounce the authority of my ascension in the announcement of the ascension in the light of certain sons of God who have prepared themselves for this hour.

Therefore, though it may come to pass in the decades or decades hence, so it is *sealed!* And it is *sealed* by the momentum of my light. For with the judgment of the betrayer, so the sons of light rise.

And I AM the resurrection and the life of every son of God.[32] And I AM the resurrection unto the damnation of the sons of perdition[33] who will no longer and no more go out to tempt or to torment the seed of light!

I, Jesus, have spoken. And I have responded to the LORD God Almighty this night—to beloved Alpha, to beloved Omega, who have sent forth the call which I have then answered, even as I have sent the call which they have answered. And therefore, I and my Father are one.[34] I and my Mother are one.

I seal this fiat of my heart. I seal it this day and date, this twelfth of May, for I AM in the victorious golden cycle of the New Day.

I *seal* it in the earth!

I *seal* it in the astral belt!

I *seal* it in the mental belt!

I *seal* it in the etheric belt!

And there is *nowhere* that the Fallen One may hide! For I AM Jesus the Christ, and I will pursue unto the finish everyone who raises his head against the living Truth throughout all cosmos.

And I AM the multiplication of my Electronic Presence, worlds without end! And you will see the coming of the New Day. As I AM THAT I AM on the earth and in the heavens, so I AM Alpha and Omega. I AM the beginning and the ending[35] and the Amen! For I AM Jesus and I contain the fullness of the LORD God Almighty. And I AM in his Presence, and he is in me. And I AM THAT I AM.

Alpha, Omega, I have come. I have spoken. I have descended to the altar on earth. I have ascended to the altar in heaven. I have confirmed thy Word. I have announced the decision of the Lords of Life, and I have sent forth the seal of my heart to carry out in the earth that which is the mandate of the LORD.

Now I seal in the heart of the messenger the carrying out of that Word. And I seal in the heart of every Keeper of the Flame the confirmation of that Word and that Life and that Love and that Truth, for I AM WHO I AM.

I AM your Brother of Light, and I will not fail thee, beloved.

Messenger's Comments:

Let us sing and hum softly our vow, "I'll walk with God," once again to the singing of Joe Feeney.

This is our answer to the Lord Jesus. Our walk with God is the confirmation of his Word and message.

These are our footprints, LORD God, in the earth, confirming thy Word, thy mandate. As it is in heaven, so on earth. Let Christ in me and thee affirm the judgment of the Lord Jesus Christ, which is the judgment of the Father and the Mother, and of the Son, and of the Holy Spirit, and of the *Amen*. Amen.

["I'll Walk with God" is played.]

As we walk from the sanctuary now, let us meditate upon the Holy City and the music of the Holy City. And let us know that these footsteps we take now are footsteps on the path that leads there.

And we see the Holy City just above the hill where our white cross is. As Jesus has placed that cross at your feet, so the cross is there as the marker of your ascension day. And above it is the glorious city of light—the Holy City in the etheric octave. And one day earth, physically and etherically, shall be one, and we will live to see the kingdom of God on earth as it is in heaven.

So walk toward the city of light, and keep silent as you meditate on this. Take your leave of your bodies when you have placed them in the place of rest. And go right to the point of that Holy City where we will continue to commune with beloved Jesus, for he has much teaching to give our souls this night.

I seal you in the sign of the Father, the Son, the Holy Spirit, and the Mother.

The sign of the Heart, the Head, and the Hand to you,
May the peace of the Presence abide with you.
The sign of the Heart, the Head, and the Hand to you,
Through days of service and nights of rest,
May the peace of the Presence keep you blest.

With the sign of the Heart, the Head, and the Hand to you,
May the cosmic cross of white fire of our own ascension
In the light watch between thee and me while we are
Absent one from the other and present with our God.
I *will* walk with God.
"I *will* walk with God!"

May 12, 1983
Camelot
Los Angeles County, California
ECP

CHAPTER 14

*The genes are the most sensitive vessel of your
entire world, and these chalices of light affect your thinking
even as your thinking affects them. You not only propagate
children by your genetic code, you propagate world
consciousness, Christ consciousness.*

YOU CAN BECOME A CHRIST!

"Your Genes Carry the Momentum of Your Consciousness"

Sons and daughters of the light, so long as ye are in the world, ye are the light of the world!

I AM He. I AM the One Sent to deliver to your hearts this day an increment of fire for the consuming of the anti-light. And my gratitude this day is to find in the earth souls mounting the very spiral of being—in the moment of love, in the moment of excellent creativity, with raised chalice.

And therefore, I pour. Bearing the light of the new dispensation, I pour the light. Vessel by vessel, I fill! Therefore I AM the light of Aquarius. I AM the one who bears the pitcher of water for the filling of hearts.

Thus, ye are the light of the world because the Father and the Son with you are that light. And therefore you, too, declare:

In the consciousness of the One and the One Sent, I AM He![1]

I AM He! I AM He! I AM He! I AM He!

Thus you have affirmed the most scientific statement of your being. *In the name of the Father, in the name of the Son, in the name of the Holy Spirit, and in the name of the Mother: Blessed is he that cometh in the name of the LORD!*

I say it unto *you,* for they did not say it unto me in Jerusalem of old. They did not say it unto me then, they do not say it unto me in the streets of Jerusalem today. But I say it unto you in the streets of Los Angeles and New York and Philadelphia and Berlin and Warsaw—and in the very heart of Taiwan. I say:

Blessed is he that cometh in the name of the LORD!

How can they deny so great a company of Christed ones? They must blind themselves, neutralize themselves, make themselves numb and dumb as cattle to fail to say:

Blessed is he that cometh in the name of the LORD!

O in His name be seated in the throne of His glory.

Not hard benches but tender petals of lotus flower—you are seated in the very heart of the great Three-in-One, the "throne room" of your own Christ Self. Seated as Maitreya, my Lord and your own, seated as and in The Lord Our Righteousness, you are centered in the heart of Christ. For this *centering* and this *empowering* I AM come this day by the Spirit of the I AM THAT I AM.

By the wind and the water and the wave and the light of the sun, I enter the heart of the earth, I enter the very heart of the sand and the sea and the waters under the sea. For I AM in the star of the I AM Presence and I AM in the soul of the bride of Christ. And I bring you into that point of Christ-discrimination, of practicality in every octave—in the physical, in the mental, in the plane of the heart, in the plane of the desire, in the flame of your cosmic memory of the ages.

For in that flame of cosmic memory, blessed ones, there you find the mighty tablets of the law of your own being. There you find, O my beloved hearts, where it is written of your fiery destiny and the commandments of the Almighty One—for all time and eternity written. It is the code of identity that *must* not, *will* not be tampered with, for I seal it—I seal it in this hour in the flame of the Holy of Holies.

THE STAMP OF YOUR IDENTITY

And I tell you, blessed hearts, before the coming of the Initiator, before the coming of the Great White Brotherhood and the sealing of souls of light as my disciples indeed, there have been hours in earth's history when this tampering with the identity has occurred. And therefore, there have evolved those anomalies and those exceptions to the inner blueprint of life that have manifested as the instrument of the Murderer and the murderous intent.

As you are the chalice of the LORD God Almighty, so there are created manipulated ones who have become, therefore, dark vessels of the dark consciousness of war and mayhem everywhere upon earth.

See, therefore, how I come with the mandate of alignment. And I tell you, the oft-repeated phrase "You are your own worst enemy" must be underscored in this hour. For you see, my beloved hearts, when you stray from the point of action, of Cosmic Christ attunement of the vibration of the heart of Helios and Vesta, and you go away from that heart and you begin to look at your brothers and sisters and you have the tilt of the head that begins to judge and question and to scorn and put down just a little bit here and a little bit there as you consider yourself superior to the humble of heart and therefore able "to analyze," as you say—beloved ones, when you are in such a frame of mind of criticism or of irritation, I tell you, that is when you are your own worst enemy. For then you are—and you are the only one who is—re-creating the molecules of the mind that reflect instantaneously in the genes.

Beloved ones, I tell you a cosmic secret. Just as beloved Kuthumi has told you that the aura is not still but moves moment by moment with the cogitations and the feelings and the movements and the health and all considerations of the lifestream,[2] so the genes themselves that carry the identity matrix also carry the momentum of consciousness.

And therefore, understand when conception may take place in anger or in lust or in worldly consciousness, in that moment of that consciousness there is transmitted to the offspring of earth that momentum of anger and that momentum of lust. And therefore, realize that the pattern of the soul and the four lower bodies is not merely set because of the marbles of the genes that never change and perpetually only contain human hereditary traits.

The genes are the most sensitive vessel of your entire world, and these chalices of light affect your thinking even as your thinking affects them. You not only propagate children by your genetic code, you propagate world consciousness, Christ consciousness by what you are and what you carry. And therefore, the stamp of your identity moment by moment goes forth!

CHANGE THE CAUSE IF YOU WOULD CHANGE THE EFFECT

There is the correcting lever of the Mediator of the Christ of your world that brings up the valleys and cuts down the mountains[3] (the peaks and the lows of karma and darkness), attempting to manifest the very best resources at hand. But those individuals, victims and subject to inner rage and darkness, having the split personality, the divided world, the absence of integration—these individuals scarcely return to an alignment whereby their capacity to multiply the *seed* of Christ and the *Word* of Christ may be given to them.

This is why momentum is important: because momentum is *reinforcement* of the will, the heart, and the mind building strong genes, not weak ones, and the strong seed of the heart and the strong egg of Omega in all planes of being and in all chakras. One cannot be engaged in that which is anti-God and then suddenly come and be a vessel for the Holy of Holies.

Therefore, understand wisdom. Understand that you are what you are, having thought what you have thought and desired what you have desired. Therefore, change the cause if you would change the effect. Genes are seen as causative, but they are the effects of your will, your Christhood, and your identity. The determination of the mind, like a sword Excalibur, will drive home the light and propagate the world Christ consciousness by the sheer will and determination.

There are hearts and minds of freedom all over the world today who are so *strong* and *determined* in their dedication to freedom that they affect *the entire planetary consciousness!* And therefore, their "genius" does affect all other genes on earth and there is an elevation and evolution of planetary man. And individuals actually increase their capacity to bear the Christ and give birth to holy children because of the will of a single consciousness of God-mastery held on a point of the Law that *will not* retreat, *will not* give up, *will not* stop until the desired end is reached.

SAINT GERMAIN, CHRISTED ONE OF THE AQUARIAN AGE, WAS FRANCIS BACON

So you begin to understand how the one mind of our beloved Francis Bacon influenced the course of Western civilization and laid the foundation for the New World, the new science, and the golden age.[4] Realize that many who walked the earth in his life* took on the very profile of his soul. Think of it, and think of the one who has in his heart the preknowledge of becoming the hierarch of the Aquarian age.

Think of your own destiny. Think how Saint Germain, therefore, did write down all of those molecules of word—coded, ciphered— demonstrating the interactions of light and darkness in the human scene and on the stage of the world.

Thus the lessons of the parables now become the plays of Shakespeare, which you ought to know far better than you do. Let lovers, therefore, of Shakespeare teach, demonstrate, act, and show the magnificence of the transmission of a teaching of the Christed One of the Aquarian age.

Realize that in the absence of Francis Bacon, this world would be several octaves lower in awareness, in enlightenment, and in illumination. This must tell you something about the genius of the

*lifetime

mind that has its correlation in the genes of the body—and the genes, focal points of the seed of Christ.

It ought to tell you about the power of God in you! It ought to tell you about the power of thought and the power of the aura! —and the negative power of idle thoughts and indulgences and nasty and subtle feelings that tear from you the momentum of your service and light and ability to change the planet.

It ought to tell you something of the meaning of the descent of Saint Germain and the ascended masters into your very presence and how the power of God is just as powerful to work evil as to work good—and it depends upon the *genes* of the mind at any given moment.

BE WARRIORS OF PEACE

There is a reason, a very good reason, to be vigilant. And it is love. Not a universal love that is difficult to define (as difficult as catching a mist or a vapor) and therefore a love that fails to specifically "love one another." No, there is a love, there is a reason in love. And it is for the very person of Saint Germain himself and for the person of the chela that you guard the heart and let it not be troubled[5] or trembling for fear.

Peace I place in your *heart* this day! Two thousand years hence from my promise, I bring Peace to the hearts of lightbearers who will sustain the vibration of Peace and not turn it to anti-Peace and the momentum of unreality and illusion concerning the sword that guards the way of Eden.[6] That ought to tell you something about Peace.

Do you think that the covering cherubim would fail to guard the ark? History illustrates that when man violated the Law, having been told not to touch the ark of the covenant, when man did so to steady that ark, he was struck dead.[7] By whom? By the covering cherubim who guard the ark and the mercy seat.[8]

Therefore, sometime, somewhere the angel of the Lord must

say: "Thus far and no farther! If you cross the line of the Holy of Holies, the fire will consume you and your malintent."

Do you think that the cherubim who guard the way of the Tree of Life with a flaming sword would fail to use that sword if confronted by the hordes of hell? Do you think that that sword is a decoration? I tell you, beloved ones, that sword, turning every way, does keep the way of the Tree of Life. And our legions know how to wield the sword.

We would make you warriors of peace.

The world has attempted to cast in the role of Gog and Magog the United States of America and the Soviet Union. I say, *Nay!* They shall not so cast America in that role, nor shall they cast the lightbearers and the freedom fighters of Mother Russia simply because the fallen ones are engaged as the Adversary in locked combat. They will not, therefore, personify Uncle Sam and lightbearers as being equally involved and in balance with the aggressions of the sinister force.

Yes, they have mounted. They have mounted their campaign against the world in the Soviet Union. This we know. But they have also mounted their campaign against the light in America.

We will not confuse the fallen ones and their archrivalries and the oneness and the union of the children of light! This nation America was dedicated by the Great White Brotherhood to bring peace and freedom, the Christ consciousness and the golden age to the world. And the Soviet Union was dedicated by the Black Brotherhood to be the force to prevent that from happening and to put down world peace.

We know that there is darkness in both nations, and we know that there are lightbearers in both nations. But so long as the malintent and the evil of the Soviet Union is as it stands, therefore it must be recognized not only as the enemy, but the *Enemy* with a capital *E* and *Darkness* with a capital *D*.

And therefore, let us cast out the betrayers of the Word in

America, and let the American people who enjoy the freedom to do so rise up and expose the betrayers of the Word in this nation, that the Union may be drawn, that the crack in the Liberty Bell might be *healed,* and the genius of freedom and creative sons of light might know the meaning of the oneness and the strength of the One Sent.

Let the members of the I AM Race worldwide, including those who yet live behind the Iron Curtain, understand the great gathering of the elect[9] and the coming to America of those light-bearers who will stand to defeat the world totalitarian movements within and without and universally manifest.

Let us draw the lines! Let us be clear in our definitions! And let not words convey metaphysical ideas that have nothing to do with God-reality. Let not the invocation of the word *Vietnam* therefore bring down upon the people a definition of "failure at war" and therefore "never again." Let not these words that describe only specific circumstances, manipulated and controlled by the fallen ones, therefore dominate the *free, disciplined,* and *inspired* thinking of the sons of God today.

We deal not with Vietnam today! We deal with the realities of life in this year in other nations—whose complexities and circumstances have naught to do with that particular moment in history.

Blessed ones, who fears to think? Who dares to overcome the automaton trembling with fear that resorts to computers to make the decisions of life and death? Who fears to be creative? Who fears to evolve a new policy of peace, a new approach?

We shall not be caught in left-wing or right-wing rhetoric! We shall not be aligned with those who think because they repeat words and slogans they have solved the problems of the age.

THE MISUSE OF LANGUAGE AND THE DARK CYCLE OF PISCES

This is an age of the misuse of language—and of violation of the Word, if it were possible. And therefore, language, instead of cups of consciousness of the angels themselves, has become a device of manipulation and conditioning. There are words in this language whose original meaning has been so lost that I would no longer use those words to convey to you mighty truths, so colored are these and so charged with hostility and "instant" ideas that are based on fear.

I tell you, the Dark Cycle in Pisces[10] has so colored and burdened the people (combined with anti-God-mastery, anti-World Teachers on that two o'clock line) as to make the children and youth of this nation bereft of a true understanding of life. Even their courses in literature and history are colored and turned and revised to reflect again the political thinking of the day.

Beloved ones, there is scarcely anything taught today that is not colored with a fear that therefore succumbs to simplistic ideas. You cannot reduce two and a half million years of karma and the betrayal of the fallen ones and the final age of Armageddon to simple ideas of peace and war, or freedom and anti-freedom.

CHILDREN OF EVERY NATION NEED TRUTH

Know this, beloved hearts: that the youth and children of every nation need truth. They need logic. They need a sound understanding of *reason* and how to move from a basic premise to a conclusion in life. The children are not taught how to think, how to analyze, how to investigate. And therefore, they move on the sea, a turbulent sea.

And who stands in the midst of the classroom in the local high schools and elementary schools? Who stands in the midst of my children to say, "Peace, be still!"?

The children are agitated when they themselves were not agitated. They are agitated by the fears of an adult world. Little ones are burdened by issues for which they are not prepared to make independent decisions. Thus, they are locked into the thinking and the decisions of their elders before they have evolved their own internal Christhood to understand "Come, let us reason together, saith the LORD."[11]

Let us understand that our laboratory of Montessori International is the most important cradle of the New Age civilization. Our correct alignment, organization of materials, fastidiousness in the creative as well as the initiatic path on behalf of these little ones is to set the course of illumination for this age. Let us spare not whatever it does take to see to it that our method, our courses, our subject matter fill the need, that these children may become shepherds, chalices, leaders because they are also followers of the living God.

Blessed hearts, you cannot lead an army with no leader. No leader ever became leader without the full training in discipleship and the hierarchy of the archangels. The dearth of leadership everywhere is the indoctrination and programming of the educational systems—of the soul away from the inner Christ. And the spirit of Luciferian independence has made every man a law unto himself.

And therefore, where is the Union? Where is the recognition of the lightbearer? We send the lightbearer, and he is maligned and condemned, for his brothers are jealous. And therefore, not acknowledging the light in him, the light within themselves is gone out.

Beloved hearts, it is not too hard a miracle for God to send shepherds and leaders! The problem is that when they are sent, they are slain, they are murdered, they are persecuted, they are tormented until their very psychology is altered and, in the course of a lifetime—unless mighty strong in the LORD—they lose either the desire, the inclination, or the ability for leadership once endowed.

How fragile, how delicate is the alchemy of the Holy Spirit working in the members of the soul. Therefore, understand that the Lord will bless you as you recognize, regardless of all attitudes of the world to the contrary, that we have endowed the messenger and the teachers and parents and all who participate with a golden flame of illumination to illumine the world's children.

Why did Gautama, our Lord, select this one flame to transmit in the hour of the passing and the ascension of the first messenger?[12] Was it not that out of understanding and the illumination of the heart and the teaching of the world's children would come a new race and a new civilization?

Why, beloved ones, *indoctrination* is the name of the game nation by nation—and a people who think they are free yet think only according to what they have been told by those whose thinking is not aligned with God.

THE PROFILE OF FREEDOM ETCHED UPON THE AMERICAN PEOPLE'S SOULS

How can a nation and a people evaluate what they see in mass programs of indoctrination and in strong visuals to move their emotions and align them with fear[13] if they have not the developed mooring within of that Cosmic Christ? Why, beloved ones, we must *skip over* these genes, undeveloped genius, and go right to the heart of the soul.

And therefore, the American people know from within. They do not even know how to articulate their own conceptions of freedom, but by the grace of Saint Germain and the indomitable will of his heart to raise up this people, the profile of freedom is etched upon their souls, and in their breast there beats a heart of freedom and a fervor. Sometimes it is misplaced, sometimes hitched to the wrong chariots, but these ones, beloved hearts, at least retain a sense of freedom when the logic of freedom has been taken from them.

Then you have outside of the schools the brainwashing and indoctrination of a false theology. This theology teaches that Armageddon will come and therefore "do not resist it"—passive expectancy. An expectancy that is a doctrine of final ends is upon a segment of this nation's body of believing Christians who have accepted the inevitability of nuclear war as being equal to and therefore the manifestation of Armageddon.

"Since Armageddon was prophesied," they say, "we can expect to see a nuclear war in our day because this is the end of the age—and until it occurs, Christ will not come." And therefore, they have *fallen* into the ditch of the *false* logic that in order for me to come in the Second Coming into their life, they must first experience a nuclear war.

This, too, is a matrix. This, too, is a pattern. How can we, therefore, give unlimited light of the Holy Spirit when it must be pressed through the mold and the sieve of this conception? Why, the more light we give to that mentality, the more it will *will* the war upon the earth and also the inevitability of mass death and the belief "There is nothing we can do about it but wait, and even if we die, we will be caught up in the rapture of the resurrection with the Lord."

This is passive expectation that puts a fiat on the earth. And therefore, the demons do fulfill the decrees of their doctrine, and these decrees go forth as a mindset, as a human will. And they are as powerful as the momentum of prayer and light that may be coursing through those individuals because of an innate devotion that does perforce draw down that light.

MAKE KNOWN THE REAL TRUTH OF MY MISSION

Thus you see how free will must be tethered to the Christ mind and that that *leap* must be assisted. The gap must be closed by embodied teachers who will explain by the logic of the Logos these steps of the Law and how they have gone astray from my original teaching.

I plead with you in this hour to make known the real truth of my mission in Galilee and Judaea and all the words that I spoke and the meaning of my parables and of the prophets who went before and of John the Baptist.

They do not understand the message and therefore they have determined that in order to update the message, they must now borrow from Karl Marx. The Pope so believes[14]—and his priests and many Protestants. As unbelievable as it might sound, you also know it is fact.

The message of the eternal God through my heart was and is complete for the Piscean dispensation. And that very message itself —not complete in the written word, but the totality of my message— is the foundation for transition into the seventh dispensation that is made known by Saint Germain.

If they would but read what they have, they would find a way out from a dead doctrine and dogma! But they cannot even read the printed word without it being precolored, preconditioned. Their minds are preconditioned—their hearts, their souls. Therefore when they hear a certain passage, beloved ones, that passage automatically means and has for them the conviction of a doctrine that has been taught since they were born.

When a doctrine is sealed, such as the phrase "Jesus died for your sins," it becomes a law that no longer has an understanding, such as proper nouns that were originally taken from words but the proper nouns no longer are thought of in the context of their original meaning because they are everyday words. Thus, everyday statements of the Bible no longer are thought through, and only those who have escaped that indoctrination freely think and understand and are receptive to the Holy Spirit—the Holy Ghost who will reveal unto them all truth[15] and give the true interpretation of holy scripture to your hearts.

DWELL IN THE REALM OF THE MIND OF GOD

The very fact that you know that I have tutored by the Holy Spirit your messenger since childhood and in previous lives, the very fact that you know that I have spoken and interpreted the Word, the fact that you know that when you hear the interpretation you *know* it is true should enable you to conclude that you also may be God-taught by the living Word with you—your own Christ Self.

It is *not* an exclusive gift, but to receive the gift requires receptivity and the pursuit, the desire, the love of the gift—therefore loving to be tutored more than all these other things and distractions.

Thus you have learned of passive expectancy as the evil that founds on earth the magnetism that magnetizes the forces of hell and their aggressive manipulations. There is only one way out of the dilemma, and you know it—and that is to skip over the push/pull action of right and left and relative good and evil. It is essential, beloved ones, that you dwell in the realm of the mind of God.

Seal yourselves, seal your lifestream from the crosscurrents of light and darkness in the relative sense. Enter the power of Almighty God and his Light, beloved hearts, and know that only the absolute Light can swallow up the absolute determination of the dark ones to destroy God on earth and in heaven. This is their design.

BECOME A PILLAR OF FIRE,
THE SEALING COVENANT OF YOUR VICTORY

Realize that the reason we teach a principle of absolute Darkness or absolute Evil is because some have chosen to embody a 100 percent determination to use their light misqualified to destroy God in his little ones. These are not petty errors or relative mistakes that are correctable. Absolute Evil incarnate is defined as the total dedication of the individual to Darkness, to Evil, and to world destruction.

They will not tell you in so many words. You will only know them by their fruits[16]—by their vibrations, by their actions. It would be well for you to be deaf or to turn off the sound of your television and to read only the vibration and cease listening to the words and then discover who is who—who is who in America, who is who in Mother Russia.

Beloved ones, I can tell you the formula. It is absolute Good as a pillar of fire where you are as the individual. It is not relative good as a good human being, but absolute God-good as Christ incarnate that does not move up and down and wane, but is steady —that takes the light and accumulates it and does not squander it.

This force in you will swallow up and defeat absolute Darkness incarnate.

Whether on the battlefield or not, wherever you are, the pillar of fire that you become allows the archangels to defeat the fallen angels who are absolute Evil incarnate. Remember this each day:

This day I AM begotten of the LORD!
This day I AM the Son of God!
This day He has said unto me:
"Thou art my beloved Son.
This day have I begotten thee."
I AM begotten of the LORD—
    the I AM THAT I AM Elohim.
I AM the Son of God in the earth.
I AM the Son of God in heaven.
I AM a pillar of fire!

I AM a fire infolding itself of the mighty I AM Presence, and therefore I AM the dissolution of worlds of evil and of absolute Evil incarnate.

This is the light of Almighty God that does defeat the Adversary by universal transmutation, by the accelerated fires of freedom, by the mighty sword that does keep the way of the Tree of Life in the garden of God.

I AM a mighty flame!
I AM the action of the flame of the ark of the covenant.
I AM the sealing light of the Almighty in the earth.
I AM the Son of God.
I AM the Holy Grail, the vessel of the Godhead.
And therefore, where I stand
ELOHIM OF GOD, ELOHIM OF GOD, ELOHIM OF GOD
do swallow up the anti-Elohim, the anti-God, the anti-Father, the anti-Son, the anti-Holy Spirit, and the anti-Mother!

Where I AM THAT I AM is the mighty pillar of fire. And so, descend, my mighty I AM Presence, my beloved Christ Self!

I accept the gift of *Peace* in my heart.

I accept the gift of *Peace* in my soul.

I accept the gift of *Peace* in my mind,
    in the science of the spoken Word.

I accept the gift of *Peace* in my throat chakra,
    in my power center.

I accept the gift of *Peace* in the all-seeing eye of God
    anchored in my third eye.

I accept the gift of *Peace* in my crown chakra as
    Cosmic Christ illumination now.

I accept the gift of *Peace* from the heart of
    Gautama Buddha in the solar plexus.

By the mighty power of the Elohim Peace and Aloha,

I AM *sealed* in the Great Sun Disc,

I AM *sealed* in the heart of Peace,

I AM *sealed* in God's desire for Peace!

And I AM the binding of war and the warring in my members
and the war of Armageddon and the warfare of Gog and Magog.
I AM THAT I AM in me is the binding of the entire planetary
momentum of war of the Nephilim gods and the fallen angels.

I AM THAT I AM.

I AM in the heart of the Prince of Peace,

And the Prince of Peace is in my heart.

I AM the manifestation of Elohim *here and now!*

I AM in Christ and Christ in me.

And therefore I AM *He!* I AM *He!* I AM *He!*

I AM the One Sent to embody that Word. And so long as
I AM in the world, I AM the light of the world!

In Jesus' name, I AM a joint heir of that universal Christ.
I AM where I AM, and I AM the Light of Almighty God—the
absolute Light of the Godhead where I AM that does swallow up
the absolute determination of the fallen ones to destroy that Light.

And therefore, it is no more! And Alpha and Omega where

I AM, *complete,* do move therefore against the Gog and Magog arrayed against one another in this world.

And I AM no part of their struggle!

I AM no part of their strife!

I will not lay down my life for them or their causes or their manipulations or their international monopolies or money funds.

I AM the determination of the Almighty God to be a freedom fighter for Saint Germain, to defend Saint Germain and the I AM Race and the light of God and the light of freedom—but I will not lay down my life for the corruption on this or that side of the ocean.

For I AM the Living Witness!

I AM the Son of God!

I AM the pillar of the resurrection fire that does swallow up death in victory, that does swallow up hell.

And therefore, I walk with God and I AM that God in manifestation, and I will not stray from the inner alignment of my own crystal cord and mighty River of Life.

And I will *listen,* I will *listen,* I will *listen* as I walk and talk with God. I will be the receptivity and the expectancy of the descent of *light! light! light!* every hour of the day, every hour of the night.

I AM *light! light! light!*

I AM light in eternal manifestation on earth as in heaven. And this world is full of light! This world is full of the light of victory because I stand, because we stand, because we are one in the Great White Brotherhood—as Above, so below.

Therefore, I declare and *we* declare the victory now!

And earth is swallowed up in victory.

Earth is swallowed up in light.

Earth is swallowed up in the mighty Cosmic Christ illumination of the age!

I AM with Maitreya in the mountain.

I AM with Saint Francis in the streets of the cities.

I AM with the Holy Kumaras, with the mothers of the world, and with the incarnating Christed ones.

I AM with Gautama Buddha for God-government in every nation, and I AM in the heart of Jesus. I AM in the heart of Jesus, and Jesus is in the heart of me.

In the name I AM THAT I AM, I seal my prayer in the heart of beloved Mother Mary this day, who will intercede for me before the throne of the Father and the Son and the Holy Spirit.

Beloved Mother Mary, so intercede in my behalf that even my own world is swallowed up in the victory of light and all remaining human creation and karma and the dweller-on-the-threshold is bound and judged and held in abeyance until the Great Law shall then take it—take it up and consume it and consume the scroll of the record—and I walk free in cosmos as a free spirit and citizen of cosmos, and time and space are no more. And I AM in me— I AM THAT I AM—is the victor over death and hell, worlds without end in the Matter cosmos.

As Above, so below—in the name of Alpha and Omega, *it is done!*

Thus I have given to you, my beloved, the sealing covenant of your victory and light and for that preparedness in the now, sharper than the two-edged sword.[17] For I, Jesus, desire that you should understand the nefarious activities of darkness in this moment to overturn this nation and the lightbearers everywhere before they become wise and disciplined and understanding that the victory is to those who maintain the perpetual watch.

YOU CAN BECOME A CHRIST

Watch and pray that ye enter not into temptation.[18] For the light given unto you must not be turned to darkness by neglect, by a thief in the night, or your own vulnerability due to ignorance and naïveté.

I do not say that any of you, my beloved, are malicious. But deeds done by ignorance can have malicious effects upon the children of light. And therefore, recognize: the most deadly enemy of all is the habit of human ignorance that rests in its own ignorance and does not desire to know and to learn and to study—to keep abreast, to be aware, and to watch and pray.

We shall have our victory as long as you remain watchmen of the night and watchmen of the day.

Through the hands of my servants, I serve you now Communion, and I bless the bread and the wine in the name of the Father, the Son, the Holy Spirit, and the Mother.

["Onward, Christian Soldiers" is played during Communion.]

You can become a Christ! This is the true message of this revolution in higher consciousness, which is in the *now* even as Maitreya is in the very chalice of the moment of the beating of your heart.

O my beloved, the essence of my teaching has always been and ever shall be: *You can become a Christ!*

I have just now proved it to you by transferring to you the bread and the wine of my Christhood, of my mission—the very heart of hearts of myself.

Take the seed and multiply it. Let it grow and come forth. Welcome the hidden man of the heart.[19] Let him be hidden no longer, for the veil in the Holy of Holies is rent in twain and standing before you is the high priest of your own Christ Self.[20] Therefore, know him face-to-face and be at peace.

My Peace I give unto you. My Peace I leave with you. My Peace I sustain. My angels of Peace are the sustaining presence of the power of Peace to seal the earth from all deadly intent. So in Peace, command:

Peace, be still!
Peace, be still!
Peace, be still!
Peace, be still!

Thus direct the command into the very core of each vibration of anti-Peace, and be not forgetful to challenge in the physical octave by the power of the word of Peace itself the very force and vibration of anti-Peace wherever you find it:

Peace, be still!

Thus, it is a mantra that the mighty Elohim has transmitted down the hierarchical chain of the Christed ones. Thus, this mantra has millions of years of momentum of the command of the LORD—Above and below.

Thus, when you recite the mantra in my name and give it as a perpetual prayer, you will find, as did my apostles, that the devils will be subject unto you.[21] Therefore, you may say and have the authority of my mantle and receive my mantle by the mantra:

In the name of Jesus Christ:
Peace, be still!
Peace, be still!
Peace, be still!
Peace, be still!

Thus, in so saying, you command the quadrants, the spirits of nature, and the angelic host will be enlisted in your service. Therefore, stand back and let the LORD be the victor in battle. Let him go before you, and watch and see his salvation with you, my beloved.

November 24, 1983
Camelot
Los Angeles County, California
ECP

CHAPTER 15

*I AM ... in this moment become a whirlwind
of sacred fire to swallow up darkness. ...
I AM the fire of Christhood and I AM congruent with
all hearts where the threefold flame does provide
a chalice for the acceleration of resurrection.*

THE MISSION OF JESUS CHRIST FULFILLED IN THE SEED OF THE WOMAN

I AM the Prince of Peace. And therefore I take dominion in the earth. Though my kingdom is not of this world, yet the kingdom that is the consciousness of my Christhood is lowered this day into this world by the chalice ye have provided, by a perpetual prayer without flaw—saving that which is intrinsic itself to the human nature.

The vessel has been filled with light—thy vessel and my own. And the turning of worlds, Above and below, is the very process whereby the kingdom does descend into the fiery hearts of the faithful. And by its presence in their hearts, they also ascend.

Thus, earth draws nigh to heaven as heaven enters earth, and in the very process there is a Mediator and there is mediation. For at that center, at the center band of the meeting ground, so the Christ consciousness does intensify. And in its intensity, there is manifest a greater judgment for the binding and the removal of that darkness that is anti-Christ and therefore can no longer dwell where it has dwelt.

For the kingdoms of this world are become the kingdoms of our Lord and of his Christ—our Lord Sanat Kumara.

You have given him the key to the city and to the kingdoms of this world. For every lifestream from every root race and every authority of group karma of the nations has ratified, *will* ratify, and will participate—past, present, and future—in this ritual for the confirmation of the white fire in the Middle East. Thus, on land and on sea, as in the ark of the covenant itself, as in the ark of Noah, so we have manifest the glory of the Lord as you have called it forth.

I AM come, therefore, as the witness of the miracle of light. And I say, O God, now I speak, now I invoke before the altar of the Mother and the altar of the Father—as Above and so below. I AM Jesus and I AM in the heart of the earth, in the heart of my disciples, and in the heart of my messenger.

Therefore I say, my causal body, through my own, does now intensify the cloud over the Middle East[1]—and in it and through it. And therefore I stand, and I AM in the full fire of the resurrection flame!

And this power of the spirit of the resurrection that I AM does, indeed, in this moment become a whirlwind of sacred fire to swallow up darkness, and legitimately by cosmic law does accelerate in this moment the casting out of the anti-resurrection forces of the laggard evolutions who have no part with the white fire and the fiery core of Alpha and Omega that is based in the Middle East,[2] that is focused by Serapis Bey, that is the great power of the ascension flame.

Therefore, at the vibration of the resurrection, at the two-thirds level of the pyramid of life, I AM the fire of Christhood and I AM congruent with all hearts where the threefold flame does provide a chalice for the acceleration of resurrection.

THE LIGHT DESCENDS FOR THE PURGING

I AM the light of the LORD God in the prophecy given unto Daniel. And I AM the awakening, by the power of the resurrection, of the souls of the earth—some to everlasting life, and some to everlasting contempt.[3]

Beloved ones, let it be as the light does descend. For so it is, so it always has been, and so it shall be that the concentration, the focalization of light is for the purging of the body of God, is for the purging of thy body and of the Holy City and of all races and of all kingdoms and nations. And thus, the righteous receive the quickening—and the wicked, also. And as they are accelerated, they are bound! And their karma does cause them to forfeit, therefore, any further opportunity to move against the light of God on earth.

Therefore, by the process of the selective judgment of the Lords of Karma, there is a binding action this day, there is the light of Elohim—and one is taken and another is left.[4] And there is the binding of those dark souls that have perpetrated and perpetuated the energy veil upon this planetary body, weaving their astral weavings through the Middle East and tying all corners of the earth to that Nephilim conspiracy and control.

Therefore they are bound! Therefore they are taken!

THE FULFILLMENT OF MY MISSION, THE SEALING OF MY CAUSAL BODY IN THE EARTH

O blessed hearts of the living flame and of the living witness, I AM THAT I AM. I AM the eternal light.

I AM the light of the Ancient of Days. And I AM standing in the earth and my Electronic Presence does intensify that of my own. And I have also placed my feet once again upon that walk of the fourteen stations of the cross in the city of Jerusalem.

For there I did anchor, two thousand years ago, my fiery coil for the judgment of all who violate the union of Alpha and Omega, the Christ and the disciple, and the Woman and her seed in each of those fourteen points of the law of the ladder of Cosmic Christ illumination unto the seed of Sanat Kumara.

Understand, therefore, that I came to the darkest point upon the planetary body to bring the light, to bring the judgment, to stand before the very fallen ones that have moved against the lightbearers ever since. Now is the ratification of that judgment of the Son by the light of the seed of the Woman—the chelas of the Guru Sanat Kumara in the earth.

Thus, Alpha has proclaimed it in me! Thus, Omega does ratify it through the messenger and the chelas!

Thus, Alpha and Omega seal now the action of my mission, and the fulfillment of the hour of that mission is come. And the hour of the fulfillment of my mission is at hand for the sealing of the judgment of the earth.

Understand, therefore, that my declaration of my cause, my witness unto Truth, my manifestation of the light of the world, my judgment, my resurrection, my healing, and the miracle of life —that very stated purpose, that very life lived is not fulfilled or completed until the two-thousand-year dispensation is sealed and is sealed in the body of lightbearers who now wait and do receive my mantle as I received it from Elijah.[5]

So now you receive it from me, from Elisha, to your very own heart. And you understand that it is the laying of the foundation for your forward movement into the age of Aquarius.

Beloved sons of the Most High God, beloved light of the eternal Great Central Sun, I therefore do make known to you this day the *sealing*, the *sealing*, the *sealing* of my causal body in the earth, as that kingdom come on earth as it is in heaven!

YOUR MISSION, AND THE DISPENSATION OF AQUARIUS

Realize, then, that your mission is founded upon the Rock of the release of my causal body, for which you have provided a vehicle, your very own vehicle, in this day and in this hour. Thus, beloved hearts of light, as you have prepared, and receive that portion that you are able to receive, so it is the passing of the torch of my dispensation unto the two witnesses, unto your lifestreams.

And now you will receive from the heart of Saint Germain the very fiery coil of the dispensation of Aquarius. And that mission, beloved ones, will not be complete until two thousand years hence, you also [to] stand as ascended beings to release unto those who yet abide as unascended ones the full-gathered momentum of your reason for being and your attainment in the higher octaves of that two-thousand-year dispensation.

And thus it is, and thus it ever has been for the fulfillment of the mission of the two witnesses of every age. And those witnesses, beloved hearts, become therefore in manifestation, signed and sealed as your own twin flames. Alpha and Omega within you witness unto the Truth, dispensation after dispensation, until you yourself stand the living Word and the living Christ to bequeath your momentum unto those who have been the vessel for your Christ attainment.

Therefore, understand the necessity for keeping the vigil and sustaining that mounting, that building, that spiraling momentum for the physical chalice to be built in these sessions of the sacred fire —to contain the cup of light and to receive a transfer not only from myself but also from other hierarchs of light whose hour is come for the fulfillment of their mission after so many thousands of years, where the Great Law does necessitate that they once again deposit that momentum of light in their unascended chelas.

Therefore, watch and pray and entertain strangers, for thereby some have entertained angels unawares.[6] Watch and pray and realize the very purpose of the vigil of the hours in the building of your own forcefield of light. For all that which you send to the nations and all that which you give must by cosmic law return to your aura. And therefore, many of you are building, as it were, the forcefield that is akin to that of the Goddess of Liberty, the Mother of the nations who does hold the flame of liberty for them.

And you will find that one day the Goddess of Liberty will also come and speak to you and deliver to the hearts prepared and uplifted that fiery torch and that Book of the Law for the nations of the earth, of the I AM Race. And you will understand why you have been called to keep the vigil of the hours by the masters of the Great White Brotherhood, by the Darjeeling Council.

In the fullness of my desiring, therefore, I have come and I AM with you, and I AM with you alway, even unto the end of the age.[7]

THE SEALING OF THE JUDGMENTS OF ALMIGHTY GOD

Uriel beloved, Gabriel beloved, Michael beloved, Zadkiel beloved, Jophiel beloved, Chamuel beloved, Raphael beloved: come forth now and let there be the sealing of the judgments of Almighty God throughout the circumference of that area known as the Middle East, which I do draw now by the power of Sanat Kumara as the electronic fire rings of the Great Central Sun.

And therefore, within that ring there shall occur, beloved hearts, the activation of light and a holding action so long as Keepers of the Flame continue to seal and ratify, *seal* and ratify, *seal* and ratify the action that has been fulfilled this day.

Therefore, these services and the recordings of these services become the matrix for the twenty-four-hour vigil of the Christ Mass and the season for the holding of the balance in the white-fire core of the earth. For it is the sign marked of the cosmic cross of white fire for the descent of the Manchild. It becomes the cradle, therefore, of the birth of the living Word, symbolically and actually, as in your very own heart.

And this is the reason for the attack of the fallen ones in that area of the earth. It was to put out the light of the Son of God, and it remains as that purpose—to put out the light of the sons of God.

And therefore, let the infant and the Christ Child be sealed! Let the mature sons of God be sealed! Let the souls of light in incarnation be sealed! And let there be the protection of the white-fire core of the Middle East.

I remind you therefore, beloved ones, that the focus of Alpha and Omega in the North American continent lies in the twin cities, and it is the counterpoint of that forcefield of light in the Middle East. Therefore let us renew and rededicate our twin focuses to the victory of the Godhead and to the holding of the balance of America —the Americas, North and South and Central America. And let this hemisphere now be bathed in the same light invoked for and on behalf of Lebanon this day. And let it take place in all continents.

And let the earth now be sealed in the light of the Keepers of the Flame. And let it be the perpetual prayer of angelic hosts and the Christ Selves of each one that earth might truly be accelerated and raised a niche in the cosmic initiation—the *i-niche-i-action*[8] of the Lord Christ and the living Word.

I, Jesus, am in the heart of the earth, in the very sacred heart and sacred fires of my disciples. Therefore be *sealed* in love! Be *sealed* in harmony! Be *sealed* in the fulfilling of the Word! Be *sealed* in Elohim!

Let not your hearts be troubled. Ye believe in me. Believe also in God. Believe also in Elohim! Believe also in the saints ascended! Believe also in your mighty I AM Presence and Christ Self as that "God with you"—the Emmanuel incarnate.[9]

So be sealed in the living light—the light of Maximus, the light of Elohim, of Central Sun Magnet—and let earth be sealed in Elohim in this hour.

In the name of the living Word, I AM Jesus Christ.

I AM alive forevermore in the mind and heart and soul of my witness in the earth, in the heaven!

I AM alive forevermore in the faithful and true witness of every disciple indeed!

December 4, 1983
Camelot
Los Angeles County, California
ECP

CHAPTER 16

*We come to assure you that every prayer and
thought and feeling, every heart's desire and effort is
rewarded exactly by the power of light and the magnetism
with which you enfire that prayer and that desire.
Thus, . . . heaven will accord to you a return,
and that also multiplied by our hearts.*

THE VOW OF THE
MINISTERING SERVANT

O eternal light, we come! For we are the Law of the One.

Sharing the office of the World Teacher, of Lord Maitreya, we do hold the balance from time to time as the Alpha-to-Omega. Serving, therefore, as the Giver and the Receiver, alternating in the mighty rhythm of life, we portray the balanced manifestation of the heavens and the earth—the knowledge of Matter, the understanding of Spirit; the Alpha descent, the Omega rising; the Master, the disciple; the Guru, the chela; and the wholeness of the divine polarity to be outpictured between yourself and the beloved one who is your Guru.

In the cradle of life, in the very alchemy of the soul's experiment in the laboratory of being, welcome to our hearts, O diligent ones! Do be seated in our love.

Jesus and Kuthumi. From not so many circles of devotees do we hear our names linked together in prayer. We are grateful, for this affirmation of our being confirms our witness and service as World Teachers. To be known as Teacher, rather than saviour (or even rabbi or guru or master) gives to us the entrance truly of those who come but to teach.

The offering of our teaching is the giving of our gift of Self and Selfhood. All that we know and are has come from Above

—and also from below in the sweet flowers of the field and the outpicturing of the stars. All that we are is all that we teach and may impart. And as we, too, empty our chalice to give of the teaching that I AM—*Elohim*—so we are also filled with the teaching of our Teachers, entrusted to us until our own disciples may be brought to the level of our table, sharing with us the Christ and the Christ consciousness, able to receive from the Source whence we derive our own offering.

We are here, therefore, to assure the students of our Ascended Master University that you will, therefore, according to the great law of the circle, always receive in return and multiplied that which you have laid upon the altar, that which you have given specifically to our hearts as sponsors of this quarter as well as to the Almighty and the universal One.

We come to assure you that every prayer and thought and feeling, every heart's desire and effort is rewarded *exactly* by the power of light and the magnetism with which you enfire that prayer and that desire. Thus, the very life and life force that you can bring to bear in the communication with heaven will accord to you a return, and that also multiplied by our hearts.

DO NOT LEAVE OFF YOUR STRIVING

As practice makes perfect, the most important instruction we can give to you is this: do not leave off your striving, your studies or your pursuit, your love-endowed decrees—dynamic in the Word. Do not leave off the search, thinking that because now you have reached a level of initiation, you have found the All.

There are many doors that you must pass through, and many keys that you must earn the right to be given and to use until one day you may find that the master key is yours because you yourself have mastered your own life and therefore wrought the key from your own heart fire.

To be given the key to one or another retreat of the Brotherhood is to be given the formula for entering in to that ascended master's consciousness. This formula may not come to you unless you yourself have in some way formed and formulated that molecule of light, that mathematical formula that equates in the negative polarity with the positive polarity of Spirit.

When the pupil is ready, the Teacher appears! When there is in your heart a certain fire, and you see him then face-to-face, and you say, "At last, you have come!" it is not really such a surprise, for, you see, we could only come into your life by the corresponding presence in you of the Disciplined One who magnetizes our love.

When you come to understand the meaning of our Word, you will see that it is possible to discover by holy prayer, by a fervent reaching to the heart of the Central Sun, that counterpart of Elohim or archangels that you might carry as a locket in your own heart. You can discover the matrix to be the counterpart of the Great Divine Director. And you can become such a ministering servant, endowed with the Holy Spirit, that people will feel our presence as the universal Christ even when you enter a room.

YOUR INDIVIDUALITY IS COMPOSED OF MANY FREEWILL CHOICES

See how it is necessary for the soul to be humble enough to desire to be the mirror of God on earth rather than to forge a separate identity and to be praised for that ingenuity. Your individuality is composed of many freewill choices to fill in on earth your selection of a vast design of your own Godhood. The random motion of the disciplined electron teaches always, by sign and symbol, the nature of freedom and free will, operative within the confines of a known formula—even though it may not be known by the observer.

Thus, beloved, there are infinite possibilities for the individualization of the God flame when that one stands beneath the Sun in his zenith, directly under the I AM Presence, and therefore without shadow, in the purity of perfection's divine flow:

Here I AM!
I AM Omega in the earth.
I AM Alpha in the heavens.
I AM *Being.*
I AM *Consciousness.*
I AM *Identity.*
I AM the One,
And I AM the twain.
And I AM the All-in-all!
I AM the sacred fire breath.
I AM the heartbeat of God and of his Cosmos.
I AM a soul swimming in the sea of Life.
I have direction—
I move by the stars!
I understand the magnetism of stellar bodies.
I AM caught up in the LORD's Spirit.
I AM found one and in that Spirit in the LORD's day.
I AM in the Love of the Father,
And the Father with me is the Love of the Son.
The Son in my heart is the true presence of
     the Holy Spirit, and his Spirit does enlighten me.
I AM in the heart of the Mother,
And the heart of the Mother is my own.
I AM a soul born to be free!
I AM a pillar of living fire!
I AM now in this hour in the heart of the bird,
And I AM truly in the heart of the Sun—
     the great Great Central Sun behind the sun.
These things I know, for I AM WHO I AM.
I stand upon the Rock of my own Christ Self.
I see my God face-to-face!
     I AM in the spherical being of the Divine Monad, and I move
in the earth as a spirit gathering more of the eternal Spirit unto itself.

I AM the instrument of God's all-consuming fire,

And I AM the consuming of world hatred where I AM.

I AM the filling of the hungry, the healing of the broken-hearted. As I AM clothed upon with His raiment, so I AM the supplier of every need.

God in me is the Doer, and I AM caught up in his doings.

In his comings and in his goings,

I AM the One and the Law of the One operative by Love.

Sealed in the chalice, I become the chalice. I become the bread and the wine. And my LORD does give of me, as Holy Communion, saints unto the saints. The Alpha, the Omega that I AM THAT I AM is given for the life of all.

I AM in Christ and Christ in me.

I AM Alpha and Omega, the beginning and the ending of my journey in time and space.

God in me is the formula for my return, my pathway, my initiations, my transfiguration—even unto the crucifixion, even unto the resurrection and the ascension to eternal life.

God has ordained my descent and he has ordained my *ascent.* Therefore I stand in the earth, one with the World Teachers, and I offer this my pledge to be the vessel of the Holy Spirit, to be the Ministering Servant—drop by drop to share the blood of Christ and the crystal fire descending, little by little to *see* the new birth of the Son of God.

In the name of Helios and Vesta, the Father-Mother of this system of worlds, I serve these evolutions by the path of the World Teachers.

I serve with Maitreya, Gautama, Sanat Kumara.

I AM my God in action!

I AM my Christ in action!

I AM here and now, God in me, the victor over death and hell! I take my vow before Almighty God in the Temple Beautiful, and I descend once again to the valleys and the cities and the nations and the dominions.

I go before the LORD to prepare his coming,
And the LORD goeth before me to show the Way.
I AM in the heart of the earth!
I AM in the heart of all who are in need—

    all who are poor, *all* who hunger, *all* who weep.

For I AM the Light of the Logos,
And God in me shall fill their cups.
I bear the pitcher of the LORD.
I AM one in the Spirit of the Aquarian avatar.
I AM in the light of the new dispensation.
I AM that dispensation!

By the authority of the World Teachers, I serve to set life free
—I serve Saint Germain. I AM born free!

And I will plant my flame in this earth as a flame flower that
shall produce after its kind until all the fields of the world's consciousness blossom with the flame flowers of the light of the
Buddha and the Christ and the Mother where I AM.

This earth shall know a better day because I walk in it in this
hour. Conscious of my God Self, in the knowledge of who I AM,
I plant the seed of Christhood and I keep the Watch.

I *will* endure unto the end of the cycles of my personal karma
—*and* of planetary karma.

I will endure with Kuan Yin!
I will endure with Mother Mary!
I will endure with the Christ Self of all!

And I *will* receive the crown of life by the grace of the living
Saviour, the Cosmic Christ of all.

I seal my vow at the altar of the Holy Grail. And I recite it in
the hour when some may falter—and perhaps when I may fear or
doubt the next step. I will take my vow to the World Teachers, and
I will affirm my being and my source as the Central Sun.

O Great Central Sun, I send the call!

I have gone forth to fulfill that vow in the beginning and

I take my vow in the ending for the return.

By the light of Omega, I AM made whole!

And I enter again the initiatic ladder of light.

O my Father, O my Mother, I AM coming Home.

Now I shall go forth to work thy works on earth—to be a Christ, to seal in love those in pain and sorrow.

I will be Thyself here until the hour of thy call, O God.

I will hear thy call!

Thou hast promised it. And I will answer.

I AM thy son, and I AM ascending to the One!

O my Father, O my Mother, I AM coming Home.

Our gift to you, each disciple of the Word, is this prayer and vow to unlock the door of thine own Selfhood. Each time it is reaffirmed, it will draw again another ring of disciples of the World Teachers. And you will see how the vow taken becomes the magnet of the Central Sun in the heart of community. And you will also see how the vow not taken and the test failed will remove that subject from the very circle of community.

There is no bond—not of community, not of star systems, not of nations, not of families—without the presence of the commitment of the soul, the dedication of the life*stream*—the stream of life as the crystal cord descending from your I AM Presence.

When you take the vow, it is the sealing of the matrix, and all of your *light* does flow through the vow! And all of the *intent* and the *willing* and the *desiring* and the *loving* and the purpose of your soul moves to fulfill, by the power of your word, that which is the very depths of your consciousness.

Therefore, beloved hearts, receive then, O students, the cape of Saint Germain and the mighty star signifying your level of initiation. Angels of the World Teachers, angels of Nada and ministering servants go with you, and with all of you who are our disciples indeed.

O living flowers, immortelles, we will leave you to grow in the earth, to show all of the beauty and the wonder of God until the call of Alpha is heard by you and by us, and this lifetime may be rolled up as a scroll. Then we will come, for this is our vow to you: to pluck the flower of your soul for another field of service—service in the LORD and service of greatest need.

ENTERING IN TO GOD'S KINGDOM

Thus, beloved, may our promise to be there in the hour of transition now take from some of you an inordinate burden as fear of death. And may you understand that our promise is that you shall see us face-to-face and know the entering in to God's kingdom.

As you sow, so shall you reap. Therefore, may your sowing be that this entering in shall be the everlasting entering of the ascension in the light. As you send forth light, so shall your harvest be. The things that shall now come to pass in your life are more your option than ours, more your free will than the Father's preordained destiny. It is all up to you, as the Omega, to decide to return to Alpha.

We have shown the Way. I AM is the Way! And the Way ye know. Enter in to heaven here and now. May your heaven be on earth. May you know the Way, find the Way, *lead* the Way, and *be* the Way.

Children of the Sun, remember always the Law of the One. Remember, you are from the Sun—from Above, and not from beneath.[1] Go not after those or imitate those who are from beneath. Their ways are not our ways.[2] Their ways are the ways of the death of the soul.

Be free! Be free! Be free!—eternally free, O my blessed.

Precious love of the heart of Maitreya, in his service we serve you. Come now, disciples of the Word. Let us be up and doing, for the cries of the needy are even at the door.

December 11, 1983
Camelot
Los Angeles County, California
ECP

CHAPTER 17

*My victory is the same yesterday and today and forever!
And that victory, as the Spirit of the LORD God, is able to
consume, as with a mighty fire, the plague of death and hell
that has been unleashed against the nations in this era.*

MY VICTORY, YOUR VICTORY

Sons and daughters of the Most High God, my brothers and my sisters, welcome to my heart of hearts this day of the LORD's resurrection within you! I AM Jesus, drawn from among you two thousand years ago that I might remain with the remnant of the called-out ones, with those who have pursued with a zeal the prophecy of my coming and its fulfillment in this age.

The centuries have turned. The fire of my heart is ever with you. And my victory *is* the same yesterday and today and forever! And that victory, as the Spirit of the LORD God, is able to consume, as with a mighty fire, the plague of death and hell that has been unleashed against the nations in this era. To what end?—that the people might behold the consequences of the actions of the wicked, and that they might know also the fruit of the worship of the one God, and that they might know that the laws of God are just. And so, that which is sown must be reaped.

The conditions in the world today are not far from those in the time of Zephaniah.[1] Let it be understood that the children of the light in every nation have gone after other gods. They have worshiped their idols who have come out of the pits of hell, who have taken incarnation from the astral abode and who have been the false gods and the pied pipers who have led them into war and the pride of ambition and the cult of the money beast and the abuse of the body by all manner of drugs and intoxicants and that which is poison and that which does stimulate and aggravate that which comes from beneath.

Beloved sons and daughters of heaven, *you* who have descended as souls of light from the mighty I AM Presence, *you* who know the meaning of the ascent of those who have descended, *hear* me! For I cry out in the midst of the city. I cry out in the midst of a people who like to rejoice and sing and play and laugh and would take now the fire of my victory as a day of rejoicing. But I say to you in the full spirit of the resurrection, it is also a day of warning, a day of inevitability of the coming of the LORD in judgment.

Those who understand the mysteries of the law of God, the mysteries of his judgment, will also understand that these infractions of the Great Law of God, of Elohim, may not go unchecked by the very law of God. This law is impersonal and yet very personal, beloved—for the LORD chastens whom he loves.

As in the time of Josiah and the imminent coming of Nebuchadnezzar and the actual destruction of the city, so there are some who have aligned themselves with the seed of the wicked, who have gone after the gods of Baal, who have sacrificed their seed in abortion, and who have unwittingly committed the rites of Satan in this act of abortion, even as they have thought that they were the liberated ones.

What shall come of an earth and a body and a people who have denied their God in these little ones—even the least of these my brethren? I have said it before, and I say it again: It is the hour, therefore, in 1984 to look to the judgment of those who are the pagan ones, those who have professed me and the name of Christ and yet have denied in action the firstfruits of that love.

Understand, therefore, that all that is different between the hour twenty-five hundred years ago and today is this: it is that the ongoing cycles of prophecy have also fulfilled my coming on earth and the deliverance of grace and the restoration[2] to all of the sons and daughters of Seth and the very remnant of Eden—the opportunity to face the Christ and live again, to receive the grace, even of my Father, even of Maitreya, Gautama, Sanat Kumara. And therefore, the fruit of the Tree of Life has been offered in my life and mission, such as you know of it.

Beloved hearts, that grace that I give unto you is sufficient unto this hour of world challenge if you will understand that for the prophecy of salvation and fulfillment and of resurrection of the whole mystical body of God upon earth to be fulfilled, it must be fulfilled on earth through my brothers and sisters, through the remnant of life who have taken the responsibility in this very hour to walk the earth as the anointed ones, *fearless* to claim Christos as their Real Self.

You who have remembered also the prophecy of Jeremiah and the coming of The Lord Our Righteousness[3] have truly and surely identified the name of the LORD—the one worship and name of the I AM and his Son with you—as that Lord Our Righteousness, your own beloved Holy Christ Self.

Now, therefore, you have seen the divine approbation of this path of light. You have seen the blessing of yourselves as a remnant and all people of light worldwide also who have followed the teaching of the Word as the remnant who would keep the sign and be an ensign unto all people of the return to their own mighty I AM Presence.

THE REMNANT WHO WOULD KNOW THEIR GOD

Beloved hearts of living fire, I now place my sacred heart one with your own, each and every one of you, that you might *feel* the burning in the heart that every true disciple must know on this day of days. And this is the fire that shall try every man's works, giving you, measure for measure, the understanding of personal karma that must be swiftly balanced by your call to the violet flame, which is the dispensation of the LORD God unto this remnant. And it has been the prophecy all along that the remnant who would know their God, keep his name, and worship according to the spirit of Truth would be saved in the hour of the LORD's day.

Blessed hearts, I give you not a timetable, but I give you an understanding of the Law itself and the mechanics of the Law. When you see these signs, the same signs of the false gods and the idolatrous generation and the rhythm and the rock out of the very pit itself and the idols taking the virgin light of the children in so many ways, when you see the wars and you see the threat of that nuclear war, and then you hear the prophecy of the devouring of the land, of man and beast so that all is consumed, recognize that it is an equation of divine love and of mercy that must utterly consume the forces of anti-God, that the children of the light might live.

Now I say to you, one and all: *Stand* in this land embodying the spirit of prophecy! *Sound* the warning, also, that this people ought to turn from their idols of materialism, their self-indulgence, their toying and destroying of their bodies in all manner of excesses and introverted practices that are the perversion of the mighty sacred fire of their God!

Let them turn and call forth the light!

For, you see, Gautama Buddha has also come. And great saints have walked the earth in these twenty-five hundred years, giving the teaching East and West for the *calling*—the calling of the people who are the sons and daughters of God to keep the sacred fire burning, that in the hour of the turning by the hand of the LORD God, when the judgment should be upon the seed of the wicked and their Cain civilization, the remnant should indeed survive.

And that remnant itself—as Moses did plead before God for mercy, as I myself have pleaded for mercy, as my Mother has pleaded, and many children in recitation of prayer have pleaded for mercy—the compelling of the light of the LORD by his own on earth does mitigate, by the mercy and grace of Christ who lives in you, that oncoming karma of the Dark Cycle of planetary momentums returning to the very point of their inception.

That energy demands resolution. It is the energy, light, and consciousness, heart and mind of God that the people themselves have gone against, that they have abused, creating out of that substance their fantasies, their illusions, their astral darkness, their imaginations and fears. All these things have created the same dark clouds at inner levels. Swirling around the earth, milling almost as cattle, these are the creations and the creatures of the minds of a people gone astray.

RECOGNIZE THAT THIS IS YOUR HOUR

The hour is an hour of a cosmic interlude. It is a moment when those who are the decisive ones may take a step, intensify the Word. Recognize that this is your hour and the *sound* of the coming of the sons and daughters of God who are co-creators with him. It is an hour when a people can rejoice in the Immanuel, can recognize the Godhead in their temple dwelling bodily as it has and ever shall within me.

It is an hour when the sons of God ought to deny their priests and ministers and rabbis who deny them that sonship, that divine oneness—by whose power the false prophets and the false preachers are cast out of the temple as the moneychangers who have no part with me or my life or my living message or my presence in the earth. For they have hid for centuries my true mission, my journeying to the Far East, my love of Maitreya, my oneness with the eternal Brotherhood of light, my own desiring for the oneness of the Teacher. And they have denied, therefore, the entire chain of light of cosmic beings who have preceded me in the demonstration of the Law.

Thus, they have drawn a circle of orthodoxy and they have kept out not only the living God but *you,* my brothers and sisters, who could no longer be stifled where there is preached another time the doctrine of the only Son of God, the doctrine of death and hell and fire and brimstone and eternal damnation for the children of God. I tell you, it is the lie of Satan and the seed of the wicked.

MY DAY IS A DAY OF RESURRECTION UNTO ALL PEOPLE OF GOD

And I take this day and this occasion to speak to the earth and to declare to you that my day is a day of resurrection unto all people of God and people of light, not by a vicarious atonement but by working the works of God, manifesting the Word, and walking this earth in the masterful presence of your own I AM THAT I AM.

Drinking the full cup of the joy of the resurrection, you shall know this same God with you that is in me. And truly I stand for the rescue of your souls that have been condemned and judged for taking the name of God, I AM, to yourself when truly it is the gift of God to you as the all-power of heaven and earth given unto every son of God.[4]

Let this be the turning of the centuries. For I send my legions of sacred fire for the *consuming* of ignorance, the *consuming* of the lies of the false priests that have been told again and again and again all through the centuries and therefore have been used to thwart, to set aside the ongoing march of victory of the lightbearers in this age—who must come to the place of dominion to turn the tide of the world karma of the fallen angels in the midst of the people, who have led them astray in the governments of every nation.

I tell you, they have led America to the very brink of self-destruction by neglect, by failure to cast out this trafficking in drugs, by failure to hold to the honor of God, to keep the temple free, to keep America strong and of strong mind and heart by a necessary and proper education, by the pure food and water and the pure religion undefiled, which has been my teaching for centuries.

Beloved hearts, this nation belongs to God and to his people.

Let strife *cease* from among those who love me, one and all! I send the mandate of Alpha and Omega. And by the power of the mandate of the LORD's host, I say, let them be bound! *Bind,* therefore, the demons out of the pits of hell who send division and schism in the churches and deny the true and the living Word!

I say, let there be the *binding* in the astral plane and the *binding* in the physical plane of those individuals who uphold the doctrine of Satan and of Antichrist and do not liberate the sons of God to manifest the pure nobility of the light of the Holy Grail!

Lo, I AM that Grail! Lo, I AM that Christ with you! I will not be silenced, and the true God of the people shall not be removed into a corner. And the true teaching of the path of your resurrection and ascension shall be made plain—*shall* be made known to you! And the people who have walked in the darkness of the false hierarchy shall see and know the great light of their own I AM Presence.

YOU CAN STAY THE HAND OF WORLD DESTRUCTION

I AM sending forth the will of God as prophecy that yet remains to be fulfilled by the science of the spoken Word affirmed by you whereby you *rejoice* in the LORD's judgment and in his Word for the stripping of all of this error and all of this doctrinal darkness that has kept the people from the real encounter with the Adversary who must be put down. For, I tell you, beloved hearts, whether in or out of government, wherever the sons and daughters of God speak his name and pronounce the Word, wherever you are in the vigil of the hours, you can stay the hand of world destruction.

You must teach the children of light the strategies of the seed of the wicked in every way: polluting the minds and bodies, hearts and souls, preventing them therefore from having the soundness of mind, the strength of soul and heart and body not only to entertain angels, not only to know the truth of the strong spiritual teachings of the age, but also to wage the warfare of the spirit with the archangels, joining them daily for the binding of the world forces of tyranny moving into this hemisphere, moving into the mountain of Almighty God.

Precious ones of the light, it surely does hang in the balance—the future of civilization—and never was free will and the exercise thereof more important unto Almighty God.

You who know what is true, what is right, what is holy, and what is the mystery of the science of the spoken Word have seen and known and observed truly that the power of God is available, that it does go forth sharper than a two-edged sword for the binding of those invisible forces as well as the very physical forces moving against the children, moving against the youth and those of every age.

Let us consider, then, that in the days of Josiah the king, in the days of Judah and the last hours of Jerusalem, there was no knowledge or presence or dispensation of the Saviour—not because my time had not yet come but because they had forsaken the truth of Moses, my preachments as Joshua, and every opportunity and dispensation and covenant that had been offered since the days of Noah! Had the people been ready, the Messiah should have appeared.

Thus, understand in this hour: The dispensations have come—and lo, the cycles have turned. It is the hour of Aquarius, and the descent of the Holy Christ Self has taken place. And the Great White Brotherhood moves among the people. But I tell you, beloved hearts, as surely as there came the rejection of my mission, as surely as Rome and the Roman church this day has *denied* the true reason for my coming, so it can come to pass that this dispensation of the I AM Presence and the Christ Self can be denied by those in the establishment of the World Council of Churches, and therefore denied to the very people who ought to rise up and be the prophesied remnant.

PROPHECY DOES TELL YOU WHAT CAN BE
IF THE PEOPLE AFFIRM GOD'S WILL

Understand the *meaning* of prophecy. Prophecy has never been a psychic prediction. It has never been ironclad. It does come to pass because the spirit of prophecy is *received* by receptive hearts who are the fulfillment of the LORD's prophecy by free will. Prophecy does tell you what *can be* if the people affirm God's will.

So it was, as I was given the opportunity to demonstrate the victory over death and hell, which had to be done in the very process of the judgment of the fallen angels who determined to destroy the Christ. Thus, I gave them my body to prove for all time and eternity that they have no power—neither over the body or the soul of my brothers and sisters who will hold steadfastly to the One and to being the mouthpiece of the One who has sent them, *even* the LORD God, *even* your mighty I AM Presence, *even* your Christ Self, *even* the Cosmic Christ and hosts of the LORD, *even* the Ancient of Days who has sent you as surely as he sent Daniel and Jeremiah and Isaiah and John the Baptist.

Lo, the Ancient of Days is present with you! Lo, his blessing upon you is here to raise you up as God's instruments! *Be* no longer burdened by the lie that you cannot, that you are a sinner, that you are not worthy, that because you have committed wrongs, you may no longer stand in honor before the LORD God. I tell you, none of it is true! For God has said, and he has kept his promise, "I will remember their sins no more."[5]

If you have sinned yesterday, then today the LORD God shall wipe clean by the sacred fire your heart and body and soul and mind. If you will go and sin no more and therefore seal your heart in his, you will make that forgiveness permanent and forever, and not a stain or a blot can be upon you, and none of the fallen angels —no, not *one* of the fallen angels—will be able to take from you the purity of your *victory* and the victory of your pure soul in God!

Let them wag their heads! Let them condemn! Let them decry!

I have heard it for centuries. They have not stopped because I have ascended. They have blamed me for the false doctrine of Christianity and for all of the sins of those who call themselves Christians.

THE SOUND AND THE POWER OF THE SPOKEN WORD ALTERS MATTER, CONSCIOUSNESS

Well, I would also like to be blamed for the victory of the light of my brothers and sisters who have recognized the truth, who have not feared the censure of the world, who have dared to open the door of the heart and of the sanctuary of the Holy Grail, to enter in, and to let the angels hear the sound of the remnant that is the sound of the mighty mantra that harks back to the ancient temples of Lemuria, Atlantis, Venus, the Central Sun, and all worlds where the body of God has gathered in commemoration of the Word made flesh.

So the sound and the power of the spoken Word *alters* matter, *alters* consciousness, and is the alchemy and the great conflagration foreseen by Peter.[6] And therefore, the elements can melt; they shall melt. But I implore you to understand the perpetual prayer and meditation and the continuing dynamic decree to forestall those things that world karma projects on the screen of world conditions.

Beloved ones, never has there been a moment in history when the sons and daughters of light have stood with the power to turn an age such as this moment. May this Easter message be an inspiration and a *command* to the resurrection from ancient doctrine, falsehoods, and a prison house of a false theology.

I call you forth from the tombs of the houses of worship this day! I call you forth to be with me the flame of the resurrection and the life to all people on this earth! I call you to rise from death and hell, to rise to the eternal dominion!

Rise with the lilies!

Rise with the angels!

Rise with the sun!

Rise this day—I cry out to you! *Rise,* children of the light, and stand and affirm your freedom now!

[Congregation rises and shouts fiats of freedom.]

Hosts of the LORD, *hear* me!

I, Jesus, *cry* to the Father!

I *cry* to the Most High God!

Send now those twelve legions of my angels! *Send,* therefore, ten thousand legions more and rescue my own! For *these* are my body, *these* are my blood, imprisoned in every house of worship and in the streets and in the alleys and throughout the valleys and the mountains.

These are my body! *These* are my blood! *These* are my own—the persecuted, the put-down, the tortured and the tormented by those who have effected a world politic, a policy that is counter to the raising up of Christ and the defeating of the fallen angels and their serpent philosophy.

O Father, I *cry* to thee! Let the dispensation come! Let angels go forth and cut *free* my own! And let these who know thee and all who know thee in every body of God on earth come apart and be separate and find the way of the Holy Grail that I AM.

GO FORTH AND LET GOD SPEAK THROUGH YOU

Father, send thy light! Set free the people of God, that the daughter of Zion might rejoice and the name of the I AM Presence be known throughout the earth. For this is indeed the prophecy of Zephaniah for this very hour, and it is the LORD's prophecy! And it is the prophecy of your mighty I AM Presence, beloved, for your soul!

God speaks to you this day to rise and take dominion. Be undaunted. Do not be put down by the accuser and the condemner that causes you to be burdened and to forget for a moment that you are my beloved, my beautiful sons, my beautiful daughters, my noble of heart, my own who are myself in embodiment.

I AM in your heart. I would not leave you, for this is the hour and the purpose to which I came. It is this moment of God's glorification within you. So he said to me, so he says to you in this hour: I have both glorified my name in you, and I will glorify my name in you again.[7]

Therefore, accept the hour of the glory of God in you, and now fear nothing—neither death nor hell nor the fallen angels, their suits, condemnations and lies. Let every one of you walk in an upright heart.

By the grace of the LORD, forgiveness is come to all of God on earth. By the grace of the Ancient of Days and your mighty I AM Presence, I empower you as I empowered my disciples: Go forth and let God speak through you.

My servants and his servants, come into my own! Come into your own fiery destiny! Come into the awareness that you are the resurrected sons and daughters of God!

Let light prevail in this earth. Stand back and see God's salvation and his judgment of the unreal and all who have aligned themselves irrefutably with unreality. For only Reality shall live in the LORD's day.

Lo, I AM Real!

Lo, I AM the fire of Reality in you!

Lo, I AM Jesus!

And I have not passed through this crucifixion for naught. I have passed through it that you might *see* and *know* the truth that God is the Victor in you in this hour over that same seed who moved against me. And in this hour it is the prophecy and the decree that the LORD's judgment will fully and finally *bind* the persecutors of Christ in you!

Therefore, as I did, so do ye. Hasten the judgment by *being* the Christ, *knowing* Christ is in you, *knowing* you are fashioned in the image, your soul is a part of me, and the universal one Christ is the common loaf of our identity in God. This do. This say and know that I AM THAT I AM.

God be with you as you take up serpents in my name.

God be with you as you raise up children of the light and love them dearly as my own.

God be with you as you look around and see none other shepherd is there to take your place.

You are *here!* You have life!

I give you my heart. Be shepherds unto my children. I pray you, as I prayed to them in the final hours, *Feed my sheep!*

Feed them, my beloved. They need me. *Show* them my true face! *Show* them the face of their mighty I AM Presence. Let them live, and send the angel Michael to their side that they might be protected in the day of the Adversary. For he shall come. His day shall be short and even shortened by the Word of the elect.

Even so, the Elect One cometh.[8] And lo, I AM with you even unto the end of the world of illusion and the dawning day of thy *eternal reality* in my Father's heart!

Amen. Amen, my own.

April 22, 1984
Camelot
Los Angeles County, California
ECP

CHAPTER 18

*When there is about to become physical through dispensation
of the Cosmic Christ the renewal of the open door whereby
souls . . . may come and go from the planes of earth
to the planes of heaven and back again,
this is the open door of the coming of the golden age.*

THE MYSTERY SCHOOL OF
LORD MAITREYA

Consider the lilies of the field, how they toil not, neither spin. Yet I say unto you again that Solomon in all his glory was not arrayed as one of these.[1]

I address you, my beloved, as lilies of the field—and that for a cosmic purpose: it is the purpose of your ascension in the light. For this is the true commemoration of the Word where I AM THAT I AM in your midst. I commemorate the place that is marked by the sign of the cross of white fire, by the sign of every cross of every hero and heroine of all ages—in Flanders Field, on every battleground and beachhead celebrated in this hour as the point of courage of the hearts of those who have stood for truth, for freedom, and for peace.[2]

I celebrate the sign of that cross repeated again and again as the inner matrix of the love of the Father-Mother God, positioned as your own marker in time and space signifying the point when and where heaven and earth shall meet in thy life. For it is preordained—*if thou will it so.* If thou wilt fulfill the divine plan according to that will that is become thine own, then the cosmic cycle shall turn and you shall be at the point of light which I celebrate.[3]

THE RECORD OF YOUR FUTURE ASCENSION

Therefore, my presence with you in this hour signifies, beloved ones, that I stand beyond your ken or awareness visibly because I stand in the future of your own lifestream. If you had the perfect awareness of your I AM Presence, you could stand in that future today, but you are somehow wed to the present, and in the web of time and space a prisoner of the moment.

But I am not. I stand at the point where God knows that we are one (in actuality) in manifestation in the very flesh form, before the soul does leave that form for higher octaves.

I stand in the moment of your Victory of the ascension!

Why do I do this, beloved ones? I will tell you. Because in my Electronic Presence focused here tonight is the *record* of your *future* ascension! You can hear the sound of ascension's flame through my aura—now pulsating around you, now accelerating the light within your being, now freely increasing the light of your heart, bringing into balance the last remaining points of the threefold flame that were out of balance.[4]

Beloved ones, by comparison the roar is almost like the sound of the modern-day rocket—as you can imagine in the inner sound of your being what would be that comparable sound of the acceleration of every atom. If you could listen to the spin of the electron, the nucleus, the worlds within, you would hear that sound that has been heard in the firing of rockets on earth—excepting that it is a spiritual sound, it is a light of Alpha and Omega, and it is truly the welcome sound. For when the light begins to purr as pure mother-of-pearl within you, beloved hearts of living flame, day by day you know that this sound of the eternal *HUM* integrated in your being does increase, does uplift, does enfold you.

THE HOUR OF THE ACCELERATION
OF THE FOUR LOWER BODIES OF MARK L. PROPHET

I remind you of the hour of the cosmic gift when beloved Lanello stood in Washington, D.C., at the very altar and the LORD

God released the dispensation for the beginning of the acceleration of his four lower bodies unto the Victory of the ascension. Such an hour it was, for it was the beginning of the "lift-off" of that soul. And so it is necessary that these preparations be given.[5]

I tell you not that that is happening to you now. I tell you that you have a "preview of coming attractions," as they say. For that attraction of the mighty Great Central Sun Magnet is truly the greatest attraction on earth, and nothing can vie with it as the most powerful experience in your life when you begin to feel the pull like the mighty winds that blow in the valley and almost push you down the street as you walk in the road of life.

As there is the mighty pull and power of the sun rays and the forces of the elements, beloved ones, know that there is a gigantic pulling action of the Great Central Sun Magnet. This is that force that does take over in your life when you yourself surrender to that mighty flow of the River of Life that descends from the highest Himalayas and from the fastnesses of the Rocky Mountains and other mountain ranges of the planetary body.

That light that flows as a pure stream of God consciousness— when taken by yourself, when you ride its momentum, when you enter it, when you fear it not, when you argue not with the voice within—when you cease your rationalization and simply decide to be God in manifestation, there comes a moment, as you have been told, when that Light which you have served turns about and serves you.

THE HOUR OF YOUR COSMIC BIRTH THROUGH YOUR THREEFOLD FLAME

Then it is that you know the tugging of the string of your heart, the very impetus of Gautama Buddha, and you feel the momentum gaining of the pulsation of his threefold flame with your own. And you know that that cosmic birth must come to pass when the Lord of the World himself will no longer sustain and intensify your threefold flame on your behalf, but you will stand in the earth, in those hours preceding your ascension, on the power of your own externalized threefold flame—on the power of your own I AM Presence with which you yourself have become one.

You see, the evolutions of this planetary body have become oh so dependent upon the sustaining power of the threefold flame of Gautama Buddha.[6] In some cases, of course, it has given them a false understanding of their own level of attainment. For they have thought it to be their own threefold flame, when, in fact, it is the crystal cord of Gautama Buddha connecting to and nourishing their own threefold flame that does give life and fortitude and strength and creativity.

But this is the compassion, the selflessness of the Buddha. This is the way of the bodhisattva—unsung and unknown. And therefore, you see, many people do not exercise their hearts, their minds, their physical bodies, their talents. They rest on the oars of the Lord of the World!

Those, then, who are on the path of initiation realize that the way of the bodhisattva is the very way of the preparation for that day when the threefold flame—which by your devotion you magnetize, sustain, and daily empower from your own I AM Presence—is sufficient to hold the flow and the matrix of God consciousness where you stand. Little by little, the reinforcement of Almighty God through your I AM Presence does allow the withdrawal of the support (the lifeline) of the Lord of the World.

These shining ones in the earth who have risen to that level of the self-sustaining grace of the I AM Presence are truly that cosmic proof on earth—are truly unascended masters who bear testimony of the unfed flame and give the glory to God and to Gautama Buddha. And therefore, the office of the Lord of the World and his function in sustaining the threefold flame of every lifestream on earth is justified before the courts of heaven.

For, you see, if this assistance did not result in the God-mastery of some souls, it might be canceled. For if it becomes a prop and one that is a substitute for self-mastery in the whole world, then what does it profit a civilization or a lifewave? I make this very requirement of the balanced and expanded threefold flame, which is in fact your Holy Christ flame (i.e., consciousness), a part of your understanding of the requirement of the Lords of Karma that there be at least one ascension from planet Earth yearly to justify the continuation of the sponsorship of earth's evolutions by the Great White Brotherhood and of the dispensation of the Mystery School of Lord Maitreya.

DEDICATION OF THE INNER RETREAT AS THE MYSTERY SCHOOL OF MAITREYA

Beloved ones, having so prefaced my address to you, I come to the reason for being of our oneness in this Heart. For we are sheltered in the heart of Lord Maitreya. And he desires me, as his pupil, to announce to you that he is dedicating this Heart of the Inner Retreat and this entire property as the Mystery School of Maitreya in this age. [Tumultuous applause]

And I say it with you:

Hail, Maitreya!

Hail, Maitreya!

Hail, Maitreya!

Hail, Maitreya!

In his name, beloved ones, in his heart flame, so be seated.

I would tell you of our great joy and of the meaning of the securing of this place for the Mystery School. You realize that the Mystery School of Maitreya was called the Garden of Eden. All of the ascended masters' endeavors and the schools of the Himalayas of the centuries have been to the end that this might occur from the etheric octave unto the physical—that the Mystery School might once again receive the souls of light who have gone forth therefrom, now who are ready to return, to submit, to bend the knee before the Cosmic Christ—my own blessed Father, Guru, Teacher, and Friend.

Beloved hearts, the realization of this God-goal and the willingness of Maitreya to accept this activity and messenger and students in sacred trust to keep the flame of the Mystery School does therefore gain for planet Earth and her evolutions a dispensation from the hierarchies of the Central Sun. For, you see, when there is about to become physical through dispensation of the Cosmic Christ the renewal of the open door whereby souls—as students of light who apprentice themselves to the Cosmic Christ—may come and go from the planes of earth to the planes of heaven and back again, this is the open door of the coming of the golden age. This is the open door of the pathway of East and West, of the bodhisattvas and the disciples.

This being so, the planetary body, therefore, has gained a new status midst all of the planetary bodies, midst all of the evolutionary homes. For once again it may be said that Maitreya is physically present, not as it was in the first Eden but by the extension of ourselves in form through the messenger and the Keepers of the Flame. And as you have been told, this mighty phenomenon of the ages does precede the stepping through the veil of the ascended masters—seeing face-to-face their students and their students beholding them.

THE ETHERIC CONSCIOUSNESS— MORE PRACTICAL, MORE DOWN-TO-EARTH

All of the ascended masters' dictations over the years have been to that end. And with the inauguration of the mission of Maitreya in this century and then again in this hour, you see that the momentum of all ascended masters' dictations gone before does increase the momentum of light and the ability of some, and *not* a few upon earth, to actually maintain an etheric consciousness.

Though they may not be aware of it, their hearts and minds

tend to gravitate to the etheric octaves so apparent in the higher altitude and in the mountains and the snowy, fiery energies of the coolness of the mountains. For this fire of coolness is a stimulant to the chakras. It is a stimulant to the mind. It creates an acceleration of fire merely by the change of temperature of the four lower bodies.

And so, the net gain of this activity and those gone before under the sponsorship of the ascended masters is that for certain lightbearers on earth, life has truly become more etheric—and therefore, I say, *more* practical and *more* down-to-earth!

As this messenger has explained to you, it is the matter of initiation in the fire of the earth and the earth of fire—Capricorn as a sign of initiation transmitting to the sign of Cancer[7] this polarity of Alpha and Omega from the crown to the base chakra, from the mountains unto the sea, from the flame of the Father unto the Mother.

Understand therefore, beloved hearts, that this messenger has also dwelt in that etheric plane. And you see the result in the effort and achievement, accomplishment of the entire organization, because the fire of the etheric plane makes practical and energizes in a tremendous momentum all those who may dip into that higher consciousness.

The etheric consciousness and that octave is a part and parcel of your own Christ Self. By entering therein, by maintaining a fiery forcefield of protection as well as harmony, you can remain secure in that vibration and hold the forces of the archangels gathered around yourself as a mighty cloak of blue flame, so that the onslaught of the world that resents the intrusion of the pillar of the etheric plane can in no way detract from your life or bring upon you untoward conditions.

And so, you see, it is not only to *meditate* into the etheric octave but it is also to *be* there by daily God-mastery, transmutation, and the overcoming of the densities of the flesh that is the be-all and end-all of your path! (To *be all* of God in action and to *end all* human strife.)

THE PUBLISHING OF ALL ASCENDED MASTER DICTATIONS GIVEN THROUGH THE MESSENGER MARK L. PROPHET

Now, beloved ones, I have explained that all of the ascended masters' dictations preceding this hour have been as a spiral staircase leading to the moment of Maitreya's return. Blessed ones, because this is so and because in every dispensation the individual must mount the stairway of that initiation step-by-step himself— each and every one—we have charged the messenger to release all of the dictations ever given by Mark Prophet that you might mount the stairway of his mantle, of his many incarnations in the exemplification of the God flame of Maitreya and myself, that you may enter the coil of the ascension flame with him in every dictation and in the causal body of every ascended master who has ever dictated through him.

Beloved ones, we have therefore begun to prepare and will release momentarily four-cassette albums containing nothing but the continuous dictations of the messenger Mark—four ninety-minute cassettes beginning in the hour of his ascension and moving backward to the very beginning of his first dictation recorded.[8]

I cannot tell you what this will mean for the earth! You must experience it for yourself. As you play these dictations in your homes and in your automobiles, and as you play them again and again even while you serve or work or sing or take care of your children, you will come to experience the writing of the law of God (as it was spoken in living fire to Mark) on your inward parts—on the mind, the soul, the heart, on every chakra of your being, and finally every cell as these cells are flushed out and cleansed by prayer and fasting.

And you will notice how the mind follows the words and the cadences, until the day will come, beloved hearts, when you find yourself reciting those dictations; for you will *know* them by heart. And then you will know the meaning, "I will write my law in their inward parts."[9]

HEARING THE SPOKEN WORD
OF THE ASCENDED MASTER THROUGH
THE VESSEL MARK PROPHET

Blessed ones, in this twentieth century, by the technology available to this planet, you can actually *hear* the Word spoken by the ascended master through the vessel Mark Prophet and therefore hear the spoken word of God's messenger as though you stood before Moses when he delivered the Word of the Almighty.

And you must realize that the advantage is this: that though you may have heard Moses in the hour that he spoke, you were then less advanced on the Path, less aware, less charged by the violet flame and the holy light. Your vessels are crystal today. By comparison, they were earthen pots in those hours—and you had much to transmute.

And so it is, beloved ones, that *the spoken Word of the Godhead through a living messenger now ascended* may enter the inner ear, and you may rehearse what took place on the ancient continent of Lemuria long before the fall of the fallen angels when the mighty Teachers and the Manus[10] sat with you, one by one, and transmitted by an oral tradition in the ear, to the inner ear, the sound of the mantra, the sound of the Law, the sound of the Word. And it did quiver upon the eardrum and vibrate in the bones and register on the blood. And you were therefore *fashioned* out of the very Word of God spoken by the Manus and the Elohim.

In this day and age, therefore, you discover that in your listening to these dictations you will be fashioned anew, reborn as a new creature by the power of the ascending scale of these dictations. They are the fundamentals. They are the building blocks. And when you have heard all of these as the joyous lilt and rippling of the flame now grown to the size of your own body temple, and all of you has become the flame, and the Word has become all of you, you will know the meaning of the foundation of that power and build upon it and comprehend more fully the complex teaching released by the light of Omega through the Mother since the ascension of your beloved Mark.

FOOTSTEPS ON THE SPIRAL STAIRCASE

Precious hearts, your own Mother with you here could hardly contain her joy and desire to shout from the housetops this wondrous dispensation for the publishing of all of the dictations given through her beloved Mark—which dictations she heard, each and every one, sitting at his feet and (in the early days) running the tape-recording equipment!

Beloved ones, realize, then, that that listening at his feet was for her own footsteps on that spiral staircase. And therefore, she was formed and re-formed as the living chela. Having passed through those initiations, she was ready to take the community forward, built on the power of Alpha and the mighty thrust of the Guru Lanello—now to be concluded by that power of Omega that must mount the full momentum of the return by the ascension current of the evolutions of this planet.

Beloved ones, some have been burdened by the complexity of the teachings given since Lanello's ascension, and yet he himself has given them as his heart is a part of every ascended master who has spoken. Now then, when you assimilate this "body and blood" of the early releases, you will discover that all that has gone on since February 26, 1973, becomes crystal clear and is waiting for you and for your attainment. And you will truly understand the individual building of your pyramid of life.

By the very economy of the life of this messenger, we could, of course, not wait for the entire movement to arrive at the Gate. For this is a mighty movement of the people of God across the desert sands, through the valleys, into the civilizations and cities of the world, thence to return to that Promised Land of the I AM Race [the United States of America] and once again to find the security, as the security of Sinai, which you discover here in the fastnesses of the Inner Retreat.

Thus, when you consider the pilgrimage of tens upon thousands, hundreds of thousands of souls, some arrive in the beginning as a caravan of light and some are in the ending. And this line of the pilgrims signifies that as each one is able to assimilate, he is also able to breathe the rarefied air. He is able to come first from the physical through the levels of the planes of desire. Passing through these, there is a sharpening of the mind and the tutoring of the heart until the call of the etheric octave and the power of fire is such a magnet of mighty dimensions as to be greater than all of the pulls of the senses and the thralldom of this world and its warring and its warfare.

So, beloved ones, when all is said and done, you will find recorded in both the spoken and the written Word all that is necessary for any individual from any root race, from any lifewave sojourning on planet Earth to find his way back up the mountain of God, that holy mountain where once long, long ago some left off from serving Him and went down the mountain[11]—*down* meaning lower in vibration in the astral plane—and lost their way.

You who have regained the vantage of the mountain, the perspective of the purity that you find here, the clarity of heart and mind, neglect not to remember your cherished ones—your brothers and sisters, beloved hearts, who are yet caught and burdened and without knowing.

You will pull them out as we continue to pull you higher. And you will know truly what is the strength of the chain of hierarchy —how each link is forged and won and how those links cannot be broken, except by free will some lifestream quit the Great White Brotherhood; and then the hand of Maitreya undoes the link, removes that link and fastens the chain together again. And therefore, the chain of hierarchy moves on.

A DISPENSATION OF
GOLDEN ILLUMINATION'S FLAME

Beloved ones, this dispensation descends. And it descends in the fashion of a giant vessel, a ship—one that you would liken to

Noah's ark or the clipper ship of Maitreya. And it is all golden illumination's flame, almost as though it were floating out of heaven, signifying that the teaching is a vessel and the means to cross over to the higher dimensions of Gautama Buddha.

If you could only see into the etheric octave now—and I open your eyes in the *imagination,* the "eye-magic" of the inner eye—all of the hills and the valleys of the Inner Retreat and all of this property aglow as if in a perpetual golden sunset! Everything is cast in the golden hue, reminding you of that ancient yellow race that derived that coloring from their concentration on the crown chakra.

Thus, Lanto and Confucius and the Brothers of the Golden Robe mightily celebrate the hour when they can participate and assist me in giving that enlightenment, that education, and that teaching that has the instantaneous power of conversion because it comes from the Holy Spirit, it comes from the Lord of the World. It restores the memory. It shows what is obvious. It clears away the brainwashing instantaneously. And the mind perceives the deception and the carefully plotted subtleties of the conspiracy of darkness. These disappear and literally melt in this golden light. Thus, we anticipate that ministering servants[12] shall become teachers on a grand scale worldwide.

CHERUBIM WITH A FLAMING SWORD KEEP THE WAY OF THE TREE OF LIFE —CAUSAL BODY OF MAITREYA— AT THE INNER RETREAT

Accompanying, therefore, the dispensation is also the wondrous presence here this night that is always there "at the east of the Garden of Eden." So long as there is a single lifestream on earth with untransmuted karma, so long as there are fallen ones, there will always be the flaming sword that does keep the way of the Tree of Life in the center of the Garden.[13]

Thus, cherubim with the flaming sword, beloved ones, are positioned not only at the East Gate of Eden but at various points throughout this property. And that sword turns every way, and it does bind and judge those who come with malintent or with lust to take the land or the light or the freedom from our bands. Realize then, beloved ones, that you may invoke the power of cherubim and the flaming sword at any hour for the judgment and the binding of any and all who assail the cosmic purposes established here for your life.

FRUIT OF INITIATION: THE POWER OF ETERNAL LIFE IN YOUR HEART FLAME

Now, you understand that the Tree of Life in the midst of the Garden is the very presence of the tree of the causal body of Maitreya. And for you that Tree of Life is represented in the messenger, through whose body and temple and heart we transmit the fruit of the Tree of Life, which is the fruit of initiation—the initiatic fruit whereby you earn once again that which was lost, the power of eternal life in your heart flame.

Prior to receiving the initiations of the Tree of Life—the power of the Godhead dwelling bodily in you—there are preliminary initiations on this golden spiral stairway that you will meet and understand as you play and replay the dictations of the ascended masters through Mark. They are all there: the footsteps, the Path, the understanding, the *keys*. Let them sink in to your subconscious.

Unlike any other school or teacher-pupil relationship on earth, when you listen to those dictations, you have solely transmitted to you the presence, the power, and the wisdom of two ascended masters —the messenger ascended and the ascended master speaking. Thus the circle is complete of Alpha and Omega, and you need not hold back or protect yourself against human creation or human momentums.* You have fully and finally the ability to open all of your chakras to the Word and the release and know that no untransmuted momentums of any earthly teacher will be passed to you.

---

*. . . as you would in the case of an earthly teacher without the mantle of the Great White Brotherhood.

This is a tremendous dispensation, beloved hearts. And I trust that you whom we count as the wise students of the World Teachers will realize what a great opportunity is upon you to make your ascension in this age.

Thus, with greater light there is greater reinforcement of protection. But likewise, beloved ones, the many trees in the Garden—many more than those listed in your present scriptures[14]—were all for the purposes of God intended for twin flames on earth and to meet all of their needs. These many trees also represent a forest of devotees of light—each and every chela and pupil of Maitreya bearing the fruit of his own tree of life, his own causal body, extending with carefulness and self-mastery that portion of God whereby he might help and support, sustain, illumine, and love another.

So you may also identify yourself and your mission with the flaming sword as you give the calls to all of the seven archangels for the protection of this property, which becomes the experiment of the Great White Brotherhood in sacred trust, that once again a group of lifestreams so dedicated can withstand all opposition to the presence of Maitreya in the earth.

Beloved hearts, I tell you that those stories that have gone forth through Benjamin Creme regarding the coming of Maitreya in a certain individual are not true but of the false hierarchy.[15] And they are designed to discredit and preempt the true coming of Maitreya in succession, as has always been in the hierarchical evolution of the ages of planet Earth.

When I was in embodiment, I was the presence of Maitreya. As much of Maitreya as could be delivered to the people, he delivered through me. And it was a mighty work and a mighty delivery that has sustained millions these two thousand years.

In this hour, due to my ascension and the acceleration of lightbearers, "He that believeth on me, the works that I do shall he do also, and greater works than these—*greater works than these*—shall he do."

Thus, in the dispensation of the presence of Maitreya as the Coming Buddha who has come at the dawn of the Aquarian age, you realize that the greater works expected also means that the Law expects a greater portion of Maitreya and myself to be delivered in this age through this messenger and through the many disciples worldwide who keep the flame and in some cases are empowered beyond that power which was held by the apostles. This, beloved ones, is due to the turning of worlds and the turning of cycles— thus, not necessarily by achievement but by the wind of the Holy Spirit in your sails, by the momentum of the Great White Brotherhood with you do you deliver the presence of Maitreya to the world.

See, then, that Maitreya truly is more physical today than ever before since the Garden of Eden. For his withdrawal into higher octaves was due to the betrayal of the fallen angels and the acts of the fallen angels against Adam and Eve and others who were a part of that Mystery School.

Thus, the long scenario of the fallen angels and their devilish practices against the pure and the innocent have ensued. And one by one, each must come to the divine conclusion of the Return. Each one is accountable for leaving the Mystery School, and each one is responsible for his own return and his making use of that which is available and accessible as the divine Word.

THE SIGN OF THE PILLAR OF FIRE
—OLD FAITHFUL—
AND THE NAME PARADISE VALLEY

Thus, Maitreya is truly with us. And Maitreya would have this announcement made prior to the coming of Helios, that Helios himself might smile the perpetual smile of the sun, might wink and be joyous in laughter, that when he places his feet on this soil he will be placing his feet on that Mystery School of the Garden of Eden come again, marked by the sign of the pillar of fire, Old Faithful, and the name recalled in the naming of the *Paradise* Valley.

O beloved hearts, if you could only know the ordinations of God and the preordaining of his will and the divine grid held in the causal body of the Great Divine Director—if you could only realize how there is such a mighty grid of light that would hold you as tenderly as a violet or a forget-me-not is held in the forests! And you have but to mount each level of the grid and fit into the blueprint to discover daily a new horizon of new octaves of light you have not seen or known before.

This is my joy in the hour when the Christian world celebrates my ascension. This is the hour, as you know, when a cloud received me from their sight.[16] And I disappeared from that view and that scene and that episode only to continue my mission, for I have never ceased to serve, both in the physical octave and from the higher planes.

I bless you now, beloved, and I return to octaves of light where I am with Maitreya preparing, oh, preparing and softening the hearts of many to receive the greater light and the teaching. It is our prayer, as you have been told, that the earth might be held in balance because many more hearts leap at the opportunity to become the vessel.

THE LIVING FOCUS OF THE HOLY GRAIL OVER THE HEART

In the name of the Holy Grail that I AM, I place now in the etheric octave over this Heart the true and living focus of the Holy Grail quested by all knights of Camelot, meditated upon in the immaculate heart by all ladies of the flame. I place it here as a shining light, a brilliant focus that none will miss seeing in their finer bodies. And it in itself is the magnet of my body and my blood. It is the magnet of the teaching and the great mystery of the flame in the bowl—Spirit infiring, enlivening, and breathing the breath of Life upon Matter.

So may you be, may you do, may you go forth in my name and in the remembrance of my sweet caress as I place my hand upon your cheek, each one, and you remember how much I have loved thee.

Cherishment . . . O Morya El, thy precious word, "Well done." For these so cherish the will of God by thy example that Maitreya may receive them now.

May 31, 1984
Heart of the Inner Retreat, Royal Teton Ranch
Park County, Montana
ECP

CHAPTER 19

*Realize that "two-by-two" may be yourself alone
with God or the ascended masters side by side with you . . .
yourself with your Christ or your mighty I AM Presence. . . .
Realize that out of the causal body there does descend
the sphere of wholeness.*

CHAPTER 19

THE ORDER OF
THE GOOD SAMARITAN

And, behold, a certain lawyer stood up and tempted him, saying, Master, what shall I do to inherit eternal life?

He said unto him, What is written in the Law? how readest thou?

And he answering said, Thou shalt love the Lord thy God with all thy heart, and with all thy soul, and with all thy strength, and with all thy mind; and thy neighbour as thyself.

And he said unto him, Thou hast answered right: this do, and thou shalt live.

But he, willing to justify himself, said unto Jesus, And who is my neighbour?

And Jesus answering said, A certain man went down from Jerusalem to Jericho and fell among thieves which stripped him of his raiment and wounded him and departed, leaving him half dead.

And by chance there came down a certain priest that way. And when he saw him, he passed by on the other side.

And likewise a Levite, when he was at the place, came and looked on him and passed by on the other side.

But a certain Samaritan, as he journeyed, came where

*he was; and when he saw him, he had compassion on him
and went to him and bound up his wounds, pouring in oil
and wine, and set him on his own beast and brought him to
an inn and took care of him.*

*And on the morrow when he departed, he took out two
pence and gave them to the host and said unto him, Take care
of him and whatsoever thou spendest more, when I come
again, I will repay thee.*

*Which now of these three, thinkest thou, was neighbour
unto him that fell among the thieves?*

*And he said, He that shewed mercy on him. Then said
Jesus unto him, Go, and do thou likewise.*

Luke 10:25–37

Beloved Jesus:

My children, my disciples, you have called unto me and
I have answered. I am Jesus, Lord and brother. And may I say that
the term "Lord," as you call me, signifies that I have embodied the
Word—the I AM THAT I AM, the I AM WHO I AM. And
therefore, the Father dwelling in me as the I AM Presence with me
is the reason of this address: LORD—the one who therefore does
incarnate the Word "I AM."

I am your brother, for I am one with you, having come forth
from the same Father and out of the same womb of the Cosmic
Virgin—the universal light. I am brother and we are one. We clasp
hands in recognition and cherishment, brother for brother, sister
unto me.

I speak to you that you might understand that my path was
not lived alone unto myself, but as the very proof that all things
that I was and became and did and did do are unto you the challenge of the hour and the very present and practical possibility.

Therefore, let us together, as elder brother with brothers and sisters on the Path, with disciples of the one ineffable Word, prove that each and every one who has descended from God[1] may in this very hour turn about and face the living Christ and become that one—that light, that Christic power, that wisdom, and that love.

Let us defeat the lie of a false theology that even in this hour would put down, by prayer itself, this servant who does preach to you the real and living doctrine of Moses and the reason for being of my life: It is for the redemption of the whole house of Israel—each one who has come forth sponsored by the very light of Sanat Kumara unto Abraham and his seed and all who are the sons of adoption[2]—that is, who have also believed on the name I AM THAT I AM[3] and accepted the transfer of light, which is the initiation of the Cosmic Christ ongoing in all generations.

And therefore, the elect are those who have elected to be that blue-flame will of God on earth and thereby, in the magnet of the flame, to draw down once again the light lost or the gift of identity in the monad of the I AM THAT I AM.

Beloved hearts of living flame, I tutor your souls. I come to worship with you. I stand with you, imparting the light of the Holy Spirit that is in this hour for your transcendence over the things of this world that are unreal—over its darkness and every foul thing pitted against the body and the soul and the mind.

THE SOUND OF THE WORD IS THE RESCUE LINE

I am here to alert your perceptions to the dangers of darkness and to alert the mind to the ever-present availability of the Cosmic Christ in answer to your call. Do not forget to make the call, my beloved. For as when drowning you cry for a lifesaver or help, therefore understand you must give the cry unto God, speak the prayer, affirm the name—for the sound of the Word is the rescue line, the vibration that quivers in cosmos.

The power of the spoken Word is the single link to eternity, forged and won through the threefold flame in your heart that does expand God's consciousness within you each and every time you speak the name I AM. Therefore say:

"In the name I AM THAT I AM, O God, Help me!"*

Therein lies the call. Therein lies the opening of the door. Thus I knock. Open the door and speak:

"In the name I AM THAT I AM, O God, Help me!"

TRUST EL MORYA AS YOU TRUST ME

Do you understand, beloved hearts, that the Holy Spirit is come as Comforter and Helper? Therefore, in the understanding of yourself as his instrument, I direct you now to the address of my own servant son, the beloved ascended master El Morya, who has been to me both son and father in many centuries of our service to earth.

Beloved ones, El Morya was himself embodied as Abraham, as you have been told, who brought the tithes to Melchizedek.[4] Beloved hearts, he was embodied many times over in the defense of the universal Christ, whether as Muslim or Jew or Buddhist or a member of the order of Zarathustra. This flaming one is indeed worthy to teach you the path of Christhood, indeed worthy to be called Father and to be known as friend of light and brother of Christ and truly as captain at the helm of The Summit Lighthouse.

I promise you that this teacher of light will never lead you astray but compel you higher only to avoid unnecessary delays and pitfalls on the Path. Thus, trust him as you trust me, for we are one.

I give you, then, the Chief of the Darjeeling Council, who would speak to you of the possibilities and duties of the hour.

Ever I remain at your side "in the garden" and in the highways of life, your brother on the Path.

---

*Fiats of the LORD here are to be used by the disciples of Christ as mantras and dynamic decrees in the science of the spoken Word. Keepers of the Flame are encouraged to compose their own affirmations based on the teachings given in the *Pearls of Wisdom.*

Beloved El Morya:

My beloved brother—my Lord and Master—I am privileged to address your own who have become my own chelas of the will of God through their devotion to your heart.

Thus, beloved, I address you and the ascended hosts of light assembled. I address Keepers of the Flame worldwide. And I have come in this hour, and this time I find you ready to receive me and I am grateful. I am grateful for your preparedness and the place prepared, which sparkles at inner levels with a certain crystal of the mind of God, signifying the coalescing in form by the process of crystallization of the ideations of God coming forth from your causal body and the inner blueprint.

Indeed, this conference in the sacred fire—the *Healing through the Emerald Matrix,* as you call it—is for the turning of worlds and the focusing on the physical octave whereby we literally leave no stone unturned in the building of the City Foursquare. For the hour of the building is nigh, and the building begins with the building of the temple of man. And you are a builder, a co-builder with the Lord of the World Gautama Buddha, with the Lord Christ, and with all of the ascended masters.

Welcome to the fraternity of the saints of heaven! Welcome to the Spirit of the Great White Brotherhood! I, El Morya, salute you from Darjeeling and from this place where I am one in the heart of the messenger and one in the heart of every devotee of the will of God present with me.

Now we come, therefore, blessed ones, to make that love of the will of God most practical in its application. And this is the meaning of delving into the physical atoms and compelling those atoms to *submit* to the will of God! And I speak of every cell and atom of the mind. I speak of the members of consciousness. I speak of your households, your affairs, your offspring, your businesses, and your livelihoods. This is the Matter universe and all attainment of the sacred fire must show forth as the abundant life and as God-mastery, even in the way of the saints who remember the vow taken of old: We seek no continuing city here.[5]

Beloved ones, the building of the pyramid of Self is an inner building, but the outer equation must comply, must show fruits, must set the example that others may follow you all the way to the heart of the Sphinx—to the very heart of the living Guru whom the Sphinx represents and to the heart of the flame within the Great Pyramid that is on the etheric octave (and is not held in the pyramid of Giza, which remains the shell of its former focus and function due to the misuse of its energy by black magicians and false gurus and false chelas).

Therefore, seek not that which is of the earth earthy[6] nor that which is of the flesh, but endow Matter with a living Spirit and compel its members and atoms to surrender the false gods and their cursings and their misuse of the science of the spoken Word.

Beloved hearts, consider the writing concerning the going forth of the other seventy.[7] Consider it in the light of the path of the ministering servant. Understand the duties and the disciplines and the self-mastery involved.

I WOULD TUTOR YOU IN THE
PATH OF DISCIPLESHIP UNDER THE LORD CHRIST

Would you be the ministering servant in answer to the call of the Ancient of Days and your own heart's love for all whom you meet? Well, then, I would tutor you in the path of discipleship under the Lord Christ. I would show you the way of the binding of serpents and of devils. I would show you the way of exorcism. I would give you a new impetus of dispensation of light—for you who have applied all the teachings that have gone before.

And for you who have first entered our doors in this hour, I say, welcome to the heart of hearts, for this is indeed a living Word and a living Work. We bid you welcome thrice—in the name of the Father, in the name of the Son, in the name of the

Holy Spirit. And we bid you welcome in the name of the universal Mother, whose handiwork thou art by the heart of Elohim.

Beloved ones, healing must be, perforce, the healing of the whole man—and this you know. But how the healing of the whole man is to take place must be set forth, for we have given it here and we have given it there. Now let the work of those becoming ministering servants be the compilation of that teaching in this hour, that all may know how to be the best servants of the universal Christ, how to be brother of Jesus, how to have the heart's oneness that is also for their protection.

It is interesting to note the great victory of these seventy and that they always went two-by-two in the action and polarity of Alpha and Omega, therefore demonstrating—as they gave forth their prayer in the science of the spoken Word as Jesus taught them —the momentum of the whole. And it is the whole that is invulnerable and inaccessible to darkness. Thus, when the two are one and the Alpha/Omega spins and there is harmony among these representatives of the Godhead, you can see how the light can descend.

You also must realize that "two-by-two" may be yourself alone with God or the ascended masters side by side with you, as Jesus and Saint Germain have promised—yourself with your Christ or your mighty I AM Presence. For you are never alone, and we seek not to limit your ministry but to give you the empowerment whereby you realize that out of the causal body there does descend the sphere of wholeness.

Beloved hearts of living flame, the preparation of the earth body for the coming of the messenger of the LORD is necessary in this hour. First and foremost, the messenger went forth stumping for the Coming Revolution in Higher Consciousness in answer to my call, clearing the way for your own service. And now you go forth, preparing again the way for a higher calling and appearance in the mighty ministry of the healing of the nations, which is upon her as our mantle of the sacred fire.

THE PATH OF THE MINISTERING SERVANT
AND THE CALL TO LOVE

Beloved ones, therefore understand the path of the ministering servant as it applies worldwide to our missionary program. Understand the path of the religious worker as the very first step which all can enter into and thereby earn their stripes and receive the full ordination at the altar of the Church Universal and Triumphant for the fulfilling of the whole law.

We begin at the beginning, then. Let us take the example of the Good Samaritan. Recognize that here is one bruised, hurt, robbed, and wounded, and therefore left half dead. Realize that humanity in a psychological sense (and many times in the physical sense of the word) are in this condition. They have been robbed by their governments, by all sorts of individuals who have set themselves in seats of power to take from them their life, their livelihood, the value of their money, their estates, their children, and so on.

Thus, all have been robbed, even as God has been robbed. And therefore, as he proclaimed: Bring ye *all* the tithes into the storehouse... and prove me herewith, if I will not pour out to you a blessing and there will not be room enough to receive it.[8]

You see, beloved hearts, the giving unto God begets the full blessing. But how can one injured and half conscious respond to a sermon or respond to a lecture—"You should be doing this, and you should be doing that, and you are in the state you are in because of your karma"?

Beloved ones, this is not the path of the living Word. This is not the path of the ministering servant. Not to condemn, not to look down upon one as though his condition of helplessness somehow were a revelation of the tarnishment of his soul, but rather to see those who are burdened and suffering as walking in the footsteps of the Lamb and bearing his stripes and living for the sake of the light.

Never mind what they have done before. We do not stop to examine, for we see all life as one and life itself worthy of succor. Therefore, one not a part of the established priesthood or the established religion of the day (which tend to become corrupted and calcinated,[9] beloved hearts, in a certain tradition and doctrine and manner of performance), but one who is free to be the universal Self—this is the one we call to the path of ministering servant and missionary unto life.

I like the term *missionary* because it bespeaks one who senses that his life is a mission—every life as a mission, as has been said.[10] And thus to define that mission and to understand that there are basics, no matter what the area of concentration or expertise, is to love the LORD thy God with all thy soul and heart and mind and thy neighbor as thyself.[11] All other callings proceed from this. There is no mastery on any of the seven rays unless God be adored and glorified and understood to be fulfilled in the service of one another. Thus—as Above, so below—the call to love precedes all other elections.

THE ORDER OF THE GOOD SAMARITAN: I AM MY BROTHER'S KEEPER

I speak, then, of the physical practicality of this missionary servant of God. Whither he should go on the highway of life, his first order of business must be to emulate the actions of the Good Samaritan.

Long ago I was called to be head of the Order of the Good Samaritans, and this I have told you;[12] and it was a part of my service and initiation on the path of the will of God. For when one pursues the will of God, one must always discover that it is not His will that any of His little ones should be lost. Proceeding from this premise, we must conclude that it is the office of the Son of man to save that which is lost or to save that which is about to be lost but for the care that must be extended.[13]

Inasmuch, then, as those who live in the physical octave cannot be found again from the state of being lost and pursue their salvation without their physical bodies, the first requirement of the Good Samaritan is to care for those in need—physical need, spiritual need, emotional need—to provide care and comfort and compassion, to go forth and to be able to intelligently help souls who are suffering from whatever dire accident or affliction has befallen them, and to be sensitive to the fact that many suffer extreme burdens of a psychological nature who also must be tended.

We begin at the beginning, then, and we desire to see the first step on the path of the ministering servant be that of one who has a new consciousness and awareness of the suffering of life and does not pass by as though it is the role of another to care, but does observe life in need and has within his heart and across his breast written the motto: I AM My Brother's Keeper!

"I AM my brother's keeper in all ways.
In heaven and on earth, I live to serve
For the keeping of the flame of life in my brother!"

Beloved hearts, in this walk of self-mastery, which is part of the discipleship of the Piscean avatar, we begin with the physical, with the outer, and move to the inner man. This is the path of the first-ray servants and those of the seventh ray. It is the power of the blue flame of the will of God and the power of freedom's flame of transmutation that restores the physical universe to be the chalice for the pristine light of the etheric octave.

We have summoned you, then, to this seminar that you might learn the very first steps—such as first aid, such as training in CPR (cardiopulmonary resuscitation)—that you might understand that the way of the Good Samaritan is to be on hand in emergencies of life and death. We have seen that this course has enabled many to save life, to restore one who could live to think again about God, to become humbled for the miracle and opportunity extended, pulling that one back from the very grips of the toiler of death.

We have seen, therefore, what good karma ordinary and extraordinary men and women have made by assisting those who are burdened, helpless, and dying. We have seen, beloved hearts, in successive stages the alleviation of burden through other means of healing, which we also outline as prerequisites for membership in the Order of the Good Samaritan—which we therefore in this hour entrust to this organization, to this staff—as a religious order of lay brothers and sisters who will identify themselves not only as their brother's keeper but as the Good Samaritan—at all times, twenty-four hours a day, responding to the call as those on duty in the fire station, on the police force, the paramedics, those who deal with emergencies in hospitals, identifying oneself always *on call:*

"I AM *on call* because I AM the Good Samaritan!"

REQUIREMENTS TO OBTAIN MEMBERSHIP IN THE ORDER OF THE GOOD SAMARITAN

And have you ever called to El Morya and failed to receive an answer, beloved? I tell you, nay. Whether you heard or did not hear, I have heard, I have answered, and the molecules of the will of God have begun to turn and to change your life. And all this would become a physical fruit were it not for the fact that sometimes you abort the spiraling into form of the blessing we send in answer to the call, by your own anxiety or temperamental behavior or even an impatience or anger that the forces of life are not serving your interests immediately as you think they ought.

Beloved ones, apropos this concept, let me say that according to the levels of density and karma, so is the definition of a descending cycle or spiral of opportunity that must pass through your four lower bodies to become physically manifest. Thus, you see, the burden of proof of the LORD's answer must be upon you, and your faith that it will be forthcoming must sustain in you faithfulness and harmony and the will to be.

Now, beloved ones, the Order of the Good Samaritans in the physical octave, having the same sponsorship and endowment as the Church Universal and Triumphant, gives to many who are not yet prepared to be ministers in the full sense of the word the opportunity to demonstrate love and service and care and to learn more about themselves and others. Thus, we see as a great means in the efficacy of the caring for the sick what shall be known as the Good Samaritan Foot Reflexology Course, to be taught here by those who have the skill and have prepared themselves to do so.

You realize that this is a treatment that can give relief to anyone. The more you know the science of it, the more you realize it is the safest form of treatment—safe for yourself, giving you protection, and also giving the person you would help protection from any unknown misuses of the laws of science or health or medical treatment.

Beloved ones, it is not necessary, therefore, to be an advanced physician in the physical sciences to be known as a brother or sister of the Order of the Good Samaritan, but it is necessary to have love and to have an awareness of what one can morally and legally administer to others and where one must refrain. It is the ability to understand, to prepare individuals slain in life or accident victims for those personnel who have the professional skills who will surely come to tend them.

Beloved ones, we are determined that you will increase in knowledge and that you will add to your awareness such things as healing with herbs or proper nutrition or the knowledge of when to use certain liquids or juices or elixirs derived from herbs for certain conditions. But in all matters you must consider yourself a lay brother—and lay in the sense of medical science—that you do not usurp the role and therefore become entangled in a most difficult circumstance by attempting to do that which it is not lawful to do and that which the Order of the Good Samaritan does not contain.

The care, the comfort and the compassion is the giving of the gift of self and the keeping of the flame. Above all, you have the science of the spoken Word and the ability to call to the ascended masters and the mighty angels on behalf of the life that you would tend.

I would see to it, therefore, that you pursue these courses during this seminar and seek to fulfill the requirements to obtain a membership card in the Order of the Good Samaritan, that wherever you go you may recognize yourself in the service of the Lord Christ to his own—being that good neighbor that is required of thee for the balancing of thy karma, being one with my order of brothers and sisters who truly meet the needs of life in every occupation. As you know that it is the motto and the way of the Red Cross to treat all and to respect not their political affiliations or their walk in life, so the Good Samaritan always serves the life of God within the individual.

I commend you to a further understanding of this order as it shall be outlined to you. I commend you to the consideration that those from many nations who desire to make their way to the central sun of this activity should consider the program of the religious worker and know that to enter it under our auspices, you must indeed be one who has fulfilled the requirements of the Order of the Good Samaritan.

THE SPIRIT OF A LIFE OF SERVICE
AS THE PERPETUAL HELPER

It is not so much requirements such as these, but rather the spirit itself—the spirit that acknowledges that one must be the Helper, the spirit that acknowledges that the coming of the Comforter and the Holy Ghost must be through the embodied sons and daughters of God—that must prevail. The Holy Spirit may contact you directly (and has contacted many servants of God), but in order for much to be done for individuals in need, the Holy Spirit must have hands and feet and one who is not only kind but skilled to render aid.

Beloved ones, when you consider the founding of the Boy Scouts of America and the Girl Scouts under the sponsorship of Saint Germain, you will realize that our Order of the Good Samaritan is an order of service for adults and those younger ones who may qualify themselves. And in its goals it is much like that of the Boy and Girl Scouts. The order, therefore, takes Boy Scouts and Girl Scouts trained to "Be Prepared" to the full maturity of a continuing life of service as Eagle Scouts and beyond—truly as the perpetual Helper.

I convey to you, then, the very spirit of the will of God. I convey to you, then, the necessity for establishing holy orders as has been throughout all ages in the churches of East and West. Realize, beloved ones, that orders are established because certain devotees desire to concentrate on a particular service, and all together learn and master that service and identify themselves as ministering ones.

This does not mean that you cannot be a member of another of our orders, such as beloved Kuthumi's Order of the Golden Robe. It does not mean, beloved hearts, that you cannot enter into the orders of the seven rays; but it does mean that through discipleship unto the ordination of the ministering servant, you must acquire the ability to render minimal lifesaving physical aid always.

I commend you, then, to the teachings of various practitioners and learned ones in the art and science of health, diet, and fasting. I commend you to study all of these rays that lead back to the one Source and to not be beset by a certain fanaticism to espouse one or the other, but to realize that all paths are given that there might be alternatives selected and the best choice made for the need at hand.

I have asked the staff of the Center for the Disciplines of Wholeness to prepare for you a sample of an ideal kit containing those preparations and bandages and ointments necessary in an hour of need when you stand alone with one injured. This will be useful to you when you have passed through the necessary courses given.

Thus, beloved ones, never without your kit but always practical, you will find yourselves in a very appropriate manner to be available.

And when you are available, somehow the angels bring to you those who have needs that you can meet. Have you ever noticed this, beloved ones? When you increase in awareness or have a certain accomplishment in a path of education, you draw unto yourself those whom you may teach and those of like mind.

Thus, suddenly you will come into a new awareness of those who are already Good Samaritans though not by name but by their very lifestyle and commitment to helping others. And I can assure you that there are many on earth and many in this country, and I, El Morya, sponsor them. And these souls of light who have prepared themselves may teach you many things and give you much understanding. And to their own devotion and attainment, you may add that which is your specialty—the whetting of the sword, the two-edged sword of the science of the spoken Word, and the drawing down of the sacred fire for healing.

Thus, when you have a flame and a bowl prepared, you are complete. Some have a bowl and a flame of devotion that must be added unto by the skill of the dynamic decree. And you yourselves who have the decree and convey such sacred fire must also have the skills, that the body and the body elemental might be given timely assistance to engage in the healing process in answer to your call.

THE VOW OF CONSECRATION
TO THE PATH OF THE OTHER SEVENTY

Many have called to me for an outline of service in the ministering servant program. I have made this, therefore, the very first requirement, for I cannot see in any way how the Lord Christ or the Darjeeling Council could sponsor anyone who neglects the physical needs of his brothers and sisters.

Beloved ones, when you meet on the path of life and when you are approved as a member of this order, you may elect to call

yourself "Brother John," "Brother Paul," or "Brother James"—or
"Sister Mary" or "Sister Joyce." Or you may elect to simply be
called as you are. It is important that you come to understand that
one who is a member of a lay religious order must act the part,
must put on the mantle, must recognize that with the mantle are
responsibilities not to go off again in riotous living or indulgences,
not to say, "Well, I may do this or that today, for I am no longer
being seen as a member of this religious group."

Beloved ones, you are a profile of the ascended masters wherever you are, and your sense of self-awareness as a member of the
Order of the Good Samaritan must give to you at all times the
sense of deference to those in need. No longer can you say, "I do
not have time," or "This is my day off," or "I am too tired," or "Get
help from another." When called upon, you answer. And thus, you
now enter into the role of the angelic hosts.

Thus, beloved, come to understand the great needs of humanity through the role of the compassionate servant. Under the ray
of God's holy will may you balance your threefold flame, for this
service is not alone for the one in need but for thyself. It is for the
development of the third ray of God's love, in all due practicality
of the Holy Spirit.

Thus, when love abounds you will find how easily wisdom
does increase and how great is the power for action. We desire to
see you become Christed ones and to fulfill this requirement of the
threefold flame. Thus, in the power of the fifth ray of the law of
Moses, you will come to know the grace of the living Christ balanced by the Trinity and the Presence of the Mother.

I have come to you that you might know and realize what is
that true and acceptable and holy calling of your lifestream and
that in the process of loving God and loving thy neighbor it is
meet for thee to enter into this service, this love, this community.

I trust that there shall return to the lightbearers of earth a new
sense of brotherhood, a new sense of being a part of the Great

White Brotherhood, a new sense of camaraderie and love, brotherly love—all a member of one great heart, the heart of Christ, all in the way of being his hands and feet.

Thus, I commend you in this vow of consecration to the path of the other seventy, to the path of the disciples, knowing that in caring for the sick or the dying that you also are casting out devils, pursuing the ritual of exorcism, and doing those things that more skilled practitioners either do not have the time to do in an emergency or may not have the knowledge or awareness of.

When you stop at the scene of an accident and you find many who are dead and dying because of drunkenness or because of drugs or because of rock and all the deadly intents of darkness, you realize how much work there is to do at inner levels for the binding and the judgment of that cause and core on the astral plane of that negative force that has devoured these youths or these children of light before they could fill their divine mission.

Thus, when there are those who have passed from the screen of life or are about to pass, being beyond help, you must escort, by prayer and invocation, their souls to the inner octaves and call with great intensity for the sword of the Divine Mother, for the power of Astrea to cut them free from the astral hordes that entrapped them and did cause some terrifying accident such as happen daily on the highways of life.

THE GOOD SHEPHERD

Realize, then, that the Good Samaritan does enter into the purposes of the Order of the Golden Lily (which was founded by the Goddess of Liberty),[14] assisting the angels and calling them forth to escort these souls to a higher domain where they might learn of their mistakes. When these things are not tended to, the astral shells, ghostlike, of the departed—and many times their souls —hover earthbound at the scene of the accident for weeks and months and sometimes even years. And thus, certain areas become areas of repeated accidents and fatalities, as increasing numbers of discarnates, together with the demons that cause the accidents, form a vortex there. And therefore, there are danger areas known.

Beloved hearts, you can go forth as a Good Samaritan to clear these. For the Good Samaritan, though he tends the physical, is ever alert to the spiritual equation and the spiritual dimension in life and understands the law of cause and effect and does not leave anyone prey to the astral denizens that desire to have them and to sift them as wheat.[15]

Thus, the Order of the Good Samaritan and your office in it as a brother or sister will be as much as you make of it. There is room for great creativity and an acceleration of skills. I merely give the basic requirements and draw with broad brushstrokes an outline of this endeavor. As every office that comes forth from God is expanded and individualized by the individual, so you must realize that within the parameters of helpfulness there is much that can be given. So do thou this, and let this order become known worldwide as an association of individuals who truly care and put that care into effective action.

I deliver you now into the heart of the living Christ Jesus who himself gave this parable because he himself descended to earth in the very role and guise of the Good Samaritan. For this is the reason for the coming of the Son of God: to save that which was lost, to go after souls maimed, marred by the fallen angels, by the sinister force. So he has come, not to leave you by the highway alone to suffer and die, but to be with you in the walk of life.

Therefore, in fact, the great archetype and the true and living Presence of our order is the Lord Jesus Christ, who himself includes in this service his brother Saint Francis and many of you who have served with them through the ages. It is a mighty order at inner levels. I come forth as the head of that order because I am the one who trains the troops. Once you have mastered what I have to give you and to teach you, beloved hearts, you will also walk as the brother and sister of Christ, needing me no longer, for you shall have become truly the heart and essence of the will of God.

Thus, I look forward to the day when brothers and sisters of the Order of the Good Samaritan may be crowned with the mantle and title "Good Shepherd"—shepherd of the sheep. Thus, the goal "feed my sheep" must well be accomplished by every member of this order, and thus you open successively the doors to Paradise and the doors of the City Foursquare.

I AM El Morya. I have opened the door of opportunity, called by Jesus so to do. May it be for you the fullness of the satisfaction of the divine within your soul that you feel ultimately and supremely useful and needed hour by hour.

Beloved hearts, can any of us endure the trials of life or its burdens except by the knowledge of that great love given to us and that which we give? . . . Because these little ones and those great and small need me, I live.

Thus, the order becomes one's reason for being. With a reason for being, you can fly, you can run—and you can ascend to God.

In the name of Mary our Mother and her immaculate heart, I seal you in the divine plan of the Goal presently manifest and to be attained in the future.

Run with God. I AM with you.

Beloved Jesus concludes this address:

You have heard from him, and the one I love. And I love him for his fastidiousness in making God's dreams come true on earth through those whom one would not necessarily suspect could be instruments of that will. Yet Morya has an eye for the single crystal in the devotee that can become the diamond heart. We cherish him, and we, too, are grateful to be members of the Darjeeling Council.

SEE YOURSELF AS A PILLAR OF PURPLE FIRE

Beloved ones, sending you forth two-by-two, sending you into the world and sending you with the mantle of the Good Samaritan—I would give you the visualization of the meaning of the alchemy of the physical body and a thoughtform for your visualization with the tube of light. It is the power of the flame that has been called the deep purple. It is the action of the seventh ray charged with the holy blue. That purple fire, beloved ones, may be visualized as a cylinder of purple within the center of the tube of light, with the more pink violet flame still burning in the center.

Look now at this focus of crystal:[16] though not fully revealing its inner light . . . yet in meditation you may find the sense of the depth of the quality of the purple-blue fire. And know this, beloved hearts—that this is the color that we visualize for the transformation of the earth element and the earth body and the physical body you wear. Its visualization is a great protection.

In fact, I, Jesus, desire you to see yourself as a pillar of purple fire moving through the earth as a crystal cylinder that cannot be violated or penetrated—all inside the tube of light. I desire you to have a very physical awareness of this color, to recall it to the mind's eye. And therefore, let its light appear through a greater display of that inner quality.

This pillar of fire, then, is a protection and an identification of the members of the Order of the Good Samaritan. Take it with you, my beloved, for it shall become a real and blessed mantle upon you when I, through the messenger, will bless you for your vow and certification in this order.

Beloved ones, the physical body corresponds to the violet flame. The violet flame, in all of its qualifications and beauty, delivers to you the means to implement your service and provides in your hand a mighty gift for healing through transmutation. We add to it, then, the color of the healing light and the emerald crystal —and *voilà!* you have before you the divine purpose ensouled of the Good Samaritan. Let it be seen. Let it be done. Because El Morya has himself espoused this cause and been God-victorious on many fronts, this order then is proclaimed this day as an opportunity to Keepers of the Flame.

I seal you in the cosmic cross of white fire. We meet in the center between worlds and beyond. I AM ever your Jesus. I have called you here. Listen, then, to my teaching through these my servants and you will discover a new vision and compartment of your own Selfhood unlocked by me and by your steadfastness in the study of the Word.

In the blessing of my Mother, Mary, and the love of Magda, I greet you, for the ever-dawning New Day is at hand.

October 7, 1984
Camelot
Los Angeles County, California
ECP

CHAPTER 20

I behold you here and now as saints: saints Above and below.
And I behold your destiny as ascended masters . . . .
I, Jesus, call you to become fishers of men in the
full knowledge that in this thy sacred labor the
requirements of thy being shall be filled.

"COME, LEAVE YOUR NETS—
I WILL MAKE YOU FISHERS OF MEN"

O Mother of the World, I AM come. I AM fulfilling light, and I AM the fulfillment of my promise unto thee and thine own gathered here in the tabernacle of the congregation.

Beloved of the light of God, I welcome you as brothers and sisters of holy flame—yes, brothers and sisters of the flame of God. This means that I hold thee in kinship with God—God the Father and God the Mother with us. For the universal Mother and her light of old, known as the Shekinah glory, is the presence of God in this universe, in this manifestation. Therefore, behold her universal light in Mary the Mother, in nature, through the Holy Spirit in thy heart and in thy messenger.

Beloved, you have heard it said, "I can do all things through Christ who strengthens me." Now understand how universal, all-pervading through and through thy very bones, is the person of the universal Mother. Understand how it is thy glory, thy discipleship to be one with this Mother.

The persecution of the believers in my Mother, Mary, is in reality an outpicturing of a deep cleavage in the subconscious, a psychological state that has been called by beloved Kuthumi "the hatred of the Mother." Sad it is that earthly mothers have sometimes quickened in their offspring this hatred of the Mother by their example that is wanting—wanting of the flow and the light of the universal matrix.

Understand how the ancients knew that the consciousness of Mother, the womb of Mother, was the matrix alchemical of that light. Thus, you see, the immaculate heart of Mother in both male and female representatives of herself must be held. For this indeed is the womb of creation where you abide, where each one is becoming Christ, being formed and re-formed in that Christ.

Understand, beloved, that each one has the dharma—truly the duty in the understanding of the universal Buddha—to be the Mother on earth, holding firmly and with strength and devotion and vision and faith the understanding of each one's potential and its fulfillment. Thus, when the Mother flame is kept, life does prosper for children are comforted, souls know the solace of love directly through your heart. And when the crystal vision of each one's ultimate Godhood is known and loved, even as one loves the soul becoming the Real Self, then the love of Mother is kindled and this love does consume and transmute the records in the subconscious of this which we have called "hatred of the Mother."

This denial of the Mother's grace divides the individual. It divides Christendom. It divides the followers of all the world's religions. It is the cause of the slaying of the firstborn in the hour of my birth and of abortion in this hour. It is the cause of the division in families and divorce and mistreatment of children and the misuse of the sacred fire. And therefore, having hated the Mother, the light is squandered.

Those who therefore deny the light of the Mother on earth before holy angels must receive the compensation of those holy angels denying them before the Godhead. Denying what? Denying their access to greater light and divinity and the onward path of initiation. Thus, the holy angels must say of such a soul: "Thus far and no farther! They shall not pass into the realm of the Father or of the Son or of the Holy Spirit or of the living Guru, Lord Maitreya!"

I come, then, in the joyous thanksgiving of the grace of our Father to admonish the sons and daughters of heaven taking up their abode on earth: Make peace with thy mother even as thou wouldst be one with our Father. The mother in the earth is the best part of thyself. By the Mother flame all avatars have come. For when thou speakest of the Word incarnate, as in me, understand that that Word is the Mother flame.

By the Mother flame, Moses communed with the I AM THAT I AM on Sinai. Had he not had quickened in him that Mother flame, the receptivity would not have been there. Thus, by the law of love whereby the Father denies those who do not love his consort, the Mother, and by the very mathematics of polarity of Alpha and Omega, those who have not the love of Mother truly have not the grace of the Son nor the magnet that will truly woo the Father and his holy angels to their side. Let us understand, therefore, that the denial of light and comfort and love to any part of Mother is a denial of her grace within thyself.

Thus, let love increase, intensify in a most practical manner for those within the congregation and those who stand waiting at the gates—waiting to be admitted, waiting to pass through when you yourselves shall have parted the Red Sea of that raging anger that exists in the astral plane that is the nonresolution with the Mother flame.

KNOW THE PERSON OF MOTHER IN HER PRESENCE

Even so, for this very initiation we send our messenger before thy face, that thou mayest know the person of Mother in her presence. For it is through the direct encounter that all things come to the surface. Thus, you may dislike and disapprove of the messenger. You may fear her as a god or condemn her for this or for that. All of these things are not objective reality but the warring of thy soul with thine own substance at subconscious levels.

It is not that the messenger is perfect in the human sense.

Who can be perfect in the human sense, since the human is not perfectible? It is rather that the mantle of the Mother is upon her. And this mantle is a holy fire acting independently even of her own human consciousness. This is in order that the Son, even the eternal Christ, might place his mantle upon thee. Thus, first the one and then the many.

Understanding this, seek direct encounter and initiation with the mantle of the messenger. Understand the meaning of the mantle as the office of the World Mother and do not become confused by the person vis-à-vis the office. You do not confuse yourself with the mantle of the Son of God; therefore, why confuse any other who does bear the mantle? There is an understanding of the limitations of our humanity. There is the understanding of the limitless opportunity of our divinity.

The great lesson of your life and the life of the messengers must always be that it is by the grace of God that both live and serve. By the grace of God the divinity descends into the humanity. And when the twain are fully one and the fire, self-consuming, does stand, there is a succession of self-transcendence. Step-by-step the veils are parted and burned away. And as they are burned away within thyself —this divinity continually raising up the soul, transcending itself— you will know God face-to-face. And the messenger will disappear and you will see me directly, even as the messenger beholds in thee the Godhead dwelling, the I AM Presence, and the smile of thy Christ —even during the tantrums of the human consciousness.

Thus, you see, ye are all God's, meaning you are all possessed of God and therefore belonging unto him. You are himself, his offspring, his creation—truly, in polarity, the manifestation of God. There is no separation, but the illusion and the lie of separation is present in this world. It is the result of the going astray from the Real Self. What you cannot see, therefore, in the anointed of God (and if every chela is anointed of God, how much more is the messenger anointed of God) you cannot, therefore, see in yourself.

THE UNIVERSAL PRESENCE OF THE MOTHER
IS THE FOUNDATION OF THE AQUARIAN AGE

Thus, seek the light in the brethren. Seek the light in the ascended masters. Seek the light in the One Sent. And then you will realize that there need not be pain or parting or sorrow or tears. For all of God with you is truly the key to present peace and happiness and future, as it would appear, immortality. Thy immortality is now. Its future destination is only an appearance of working out in the cycles of life the unfoldment of Self.

Upon this premise of understanding of the permeation of the universal presence of the Mother is the foundation of the Aquarian age built. Every saint of God, every teacher and prophet comes home to the Western Shamballa in the great desiring to raise up truly the tabernacle of the witness unto the opening of the portals of heaven, where angels freely ascend and descend and where those who have appeared to be mortals suddenly appear in the immortal state. Whether in the body or out of the body, it matters not. For immortality is a condition of being and of overcoming and of the Word and the Work of the LORD.

"Come now, let us reason together," saith the LORD. "Though your sins be as scarlet, I will make them white as snow."

Consider, then, the lilies of the field and the eternal whiteness of the Mother's blooming in thy heart, O child of love. Consider, then, and understand that God has called thee to a mighty purpose —not forever to be engaged in the transmutation of sin, but to do so with joy and all Godspeed, knowing that this is not the end! No, the goal that is set for thee is another.

Let us study the teaching and become it and not forever be learners, never coming to the knowledge of truth. For this, too, is not the end—all things converging through the assimilation of the Body and Blood of Christ, the universality of the Father-Mother God; all things coming to the quintessence of thy being.

THE GOAL—BE OUR MAGNET IN THE EARTH

What is this goal of thy being—cleansed, purified, God-taught, truly the Word present? The goal, beloved, is that thou thyself be our magnet in the earth, magnetizing the little ones, the ones who are caught—caught truly in the intense tide of the temptations of the world, caught up in the magnetism of the senses. They are not fed by God. They have not the wholeness of the Holy Spirit. They seek it by outer means.

Beloved ones, you who know the temptations and the experiences of life understand full well what is this pull of which I speak. It is a counterweight and an antimagnet, consisting of the entire momentum of nihilism—the denial of God the Father, the Son, the Holy Spirit, and the Mother—the entire counterweight of those who have chosen the left-handed path and stolen the light of the Mother to enshrine it as a way of death to be followed by the many.

Understand, therefore, that to rescue the souls from this pull and tide of the world and the mass consciousness requires pillars of eternity, the polestar, the magnet of the Central Sun, as *you* (as your heart, your chakras, your soul, your spirit), that when you encounter souls on the path of life and they come into your orbit, they are drawn mightily by archangels and the I AM Presence for realignment to Reality.

This, beloved, is known as the power of conversion—the power of conversion whereby I converted Saul of Tarsus on the road to Damascus, raising him up to be the apostle Paul and thus giving to him also these teachings and this lesson whereby he became that magnet and became the LORD's instrument, a converter of souls—turning around, demagnetizing them from error and evil and maya, fastening them to God by the mighty cross of Christ. This is the goal of thy striving, thy work, thy service, thy learning, thy purification, thy preparation.

Let us not be caught up in the ritual. Let us not allow the ritual to become rote. Let us not forever dally in the process itself, but understand that we are on the highway of our God. We move on! We internalize truth. We do so quickly, for souls are caught in the downstream current and they need to be rescued.

I COME AND I CALL YOU

Therefore, I come this Thanksgiving Day 1984 and I speak to you personally, spirits of the living fire, brothers and sisters of the eternal flame of Zarathustra, Melchizedek, Helios, Seraphim of God. All saints are worshipers of the sacred fire. And in this heart, I come—I come and I call you. I call you fervently as Jesus, your brother and your loved one.

I AM the Beloved and I AM the Rose of Sharon, and I ensconce myself firmly, one with your messenger. Have no fear, for I shall be —and she in me shall be—the instrument for the raising up of the nations of the earth, for doing all those things that are promised. Fear not—fear not the fulfillment of my mission through this vessel. For it is come to pass and it shall be and none shall turn it. But fear this, O soul: Fear that thou mayest miss thine own calling to also be myself.

Fear, then, that in the hour of the fulfillment of God's holy purpose through this mission of the Mother of the World that thou might be set aback by the darkness rising from the mists of the unconscious. Fear, then, and know that this fear is the sense of the awe and the holiness of God in thy Presence eternally. And have the sense of the honor of God, trembling before the sacred fire of Sinai and knowing that in this hour the LORD thy God does require of thee the fulfillment of thy holy purpose. This is the reason for thy calling, for thy blessing, for our love to thee.

For angels have gone forth from the Keeper of the Scrolls, reading unto us, the ascended masters, the names of those of whom the LORD does require answer in this hour and decade and century. And to each and every one of these we have sent forth legions of light to draw them to the fount of this wisdom, this path, and this teaching.

For it is written in the Book of Life that the LORD thy God does require of thee in this hour the fulfillment of thy holy purpose and thy calling.

Thy choice to be here is the choice to fulfill a fiery destiny that cannot be delayed any longer, will not be set back! Thus the open door of opportunity is given to the world of lightbearers whose names are written in the Book of Life and to many others whose names are not written therein—that they might be converted, that they might be drawn back to the original Creator, to the Elohim, and repent and be saved and therefore fulfill the requirement to become God instead of the anti-God.

It is the hour of the LORD's requiring of the law of thy being. Thus, in the case of those who have deified evil as an "energy veil," the LORD God does require of them this day also that they fulfill their reason for being. Thus, there is outpictured and outplayed in their world, beloved hearts of living fire, before their very eyes, from the beginning unto the ending (as there does flash before the one drowning), the entire record of the sowing of the seeds of the flowers of evil.

And they may choose to live in the grace of God and be converted and come under the rod and the shadow of the Almighty through the I AM Presence and the LORD's anointed and the Mother flame and the one who holds it. And if they do not accept the conversion of the Holy Ghost and the holy angels and the holy Mother, then the requirement of the Law shall be unto them as a searing fire of judgment as they and their works must stand the trial by fire and be consumed.

Understand, beloved hearts, that the opportunity of the lightbearers to be all that they truly are is an opportunity that has a cycle and a season. And to each one it is given seven days, seven months, seven years, seven centuries. But in the end of the cycle, beloved hearts, if those unto whom the LORD has required the fulfillment of Sonship deny that Sonship, its source in the Mother and in the Father, then the Law shall require of them every jot and tittle of their karma, every jot and tittle of their evil sowing.

IS NOT GOD THE KEEPER OF HIS UNIVERSE?

This is the law of the ages. But in the hour of its speaking through the messenger, it becomes a physical binding—a binding of the soul to God for his liberation or the binding of the soul to God for his undoing. Understand, blessed ones, that for some the binding of the soul to God is a gross inconvenience, an uncomfortability, and they lash and they thrash. And they lash out against the great light. Therefore, this resistance to the impelling force of love becomes their undoing.

Is not God the keeper of his universe? Is this not God's universe? Then does not the LORD thy God, the Holy One of Israel, have therefore the God-freedom to determine the cycles of the appearing of his sons and daughters and to require fruits of a harvest long overdue and to deliver his people from this ongoing struggle with forces of darkness beyond their ability to overcome? Is not God in his temple through Sanat Kumara and through the hearts of his own? God, therefore, the knower of all things, does call the cycles. And happy are ye who live in the fulfillment of my age and in the inauguration of the age of the seventh angel.

Therefore, on this day, in the full knowledge and the profound awareness of the Law behind these words, I say to all entangled in karma, in the personality cult, and in the pull of the world: *Come, leave your nets! I will make you fishers of men.*

This is a calling directly to the heart of every student of the ascended masters. In Maitreya's name I come to teach you the way of Maitreya's path, to teach you the way of being the Mediator, as Moses is the eternal Mediator; the way of your Christ Self, as your Christ Self is the way of the eternal Mediator; the way of the Shepherd and the way of the magnet of the Central Sun—the way of being the pillar in the temple of my God (which signifies the

Alpha-Omega polarity of the magnet), the way of being the instrument of the Holy Ghost that through thee none may resist my presence.

BE INSTRUMENTS OF MY LOVE

I AM Jesus, the Saviour of all men. I bring opportunity for your salvation—the true elevation of the Real Self within you—that you might be the instruments of the Saviour of all men. I ask that you discontinue to separate me from my messenger but remember that heaven is much closer than this.

You may count on my Word, not upon the outer person of anyone. You may count on my Word and the Word made flesh. And you may know that as you become the Rock and reach for "the Rock," as it was said, "that is higher than I," you shall also be instruments of my love.

May you recognize the calling and know that there is a cycle to leave the nets of the world and come apart. And when the calling goes forth, those who answer receive ministering angels to assist. The world must be served notice through the messenger and through yourselves in the indomitable will of God that the hour of repentance and eternal life is at hand, that the hour of the opening of the twelve gates of the city is at hand, that the hour of Truth is come.

This dispensation is now extended to all, everywhere on earth. May they hear it through your lips and hearts, through your consciousness in stern meditation upon the Word, in unswerving concentration. May the devils tremble! And indeed, they do tremble at the sound of my footstep through ye all. And may your hearts not tremble for fear but rejoice and give a mighty shout that God shall deliver you in every instance from the tempter.

Know the Word. Know the secrets. Write them in thy heart. And then, when the devil does assail thee in the way and in the hour of the fasting and the prayer and the service, thou wilt have the answer. It is written: "Man shall not live by bread alone, but by every word that proceedeth out of the mouth of God." This is thy sacred trust: that all "these things," as bread, are as naught. For the Word is Life and the Word giveth Life and the Word giveth all these things to those who require them.

No other hand shall feed thee but my own. No other hand shall teach thee. No other heart shall love thee. No other mind shall confound thee, but the mind of Christ shall be with thee. It is the principle of the Law of the One.

STRIVE TO BE THE PRESENCE, TO BE THE CHRIST

I the LORD thy God am a jealous God. I deserve and desire all of thy desiring and thy love and thy life—not half, but all. When thou givest all of thyself, I give all of myself. And the Father and the Son shall live in thy temple. This means, beloved, thou shalt walk the earth no longer the Presence above thee, the Christ Self above thee; but the Father in heaven and myself, through the I AM Presence and Christ Self, shall dwell bodily within you. Until this shall occur, the Holy Spirit in the full power of the Godhead cannot come upon thee.

Thus, strive to *be* the Presence, to be the Christ. And listen to the inner voice that does guide thee. Before thou speakest in an ungodly manner, the Presence does warn: Refrain thy speech; it is not pleasing unto the LORD. Each act, each desiring, each contemplation of deceit or ambition as it does come from the tempter is rebuked by the Christ. Listen to the inner voice and obey, and all shall be well with thee and the bliss of God shall be upon thee. And the holy angels will see that not a hair on thy head is touched.

Be at peace in the calling. Let those who would be tutored in the path of fishers of men fear not the Word of the LORD and fear not his Work. We have enshrined this place for the full appearing of that Word and Work in ye all. And I say *full* appearing. And when I say it, understand that the fullness of God has need of thousands upon thousands of instruments, each one showing a shining facet of the treasure of heaven. Thus, we assemble the mighty, the eagles, as well as the meek of the earth. Let the Word and the Work of God in you be a monument to the testimony of the Great White Brotherhood through the messengers and yourselves —a temple built without hands, eternal forever.

I behold you here and now as saints: saints Above and below. And I behold your destiny as ascended masters of the Great White Brotherhood. I, Jesus, call you to become fishers of men in the full knowledge that in this thy sacred labor the requirements of thy being shall be filled. And I consecrate our messenger to tend to the hearts of those so inclined, for in this answer ye are my disciples indeed.

Let the world know that God is in the earth and he has given his power unto his own. And let his own guard the power and keep the sanctity of this face-to-face communion. Give it not to the profane, but guard it for those who come seeking entrance.

FOR THE SAVING OF EVERY SOUL GONE ASTRAY

My precious friends, I speak in your very heart of hearts that you might hear me now in each heartbeat, in your very breath. Know my voice and understand. I come to change the prophecy of Fátima. I come to undo the dire predictions. I come to work through you for the saving of every soul that is gone astray.

This is a dispensation of the moment, the hour, and the decade. Work in this wise while ye have the light. For should the dark night come to the planet, and we pray God it shall not, but should it come, in that hour my own must be safe in the arms of the universal Mother, that they be not torn from eternal life by any condition whatsoever.

I, Jesus, stamp the stamp of holiness upon my own across the earth. And I send forth our Mother in the physical octave to bear my tidings and thine own of the joyous Word and Work of the

LORD that is here. I pray and I ask every Keeper of the Flame worldwide to keep the strong flame of faith, protection, and freedom as she is sent forth to touch those souls and bring them Home. And in that hour thou shalt rejoice, for thou shalt know and recognize dear hearts long lost, long since forgotten. Truly it is the harvest, and we gather the wheat.

Truly it is also the harvest; expect, then, the harvesting of the tares of consciousness. Expect to cast into the fire the unsuccessful experiments of thy soul in the Matter cosmos. Cast them into the flame with the joy of nonattachment, knowing that the essence of God's light so misused does immediately return for thy building of the new spirit in Christ born again after the flame of eternity.

KEEP THE FLAME OF GOD-GOVERNMENT

Brothers and sisters of the sacred fire, I have come this day to send fire on the earth. I have spoken to you my message of joy and thanksgiving. Now I charge you to keep the flame of this God-government, to pray earnestly for the freeing of your president, for the binding of the forces that would control him through the Order, through all other conspiratorial organizations seeking to amass world power. Pray for his strength and independence by the holy angels every day, that right decision might be manifest without fear and without harm to him.

Let him be encouraged by your calls and by your letters to stand for the right and fulfill the highest goals. He also is a chalice, as every man and woman is a chalice. Protect the chalice, fill it with light, and each one may be seen a better and more loyal servant. Prayer maketh the difference.

Come now, fishers of men, for there are many ways to catch souls into the net of God. It is a divine net. And each one must come because he savors the offering and is drawn by that special sweetness, that special preparation of your heart with my heart. We two walking together—behold, let us convert the world!

I AM with you always, even unto the end of this state of world consciousness and unrest. And truly, beloved, it shall end! The question is when. The answer from you will determine and make the difference.

Come unto me, ye who labor and are heavy laden. My burden is light. My yoke is easy.

Come, disciples of the eternal Word. *Come, leave your nets. I will make you fishers of men.* We *shall* convert a world!

In the name of the Mother, I AM come. In the name of the heart of the Mother, I AM come. In the name of the life, the mind, the soul, and the purity of the Mother, I AM come.

November 22, 1984
Royal Teton Ranch, North
Park County, Montana
ECP

CHAPTER 21

Realize that you were created to become an avatar.
You were created to become a Christ.
You were sent forth to take on the world consciousness
of the Lord of the World and to have your affairs
and your energies so in order that you could give
a more than ordinary service.

A TORCH OF RESPONSIBILITY

REMEMBERING THE ODYSSEY OF TWIN FLAMES

Most beautiful ones of the light, I beheld you in the beginning, I behold you now—and the glory of the light of God is upon you.

When you first came forth and had placed upon you the garments for your realization of identity in octaves below the causal body, your raiment was transparent, your heart flames visible, and the jewels you wore were solely the jewels of the chakras that appeared. (Contrary to some belief systems on earth, the colors of the chakras we have released in this order constitute the immaculate matrix for the seven stars of Elohim appearing in thy temple.[1])

I am Lanello, delivering to you now through our Mother's vessel the dictation of beloved Jesus for the fulfillment of your path in this season of striving and in the light appearing.

Remember, then, the firstborn Son.

Remember, then, thy ordination as king and queen, Father-Mother Presence—thou and thy twin flame.

Remember, then, the odyssey of the pearl and the mystery of the star sapphire lost beneath the waves of doubt and fear, and the soul forever diving to the depths to find the lost pearl and the lost sapphire.

Thus, understand: The pearl is always the symbol of the soul, and the sapphire of the Great Blue Causal Body Star in the heavens.

Thus, the glory that was with you in the beginning is a glory that has receded from the lower form.

I have described your appearance in golden-age cities, etheric cities of light on Venus and other planetary homes. The descent below the etheric matrix and garment has been fraught with despair, deprivation, loss of memory, the going out of the Way.

MY ADMONISHMENT AND MY REBUKE

Children of the Sun, I, Jesus, summon you through our messengers—twin flames who hold now the arc and the flame on this altar of myself and dearest Magda:

Understand the wholeness as Above and so below, and receive my admonishment and my rebuke. For I must rebuke the wayward self that has gotten itself so far out of the way of the divinity of the sapphire star. And I must rebuke the self that still persists in the selfish pursuits after having seen and heard and listened to the light of the Word descending.

Thus, I caution you to reckon with the equation. How easily the light is lost, how easily it slips through the fingers and through the body temple. That which is gained seemingly so easily is not, in fact, so easily gained.

WE HAVE PAID THE PRICE, NOW YOU MUST PAY THE PRICE

I, Jesus, have paid the price. Magda has paid the price. And these two witnesses have paid the price. Beloved, understand that the gifts so naturally, *divinely naturally* received have been hardearned and won by those who stand as your sponsors.

Thus, recognize that the conclusion of a quarter of Summit University is the transfer of a torch of responsibility. For these weeks together, these many weeks, as in the prophecy of Daniel[2] (weeks, then, being the division of time and space in the number seven of Elohim and the seven chakras) represent a finite segment of eternity, even as they represent eternity itself, for you have passed through the eternality of thy causal body. Thus, you have ascended to eternal life and descended to the scene of accountability—the scene of karma.

Now understand, beloved, that the passing of the torch [as it were, a mantle] is from our shoulders to your own and to those of your own Christ Self. When you are released this Monday morning from our tutelage, know that you go forth with the wherewithal, the know-how, and our momentum that *you* might begin to pay the price. And that is the responsibility for the descent from the etheric octave; for all karma is made in the mental, carnal, fleshly, emotional levels of being.

Understand, therefore, that this opportunity of my grace upon you, the grace of Magda and our beloved Mother Mary, is a consummate gift. It is the launching of a star, if you will it so. And if you choose to take that star as a football under your arm and run once again on the playing fields of the world saying, "Shall I do this? Shall I do that?" you will come to the understanding that football is a serious game, fraught with danger and broken bones— it is where you roll in the mud. And this is the way of earth.

Thus, understand it is meet for thee to reinforce the light we have given that you might, when sure of that accountability—sure and understanding of the very posture of the body and the very attitude of being on the defense simultaneously with being on the offense—when you have internalized and crystalized a certain fortitude of your own Christhood, then, then it is safe to go forth among the people and do those things that are a fulfillment of the great descending cycle of the Great Divine Director.

REACHING OUT TO YOUR TWIN FLAMES EACH TWO THOUSAND YEARS

Beloved ones, I must give you the understanding, lest you lose the precious pearl and the precious sapphire, that during past ages, after your leaving off from the place of perfection, each two thousand years we have come with a profound message and sacrifice of our very life to reach out to your twin flames, to woo you back to the great temples of the Brotherhood and to the school of Maitreya.

You must understand that your father and mother, even Adam and Eve, are in a sense the archetypal pattern of many twin flames who went forth from the mystery school, lured by the temptations of great interest and dominion in the political, economic, and social realms that were presented by the Serpent, representing that band of angels who are the scribes, who are the sophists, who pose as the sages but are not the true wise men from the East.

Thus, you see, there will always be the temptation to master another round of worldly knowledge that is seen as the key to enlightenment, the key to the resolution of the world's problems.

Blessed hearts, people have had great knowledge and science and invention for tens of thousands of years. Have they saved the world from self-destruction? Have they got to the very core of life and being? Recognize a long, long history of millions of years of trying to solve the problems of the Matter equation without, *sans*, the garment of the etheric temple.

WEAVE THE DEATHLESS SOLAR BODY

I admonish you then, first and foremost, to weave the deathless solar body. If the people of India had known that the noxious gas was to come, would they not have put on themselves protective garments and oxygen masks, or would they not have removed themselves?[3]

Understand that when you go forth without the wedding garment, without the deathless solar body, you are subject and prey to the noxious gases of the astral plane that are spewing out the world around. Believe me, it is easier to slip and fall than it is to navigate oneself safely across the dark passages of the astral plane without the wedding garment.

Thus, do not take so lightly so great a salvation.

We have deliberated, our Mother, the Virgin Mary, with us— Magda and I—concerning what we might give to you of the highest and best fruits of our own wisdom and experience, seeing as we see the long continuity of the evolution of thy soul and all that we have encountered. Blessed ones, if it were not so treacherous, the earth would be in the golden age today and you would be walking as masters among men.

We speak, then, of the treachery of the ways of the world and the subtlety of the loss of light and of the many who have come through these halls and gone forth almost drunken with the new wine of the Spirit and therefore not on guard.

THE CHALLENGE TO RETAIN THE LIGHT

I say with Saint Germain and the Goddess of Liberty: Hold fast what thou hast received! Value it above all else, and know that now the challenge begins to retain that light so easily gained by the overshadowing of those who gladly and joyfully make their presence felt in the halls of Summit University.

This is the beginning of a trek for each one of you. This is the beginning of a life wherein you daily face in an accelerated manner the returning cycles of past karma. All who are ardent chelas, who understand the meaning of the gift of the ascension to a planet, will surely avail themselves of the highest and best opportunity to serve and, by way of serving, to gain greater strength in the light.

Your own messengers would confess to you in this hour their own frailty in the very beginning of their search and their own frailty on the Path as they did encounter the most difficult karmic situations, which always must be brought to the fore in one's final embodiment. And this messenger Mark, through whom I speak in this moment, would tell you that without the overshadowing and care and compassion and wisdom of Mother Mary, he considers that he would not have made it on the Path.

THE SEARCH IS ENDED—
THE PATH OF SELF-MASTERY IS BEGUN

Thus, beloved ones, you were magnetized here because you are among the old souls of the earth who must have an understanding, who have a driving inner desire to know where they have come from and why they have an understanding of life beyond a narrow spectrum of physicality and empirical testimony.

Beloved ones, you have sought and you have found. Some are caught up with the hypnotism of the search itself. They prefer to keep on seeking and therefore, in not finding, to have the excuse for not settling down to the mighty work of the ages.

I trust you will know and hear me—that I AM the Witness, that you no longer have the excuse not to apply the Truth for you have reached the goal, the search is ended, and the path of self-mastery is begun.

We have provided what we consider to be the safest matrix here and at the Royal Teton Ranch for your building of the temple, for the resolution of inequities within you, for the mastery of your psychology and, thus, the building of the deathless solar body.

You see, at this moment you are not all [entirely] tethered to the etheric body because of rents in the garments of the lower vehicles. That etheric body is the deathless solar body. It is now become a part of thy Christ Self—that higher manifestation of it. And if you would avail yourself of its complete enfoldment and protection, you must anchor in the light and raise that light and know the meaning of the burning of the sacred fire in the spine and in the chakras, burning the debris and rising, rising, rising until literally the crown itself is on fire.

You ought to have this as the goal and realize that unless and until the sacred fire is actually burning in the temple, you have not attained to that point of equilibrium where your immortality is secured, as in heaven so on earth.

HUMAN ERROR AND ANGELIC INTERCESSION

Beloved ones, it ought to be a sign to the whole evolution of the planet how easily an error of those individuals who do not necessarily represent our Brotherhood can result in mass death and confusion. Do you realize how many areas there are on earth this day in the physical octave which, if they were upset or triggered, would cause death to millions and tens of millions?

Think of all of the installations of nuclear weapons. Think of the many plants that generate electricity by nuclear power. Think of the many plants that manufacture poisons. Think of the coming of earthquakes or cataclysm and the rupturing of pipes and systems and, in serious cataclysm, the setting off of those weapons that are positioned around the globe. Then you will begin to understand that, physically speaking, you are dwelling on a literal powder keg.

Consider that it is the intercession of the angelic hosts and the Great White Brotherhood through the dynamic decrees of the chelas that actually sustains the balance and has prevented that cataclysm—even prophesied by certain psychics—from taking place. Beloved ones, they cannot figure out the timetables because the timetables are governed by the cycles of the degrees and the cycles of the decrees of the chelas of the sacred fire.

Thus, come to an understanding of the value of thy position as a pillar in the temple of my God. Recognize the value of the altar and the value of the casting into the flame of those obstructions and inner conflicts and inner knots that are present to thwart the divine plan.

THE GREAT GIFT OF OUR HEART: THE COIL OF FIRE

Now I come with Magda and we offer unto you the great gift of our heart. And we desire, therefore, to explain this gift. In the past we have noted that some who have desired to give of themselves were not fitting candidates because of momentums of the human consciousness. A portion of the self desires to serve; the other portion of the self desires to be in the world, whether because of its karma or because of habit or because of desire—all of which amount to the same thing: the cause-effect cycles in Matter.

Thus, there is an expression of a willing heart. Thus, there is the pulling back from the level of the subconscious by the not-self that will not say die. And the soul betwixt the two is not able to resolve the dilemma. And therefore, because of the pressure of its own karma, the soul must go forth—out the door, out the gate. It must separate itself from the fiery altar because the very not-self is so resistant to the descent of the Great God Self.

Now, beloved ones, this presents a serious problem for the community as well as for the messengers. For the messengers have no desire to wrestle with those who have not wrestled with themselves. And therefore, they cannot retain as a part of their staff and as a part of the community of co-workers those who have these unalterable divisions and these dichotomies.

This, therefore, is our commitment and our gift—that those who find they have the division within the members, pulling this way and that—which the apostle Paul spoke of so understandingly, so personally and so poignantly[4]—may then call to us and ask for the transfer of the coil of fire.

Note the word: *coil of fire*—the coil of myself and of beloved Magda representing the Alpha, the Omega. When these are meshed, they form the divine caduceus. These two coils are of gold. They are of gold as you would visualize golden wire of the purest, finest quality of gold with no alloy.

Thus, this brilliant, sun-fire gold coil meshed together forms the caduceus of Alpha and Omega. It is not large. These coils are precisely the size large enough to surround each one's physical spinal column from the base unto the crown.

Now, those sincerely desiring to pass over the dark night and the astral plane of their karma and downward momentums, those who desire to transmute all of this through divine service and chelaship, those who would vow the vow of obedience, chastity, and poverty may therefore appeal for this gift.[5] We will supply it.

And by the coil of gold, by this coil of fire, beloved hearts, and by your pursuing the path of the novitiate, of the holy brother and the holy sister of the divine order, you may reach that point, by the coil and by service, of the transmutation of those elements of being that pull in all directions as horses going in diverse corners who will not submit to the discipline of the driver.

Beloved hearts, this has been the knotty problem. This has been the point of confusion. Thus, those who desire to give the most, often have the least to give because there is not this resolution. On the other hand, those who have the most to give and the greatest developed potential professionally often desire not to stay because their desires are to capitalize upon their attainment in the world itself. So you see, beloved hearts, there is a realization that outer attainment is a temptation away from the central altar and the central flame.

Now, we would not interfere with free will by our message this day. We come in answer to your calls to enable you to better come into alignment with your free will by having a superior knowledge and a wisdom, a perspective spanning the ages, and a rightful equation of what truly is in the world.

THE EQUATION OF THE MYSTICAL BODY OF GOD

Souls are being lost at a rapid rate today. Souls are truly being lost and extinguished. This is the burden of the heart of my Mother. This is the burden of the heart of the Fátima message.

The prayers of the righteous and the work of the labor of love of the Keepers of the Flame can and shall save the earth. But I must tell you, it is also an equation of number. This number is not many numbers. It is of the number one.

The One is the mystical body of God. The body of God has its components, its cells and organs. From the head to the feet, ye are the mystical body of God. God requires all of his members to be in manifestation. Thus, the numbers are always one. You are the One, I AM the One—we are one, and you form one Circle of Light.

THE GIFT OF MOTHER MARY'S CIRCLE OF LIGHT

I would comment to you, then, upon the power of the gift of the Circle of Light from the heart of my Mother initiated in this quarter.[6] This Circle of Light was retained for you unto the end that you might receive the maximum initiation and light that your bodies could bear. This, then, was accomplished magnificently last eve, and I desire to witness to the great beauty and power and alchemy that has occurred over Washington, D.C., and at inner levels.

You must understand that this formation of the Circle of Light by the messenger and devotees was and always will be an exercise in consciously ascending to the plane of the etheric body—leaving, therefore, the lesser bodies under the automated control of systems set in motion—and journeying consciously through the etheric body (again, the deathless solar body) to various places on earth for the completion of the work at hand.

This vital service cannot be overly praised, nor should it be underestimated. When you come into a realization of the all-power of God within you and its potential to change the world, I trust you will have the perspective to put all things in their proper place and arrive at the conclusion of the I AM Law of Life for your life.

WHERE ARE THE TEMPLE BUILDERS?

Thus, beloved ones, we have already outlined the divine plan and the destiny for the spiritual path and the life of lightbearers. We have pointed to the highest way and the highest goal. The temple must be built. Where are the temple builders? The land must be farmed and tilled and the Ranch must be tended and all must be in readiness for the descent of avatars and for earth changes that I trust will come about as smoothly as the violet flame can be smooth.

Beloved ones, there is an urgency in your individual lifestreams for the seizing of the torch of victory, and there is an urgency on the planet. I point out once again that those things that hang by a thread that are dangerous to mankind are only one category of danger. All other categories—of the economy, the political equation, et cetera—also hang by the thread.

OUR VISION AND OUR DESIRE

Our vision is to see now the mighty [Victory's] Temple of Light[7] and the cathedral built at the Inner Retreat and to have there twenty-four hours a day services for the nations.

We desire to see representatives from every nation who are the highest lightbearers eventually arrive there, once they have scoured the very earth itself to give the teachings to every lightbearer.

We desire to see the manifestation of the *SUN* itself in the *s*piritual *u*nity of *n*ations.

We desire to see the call and the Word and the ancient intonations resumed that were given in the early days of Atlantis and Lemuria.

TAKING HEAVEN BY FORCE
THROUGH GENETIC ENGINEERING

Even now, in the realm of genetic engineering, what is proposed—to engage now the human genes and to give them to animal genes and to combine the species—is abhorrent to the LORD God.[8] For the imprisoning of human genes in animal form is the imprisoning of a portion of the race itself, a portion of those genes that are actually endowed with a certain formula by the I AM Presence.

Thus, this is the taking of heaven by the violent who take it by force. And they take it by force through genetic engineering. And thus you see the prophecy of Daniel coming to pass in many areas—the abomination of desolation standing in the holy place where it ought not.[9] This statement from the Old Testament has numerous interpretations connected with the violation of the temple in those eras. But I speak to you today of the violation of the temple of man and the abomination in the violation of the genes and the DNA chain.

Beloved ones, these things are not merely on the drawing board. These experiments are being conducted and they are a living fact of today. Realize, then, that one of the causes for the Flood and the sinking of Atlantis was the combining of these genes in such a horrendous manner as to create half-man/half-goat creatures, et cetera. And these things became proliferated to such an extent that the very wombs of women were used as experimental laboratories for the bringing forth of all kinds of grotesque creatures. And the hour is coming in the earth when, through the absence of the standard of the Christ mind, women shall be offering their bodies in all manner of foul experimentation.

The creation of life without the God flame in the test tube and all manner of implantation of animal parts within the human body is the collective degeneration of consciousness that all might become animals once again.

WHERE WILL THE LIGHTBEARERS POSITION THEMSELVES?

And therefore, where do the lightbearers position themselves? How can you in any way allow your seed or your blood to be mixed with those evolutions who are of the animal creation? They are already in the earth. You have called them the godless. They are without the threefold flame. Therefore the cry went forth from the ancient prophets: Come apart and be a separate people elect unto God!

The separation of the seed of Christ must come. For, you see, the giving of the seed of Christ in experimentation is truly the end of evolution. And thus, cataclysm can be held back for the lightbearers, it can be held back for the coming of the golden age, but it cannot be held back when these practices are allowed to continue. There is no further purpose to an evolution that then consists of half-animal/half-human and is endowed with a divine spark by those children of the Sun, the profligate ones, who have abandoned their divine calling and who have gone to lie with the animals.

Beloved hearts, the desolation of the world and the outpicturing of death and hell in the quarters of this planet, in the quarters of the nations, is unbelievable. It is beyond belief. You have no awareness of how our angels must look upon the degradations, the sodomy, the perversion of the life force, bringing upon it the act of karma itself of this AIDS disease. Beloved ones, this failure of the immune system is due to the violation, the denial, and the hatred of the Mother light. And this disease itself becomes a threat to the race.

Thus, the karma descends for infamy. Where shall the lightbearers appear? Where shall we multiply the race of the I AM lightbearers? You must see the handwriting on the wall. You must look at what is happening today and you must ask yourselves as you consider yourselves in the office of the Lords of Karma:

What will you do with this planet in thirty years or fifty years? What will happen to a planetary home where this runs rampant and there is no stopping to the development of nuclear weapons that hang from satellites threatening every man, woman, and child? Every dumb beast, every fowl of the air and fish of the sea is threatened with the revolving of these satellites.

TO SECURE A PROTECTED PLATFORM
FOR THE I AM RACE

Beloved ones, I come with a plea from my heart and I say, set aside the desire for personal indulgence and achievement and recognize that the goal at the present hour is to secure a protected platform for those who recognize themselves as being of the I AM Race from every evolution on earth, those who recognize how precious it is to have the divine spark and those who desire ultimately that this divine spark shall not go out on earth again.

I tell you, if this planet goes down to the level it was before Sanat Kumara came to reinstate the path of the lightbearers, there shall not be given a second opportunity. The edict that went forth, which Sanat Kumara stopped—that the earth should be extinguished—*will go forth.* Beloved ones, it is a serious crossroads in the life of a planet and a solar system, and we must lay bare before you these facts so that you can make right choices.

I assure you that I withdraw in this moment all tension and all pressure you may feel from my message. I cannot withhold the Truth. I am sent by the Lords of Karma, I am sponsored by the Lord of the World. And the reason we have several masters sponsoring each quarter in these times is because of the great darkness abroad in the land.

Beloved hearts, let me assure you that if this work were not going forth and this organization were not solvent and able to deal as it deals justly with all those who desire the light, if we did not have a messenger and you could not receive initiations, the history of this earth would be markedly different in this hour. You must understand that *you* are a part of the pillars of eternity.[10] *You* are a pillar in the temple of my God. The ascended masters can do nothing for the planet without willing instruments.

Thus, you have chosen to answer our call. We have chosen to call; you have chosen to answer. There is a meeting of hearts. There is a divine embrace. We give you our love and we desire you to understand that, above all, we determine to secure the safety of the soul of each and every one of you.

Having secured the safety of the soul, we desire to secure the safety of the mental body, the functioning of the mind as a cogent identity. Then we desire to preserve the functioning of the desire body that you might retain the desire to be who you are. Then we must secure the safety of the physical body that all of these may be secured in the physical octave, which is the scene of your karma where you must be to balance that karma.

CATACLYSM SHOCKS THE PSYCHE, DAMAGES THE INNER BODIES

Beloved hearts, you may wonder why I speak in this wise. You see, cataclysm of a severe kind—the rise and fall of continents or nuclear war—is such a shock to the entire system and the psyche (which term I mean to indicate the soul) that in fact there is damage to the inner bodies when an individual goes through such calamity.

Some of the setbacks you have experienced have been because you have been on the scene and been in the situation of being a victim of types of holocaust and cataclysm that have occurred on the planet due to just the very experiments of the black magicians that are occurring today. They are determined to experiment with the nucleus of the atom and with the very nucleus of the genes.

Thus, whether in organic or inorganic matter, there is the manipulation of the sacred fire that is intended to be sealed and opened only by meditation and by the love of the heart. Understand my words—that "the kingdom of heaven suffereth violence, and the violent take it by force."[11]

Understand that there are those who force the chakras, force the light, extract all that they can from the bodies of the lightbearers. These are the black magicians who come as the rock stars. These are the black magicians who come purveying their chemicals for the destruction of the body through all manner of drugs and dope.

Beloved ones, it is almost a cause of the reeling of the mind and the senses to contemplate what actually is taking place on earth—the rapid devouring of souls, city by city, nation by nation. From the jungles to the most icy climes, this consciousness travels.

THE NEED FOR PERPETUAL PRAYER AND MEDITATION: BECOME AWARE OF WORLD PAIN

Thus, how do you survive? You survive in a cylinder of self-protection—the noninvolvement by refusing to consider these things too often. This is natural. All people do it, tending to focus on what they are able to give and able to do, what their personal responsibilities are, what their personal karma is. Understand, therefore, that to become aware, as the messengers are aware, of the pain of a planet demands that one alter one's lifestyle. This is why it is necessary to come apart.

If you are to be sensitive, if you are to make the perpetual call, if you are to spare the messenger and her four lower bodies in being on the altar, if you are to be there with the solar ring, then, beloved hearts, you will begin to become more and more sensitive, more and more aware of the need for perpetual prayer and meditation.

Will you not, then, take the book of myself with Kuthumi to study the perpetual practice of this art?[12] Prayer, meditation, and dynamic decree—a living ritual of the Trinity in your life.

Will you not begin to be aware, then, that you were created as an individual and a God-identity for more than just self-concern and the living of a reasonable life of happiness, privacy, the pursuit of the professions, and so forth?

PILGRIMS SEEKING NO CONTINUING CITY

Realize that you were created to become an avatar. You were created to become a Christ. You were sent forth to take on the world consciousness of the Lord of the World and to have your affairs and your energies so in order that you could give a more than ordinary service.

I must tell you these things, beloved hearts, because you will ask me in the hour of your transition why I did not make it plain, why I did not speak forthrightly, why I did not determine to take hold of you and remind you that you descended to this planet in order to ascend—for that reason alone! And in having avowed that solemn destiny, you must be reminded and called out of the very weight and density that you went forth to consume.

Beloved ones, each day the balancing of karma finds you a little higher in vibration and consciousness until all of you—all of your identity, all of your individuality—is one day in the etheric octave and you are there and secure and need no more to go out from the central altar of being. This is the only safety that can truly be considered as permanent and as ultimately secure.

All things are in transition.

I urge you and I encourage you to consider your position on this planet as temporary. I urge you to consider yourself as a pilgrim, to seek no continuing city[13] save that which is necessary as a dispensary of the teachings and the Path, to consider yourself here for a moment in eternity and to consider that everything on the earth hangs in the balance according to your decision.

This is the Truth. This is the Reality. I shirk not from its statement to you, beloved hearts, for the fallen ones who have raised themselves up in the positions of psychology and being cult watchers have accused anyone who cries out with the message of the Messiah to be truly attempting to brainwash, to control.

I tell you that if you should so interpret my message, you will lose the greatest opportunity that you have had in ten thousand years and more!

SEEK UNION WITH GOD, WITH TWIN FLAME, WITH THE MESSENGERS

I, Jesus, come as your brother. I come, if you will, as your equal, as your co-servant. I lay aside my garments. I wash your feet. I embrace you. I hold you close to my heart and Magda adorns you with roses and floral offerings. You are a part of us and a part of our bands and those of Sanat Kumara, and we will not leave you alone!

As long as you place yourself in our aura, we will remind you of all that we have passed through to gain a victory and to pay the price for you. We will remind you that there are just as many who will follow on the coattails of your Christhood as there are who follow us.

Thus, seek the union with God, with twin flame. Visualize the sphere of wholeness. Enter it and be a fireball for God on earth, and watch how the planet will change.

If there is any distress to the messenger, it is the absolute knowledge that where the call is made by her, there is change—the distress being that she cannot be perpetually at the altar to make those calls.

You are also the hands and feet of the ascended masters. You are also the hands and feet of the messengers. *You* can make the call in the name of the two witnesses. You *should* make the call by the authority of the mantle and the office and the protection of the messengers of the Great White Brotherhood that no harm may come upon thee.

Thus, this office of the two witnesses is safeguarded, and all who speak in the name of that office receive the angelic hosts who guard it as a protection of their lifestream and their service. You may also call and should call for the armor of Archangel Michael's legions and the seraphim of God.

Beloved ones, every call is answered. Let us roll back the time-tables of the dark ones and let us secure the victory for the light!

Now beloved Saint Germain comes to place upon your shoulders that mantle which signifies you have completed this level and, in so signifying, gives to you the momentum of his own determination, protection, and wisdom.

May you see your Teachers face-to-face. May you see the supernal spheres and inner octaves. May you see what lies ahead. May you see your beloved twin flame. May you look up and see the face of your I AM Presence. May you know your Christ Self.

KNOW ME AS YOUR BROTHER AND FRIEND, AND BE LIKE ME

I, Jesus, had my victory. This is your hour and the fulfillment of the prophecy that went forth in the beginning that thou shouldst return to the heart of the Father.

Oh, study my life—the records that you have of me, both in these writings as well as in that which has come forth in my dictations and from others of the ascended hosts. Truly gather, as you gather the most magnificent wildflowers in summer at the Inner Retreat—gather the precepts, gather the understanding.

For once you know me as your brother and friend, once you understand your present capacity to be just like me, your life will gain that intensity that comes with the new birth, with the infilling of the Holy Spirit, and with the igniting of your threefold flame with my own. These things are the promises of my Father through me unto those who truly love.

Blessed hearts, I plead with you. I plead again. Feed my sheep! Feed my sheep across the earth. Feed them before it is too late.

We release the breath of the eternal spring that is hope eternal for all life. In *you* lies our greatest hope for the world. May it be consummated by love and by faith.

I shall now use the Emerald Matrix used to transfer the blessing of Omega to bless you also from the heart of Magda and Mary.

Let us continue the Path we have begun and which we have determined to finish. I turn to the last page that shall be written by you in your book of life on earth, and I inscribe at the last page *F-I-N-I-S*. I put the seal of the finish upon this book that you may know that I am holding the flame for the fulfillment of all cycles. And I hold the immaculate heart matrix for the completion of thy round.

THE LORD'S PRAYER
AT THE ALTAR OF THE HOLY GRAIL

O Seraphim of God, O legions of angels of the Father, come now to earth and help my own in every walk of life.

I pray to Thee, O Father. Hear my call in this hour of desperation on earth. I, Jesus, pray that through these hearts they may be saved.

Send the twelve legions from the heart of the Central Sun, O Father! And send twelve legions again until every lightbearer on earth has a new angel and a new face in heaven to contemplate.

O God, let them not become overconfident but supremely aware and therefore always positive in the present victory.

Mighty Victory, I call to you with your legions of light. Come again! Come again and assist these, my beloved. Secure the divine plan for them.

I stand at the Altar of the Holy Grail physically in the very heart of my twin messengers and I deliver to you the very heart and essence of my lifeblood.

O earth, hear my call and respond! Hear my call, O earth, and respond in the name of Alpha and Omega.

I bow to the light of God within these hearts and the light of God within the heart of every servant son on earth.

I bow to the light. I breathe upon it the breath of the Holy Spirit.

I intensify that flame, for I AM determined, O Father, that this earth shall be brought Home through these, thy blessed ones.

December 7, 1984
Camelot
Los Angeles County, California
Lanello through ECP

NOTES*

FOREWORD

1. Gal. 1:12.
2. Rev. 1:1.
3. Luke 17:21.
4. Matt. 24.
5. John 14:12.

CHAPTER 1:   The Mystery of the Mother Flame within Thee: The Woman Crucified within the Chamber of Thy Heart . . . and Her Resurrection

1. Ezek. 34; John 10:1–16.
2. Isa. 53:6, 7; Matt. 26:53, 54.
3. Matt. 11:12.
4. John 1:1–9; Matt. 2:13–21; 3:7–12.
5. The poet whom I sponsored refers to Henry Wadsworth Longfellow. Prior to this dictation, the messenger read "Before the Gates of Machaerus," "Herod's Banquet-Hall," and "Under the Walls of Machaerus," from *Christus: A Mystery,* part 1: "The Divine Tragedy."
6. Matt. 17:10–13; Luke 1:13–17; John 1:15, 26–31.
7. Luke 22:53.
8. Mark 6:17–29; Matt. 27:1–54; John 18:28–40; 19:1–37.
9. John 6:29; I Cor. 3:16; 6:19; II Cor. 6:16.
10. John 15:17–27; 16:1–11.
11. Matt. 27:62–66; 28:1, 2.
12. Deut. 32:4; Matt. 16:18; I Cor. 10:4.
13. Ezek. 7:19; 14:3–8.
14. Mark 6:17, 18.
15. Isa. 40:3; Mal. 3:1; Mark 1:2–4; Luke 1:17, 76; John 3:28.
16. Matt. 3:13–17; 4:1–11; Rev. 12:1–9, 13–17.

---

*N.B. Books listed here are published by Summit University Press unless otherwise noted.

17. Dan. 12:3.
18. II Kings 2:1–15; Matt. 11:7–14; 17:11–13.
19. Mark 6:7; Luke 9:52; 10:1, 38, 39; John 12:1–3.
20. Matt. 26:26–28; Heb. 9:22.
21. Josh. 24:15.
22. Dan. 12:7; Rev. 12:14.
23. John 10:15–18.
24. John 3:28–30.
25. Acts 1:3.
26. John 10:10.
27. John 17:1–26.
28. Isa. 53:7; Acts 8:30–35.
29. John 21:15–17.
30. Rev. 12:1.
31. Luke 6:17–19; 8:43–48.
32. Alpha, "The Time Is Short," 1981 *Pearls of Wisdom,* vol. 24, no. 19, pp. 221–24.
33. Isa. 6:5–7.
34. Matt. 17:19, 20; Mark 4:30–32.
35. Rev. 6:8; 20:13, 14.

CHAPTER 2: **O Lord, Receive Thy Bride in Perfect Love!**

1. Isa. 61:10, 11.
2. *Hephzibah:* lit., "My delight is in her."
3. *Beulah:* lit., "married."
4. Isa. 62:3–12.
5. *Community* (U.S.A.: Agni Yoga Society, 1951), pp. 97–99.
6. Rev. 19:7–9.
7. Rev. 21:1–11.
8. Rev. 21:22–27.
9. St. Teresa of Avila, *Interior Castle,* in *The Complete Works of St Teresa of Jesus,* II, ed. and trans. E. Allison Peers (London: Sheed and Ward, 1975), pp. 334–36.
10. St. John of the Cross, *The Spiritual Canticle,* in *The Collected Works of St. John of the Cross,* trans. Kieran Kavanaugh and Otilio Rodriguez (Washington, D.C.: ICS Publications, 1973), pp. 410–15.
11. Gen. 2:9; 3:22, 24; Rev. 2:7; 22:2, 14.
12. The writings of Saint John of the Cross refers to Elizabeth Clare Prophet's lecture series on the *Living Flame of Love* (by Saint John of the Cross), delivered to the students of Summit University spring quarter 1977. See *Living Flame of Love,* 2 MP3 audio CDs,

containing 8 lectures by Mrs. Prophet and a dictation by Jesus the Christ, "The Marriage of Your Soul unto the Lamb of God."

13. Teachings of Sanat Kumara. See *The Opening of the Seventh Seal: Sanat Kumara on the Path of the Ruby Ray*, by Elizabeth Clare Prophet; see also 1979 *Pearls of Wisdom*, vol. 22.

14. John 6:29.

15. Serapis Bey's dispensation of love refers to the fourteen-month cycle of ascension's flame, first initiated by Serapis Bey at winter solstice 1978. The current cycle of love was announced by Serapis Bey on April 19, 1981. "Blessed ones, in this fourteen-month spire abuilding from the spiral of our heart, there is the opportunity for you to enter a path of initiation whereby love is perfected in love." See Serapis Bey, "Love That Has the Courage to Be," 1981 *Pearls of Wisdom*, vol. 24, no. 25, pp. 265–72.

16. Rev. 21:16.

17. On May 3, 1981, Saint Germain dedicated the Inner Retreat to the Assumption of the Blessed Virgin. See Saint Germain, "The Mosaic of Life," 1981 *Pearls of Wisdom*, vol. 24, no. 27, pp. 283, 293–94.

18. Prior to his final incarnation as the Nazarene Master, the soul of Jesus was embodied as David, king of all Israel and author of the Psalms.

CHAPTER 3: Seeds Not Watered or Planted

1. John 6:32–35, 48–51.

2. Acts 17:26.

3. Measuring the components of the capstone. See Cyclopea, "The Components of the Capstone" and "The Mystery of the Capstone," 1980 *Pearls of Wisdom*, vol. 23, no. 13, pp. 71, 73–74.

4. II Pet. 1:19.

5. Ps. 110:4; Heb. 5:5–10; 6:20; 7.

6. Rev. 21:16.

7. The Inner Retreat, over 12,000 acres of Montana ranchland, is approximately 78 nautical miles north of Grand Teton mountain (focus of the physical/etheric Royal Teton Retreat) and borders Yellowstone National Park.

8. Paul the Venetian. In the book *Lords of the Seven Rays: Mirror of Consciousness,* Paul the Venetian describes a magnificent chalice he was working on: "For a period of seventeen years I have been at work at inner levels in constructing a beautiful chalice to present to the Maha Chohan. And this very day it has been taken to him in his home in Ceylon. There it stands in his retreat. The base of this magnificent chalice—which, incidentally, is snow-white in color—is set

with three rings of precious stones . . . charged with the wisdom of God, the will of God, and the love of God. . . . I ask those of you who are spiritually perceptive and love the Father to call unto God with fervor and determination until, while you sleep at night, God himself shall direct your journey unto the . . . Temple of Comfort in Ceylon; and your own eye shall behold the work of my hands." (Mark L. Prophet and Elizabeth Clare Prophet, *Lords of the Seven Rays*, Book 1, chap. 3, pp. 133–34, 136)

9. John 6:29.
10. Rev. 14:6. See "The Everlasting Gospel Foursquare," chapter 21, in *The Opening of the Seventh Seal: Sanat Kumara on the Path of the Ruby Ray*, pp. 159–69.
11. John 9:5.
12. The soul of Jesus Christ was incarnated as Joseph, youngest and most favored son of Jacob, whose two sons (Ephraim and Manasseh) were blessed by Jacob as his own. The seed of Ephraim and Manasseh, reincarnated in the U.S. and Britain, therefore, carry not only the flame of the twelve tribes of Israel but also—and, most importantly— of their true Father the Lord Jesus Christ.
13. The flame of the Divine Mother in this weekend seminar refers to the Summit University seminar *On the Mother,* November 27–29, 1981, Camelot.
14. Decree 30.02, "Introit to the Holy Christ Flame," in *Prayers, Meditations and Dynamic Decrees for Personal and World Transformation.*
15. II Pet. 1:10.
16. Mark 16:18; Luke 10:19.
17. John 6:53–58.

CHAPTER 4: "God Has Provided the Recompense"

1. Refers to the Declaration of International Interdependence of the Sons and Daughters of God apart from Their Political, Economic, and Military Oppressors in Every Nation on Earth, a nonpartisan document delivered by the messenger Elizabeth Clare Prophet preceding this dictation. The Declaration, written in the spirit of the Declaration of Independence, presents a legal argument against the terms and conditions set forth in the Yalta, Potsdam, and Helsinki agreements and their subsequent violations. It enumerates specific grievances and injustices as an indictment of the Soviet Union and the World Communist movement. The concluding statement is a formal nullification of the aforementioned international agreements and a call for complete sanctions against oppressive governments who

deny their citizenry basic human rights. The document was prepared in response to the December 13, 1981, imposition of martial law in Poland. See 1982 *Pearls of Wisdom*, vol. 25, no. 2, p. 22 n. 2. To read the Declaration, see vol. 25, no. 5, pp. 41–48.

2. Jesus Christ, Lord Maitreya, Gautama Buddha, and Sanat Kumara are initiators on the path of the ruby ray. See *The Opening of the Seventh Seal: Sanat Kumara on the Path of the Ruby Ray*, chapters 1 and 9. Also in 1979 *Pearls of Wisdom*, Book I, vol. 22, p. 73ff.

3. Rev. 14:1, 6.

4. Rev. 15:6–8; 16. See also *Vials of the Seven Last Plagues*.

5. Rev. 19:11, 14.

6. John 1:1–3.

7. John 1:14.

8. John 1:11.

9. Rev. 9:1–11; 11:7; 17:1, 5, 8, 16; 18:2, 10, 21; 19:2, 20.

10. Saint Germain was incarnated as Saint Joseph, Patron of the Universal Church.

11. Rev. 12:1.

12. The Royal Teton Retreat is located in the Grand Teton, Teton Range, Wyoming.

13. Isa. 55:11.

14. See *The Opening of the Seventh Seal: Sanat Kumara on the Path of the Ruby Ray*, "Worthy Is the Lamb," chapter 13; "The Word and Work of the Saints on the West Gate," chapter 18; "Seven Initiations of the Saints Who Follow the Lamb," chapter 29; "The Vow to Save the Woman and Her Seed," chapter 33.

15. John 1:1–18.

CHAPTER 5: The Final Judgment of Satan

The messenger's invocations preceding and following this dictation are included in the text so that devotees of the sacred fire may recite them as often as they will, to bring the consonance of the Word to their own souls, poised in the worship of the Holy Spirit.

1. Matt. 10:6; 15:24.

2. Rev. 20:2, 3. Satan was seized and bound by Archangel Michael in 1968.

3. Isa. 14:12. On April 26, 1975, Lucifer was sentenced to the second death. His final judgment was announced by Alpha on July 5, 1975. See Alpha, "The Judgment: The Sealing of the Lifewaves throughout the Galaxy," and Elizabeth Clare Prophet, "Antichrist: The Dragon, the Beast, the False Prophet, and the Great Whore," chapters 19 and 20

in *The Great White Brotherhood in the Culture, History, and Religion of America,* by Elizabeth Clare Prophet.

4. Rev. 19:7; 21:9.
5. Rev. 18:10. Prior to this dictation, the messenger read Rev. 18; 19:1–5; following the dictation, Rev. 19:5, 6.
6. Mark 13:20.
7. Rev. 18:2, 4.
8. Mal. 3:2; Rev. 6:17.
9. Mark 16:17. See Sanat Kumara, "In My Name, Cast Out Devils!" in *The Opening of the Seventh Seal: Sanat Kumara on the Path of the Ruby Ray,* chapter 25.
10. Mark 5:15.
11. Matt. 28:20.

CHAPTER 6: **Believability**

Prior to this dictation, the messenger read Luke 7:36–8:3.

1. John 20:16.
2. John 12:44, 45.
3. Rev. 19:7; 21:9.
4. Mark 16:9; Luke 8:2.
5. Aimee Semple McPherson. Born Aimee Kennedy, October 9, 1890, near Ingersoll, Ontario, Canada, to devout Methodists. At age 4, she could recite Bible stories as others her age recited nursery rhymes. Aimee remembers Sunday school as the most exciting event of childhood. In 1907, she attended a prayer meeting conducted by Irish evangelist Robert Semple. This was a turning point in her life. She wrote: "Suddenly, in the midst of his sermon the evangelist closed his eyes and with radiant face began to speak in a language that was not his own. To me this Spirit-prompted utterance was like the voice of God thundering into my soul." While caught in a blizzard at the home of a family who conducted the local prayer meetings, Aimee beseeched God to fill her with his "promised Spirit of power." After a week of fervent prayer, she received answer. "Ripples, waves, billows, oceans, cloudbursts of blessing" flooded her being. A few weeks later, Robert Semple proposed to Aimee and she accepted. They were married on August 12, 1908. Robert was soon called to preach in London, Ontario. In 1910, the couple went to Chicago. Six weeks later, they returned to Canada and set sail from St. Johns, New Brunswick, to bring the gospel to China. En route to the Orient, Aimee preached her first sermon in London, England. Robert died from dysentery on August 19, 1910, shortly after arriving in China,

leaving Aimee pregnant and without financial support. Following the
birth of daughter, Roberta Star, Aimee went to New York to join her
mother, who worked as solicitor for the Salvation Army, and later to
Chicago. There, on February 28, 1912, she married Harold McPherson, under the stipulation that if at any time she should receive the
call to resume active ministry, she must obey God first of all. Later
Aimee accepted an offer to work for the Salvation Army in New York
to supplement their family income. "Dutifully I walked the beat
between Columbus Circle and the Battery" until right before her son,
Rolf, was born. During this time, Aimee remembers, "a voice kept
hammering at the doorway of my heart" to "preach the Word!" Following the birth of her son, Aimee underwent a serious operation.
She knew her choice was of either "going into the grave or out into
the field with the gospel." When she chose the latter, she was healed
by Jesus and determined to preach. One night at 11 o'clock, she
called for a taxi, packed her belongings, gathered her children under
her arms, and left for her parents' farm in Canada. She wired her
husband: "I have tried to walk your way and failed. Won't you come
now and walk my way? I am sure we will be happy." He joined her
for a time but then returned to the business world, later divorcing
her and remarrying. Aimee began preaching in tents and churches in
Canada and the United States along the Atlantic seaboard. In 1916,
while conducting a revival meeting in New York, Aimee prayed for
and God through her healed Louise Messnick, a young woman
severely crippled by rheumatoid arthritis. In the winter of 1916–17,
she carried her ministry to the South and began to edit her monthly
magazine, *Bridal Call.* In July 1917, a nationwide camp meeting in
Philadelphia was disrupted by a group of young men who stood
around the edges of the tent and mocked anyone who spoke, sang,
or prayed. Aimee describes the event: "As I praised the Lord, I seemed
to see a lot of demons with outspread, batlike wings, each of which
was interlocked with that of his neighbor, surrounding the tabernacle. But every time I cried 'Praise the Lord!' I noted that the demonic
forces took a step backward until finally back, back, back, they disappeared amid the trees. But now that I had once begun it was difficult to stop, so I continued shouting, 'Glory to Jesus! Hallelujah!
Praise the Lord!' Suddenly I noticed that from the place where the
powers of darkness had been lost to view a great square of white-robed angels were advancing with outspread wings, each of which
likewise was interlocked with that of his neighbor. Bless the Lord!
With each 'Praise the Lord,' the angels took a step forward. On, on,
on they came until they entirely surrounded the outer edges of my

canvas cathedral. Startled, I opened my eyes and looked about me. The young men who had been our tormentors were still there, but now they stood as quiet as mice . . . ." In 1918, Aimee's daughter became severely ill and she prayed to Jesus to spare her life. In answer to the prayer, Jesus spoke to her, saying, "Fear not. Your little one shall live and not die. Moreover, I will give you a home in California." Aimee journeyed to California with her two children, her mother, and stenographer, conducting revivals and working on her magazine as she went. She settled in Los Angeles, but continued to travel to other parts of the United States to preach. In 1919, prior to a sermon in Baltimore, Maryland, Jesus spoke to her about her ministry: "When you lay your hands on them, I will lay my hands on yours. And all the time you are standing there, I will be standing right back of you. And when you speak the Word, I will send the power of the Holy Ghost. You are simply the mouthpiece of the telephone. You are the key on the typewriter. You are only a mouth through which the Holy Ghost can speak." In Oakland, California, July 1922, Aimee presented a sermon "The Vision of Ezekiel" and received the inspiration from Jesus to call his message "the Foursquare Gospel" of Jesus the Saviour, Jesus the Baptizer with the Holy Spirit, Jesus the Healer, and Jesus the Coming King. On January 1, 1923, she opened the Angelus Temple in Los Angeles, her international headquarters. There she preached to thousands, sometimes in a costume designed to express the theme of her sermon. (For the sermon "God's Law" she dressed in a police uniform.) From 1923–26, Aimee stayed close to the Angelus Temple. She opened her 24-hour-a-day Prayer Tower, LIFE (Lighthouse of International Foursquare Evangelism) Bible College, and her radio station KFSG (Kall Four Square Gospel). On May 18, 1926, at the height of her career, Sister Aimee disappeared from a Pacific Coast beach. Thousands searched for her, suspecting that she had drowned; several gave their lives trying to recover her body. Thirty-two days later she reappeared in the Mexican border town of Agua Prieta where she recounted the story of her kidnapping. She told how she was approached on the beach by two strangers who asked her to pray for their sick baby. When she reached their car, she was asked to get in, then forcibly pushed inside and taken to a house, later to a desert shack. Aimee escaped and set out across the desert until she reached the border. Los Angeles district attorney Asa Keyes launched a full-scale investigation into charges of conspiracy between Aimee and her mother, misappropriating church funds by staging a phony kidnapping. Newspapers spread rumors whispered by eyewitnesses, who testified that they had seen Aimee with the married operator of her radio station, Kenneth Ormiston, during the five weeks she was missing. Keyes was ready to begin criminal proceedings. But publishing tycoon William Randolph Hearst intervened on Aimee's behalf, and charges were dropped. Aimee recalls: "Though unbelievable and wildly inconsistent, so persistent were these stories . . . that some people who did not know me or know my life could not be blamed for believing this absurd, paper-selling propaganda." In 1927, following her vindication, she once again devoted her life to preaching. A brief marriage to David Hutton ended in divorce in 1933. On September 27, 1944, she was found unconscious in her hotel room in Oakland and died a few hours later. Following her death, her son, Rolf, succeeded her as church leader. By the late sixties, Foursquare membership grew to nearly 90,000. During her entire ministry, Aimee lived in anticipation that Jesus would come and receive her as his waiting bride. The theme of her preaching was always "Jesus Christ the same yesterday, and to day, and for ever." See *Aimee: Life Story of Aimee Semple McPherson* (Los Angeles: Foursquare Publications, 1979); *This Is That* (Los Angeles: Echo Park Evangelistic Assoc., 1923).

6. John 14:10.

7. Cain and Abel, sons of Adam and Eve, brought offerings to the Lord. Abel, who was a keeper of sheep, brought a burnt offering from the firstlings of his flock; while Cain, a tiller of the ground, offered fruit. When Abel's sacrifice was found acceptable and Cain's was rejected, Cain was very wroth. And the Lord said unto him, "Why art thou wroth. . . . If thou doest well, shalt thou not be accepted? and if thou doest not well, sin lieth at the door." Cain then slew his brother (Gen. 4:1–8). According to the rabbinical tradition recorded in the Zohar, the motivation for the murder was that "Cain was jealous of the twin sister that was born with Abel."

8. After Cain killed his brother Abel, God gave to Adam and Eve another son, Seth, whose name is interpreted "consolation." "He shall be the blessed seed, and the head of patriarchs, and shall be a comfort unto thee." (*The Uncanonical Writings of the Old Testament*) "And to Seth, to him also there was born a son; and he called his name Enos: then began men to call upon the name of the Lord." (Gen. 4:25, 26) The ascended masters teach that the relative good and evil of the Cain/Abel consciousness must be transcended through the Christ typified in Seth, the Son of promise. It is through the person of Christ that men begin to call upon the name of the Lord, I AM THAT I AM. Only from that point of the Real Self can the true path of attainment be entered and won.

9. Refers to lectures on the "Corona Class Lessons" by Jesus and Kuthumi. See "Habit" in *Corona Class Lessons...for those who would teach men the Way.*
10. John 8:32.
11. See Michael Baigent, Richard Leigh, and Henry Lincoln, *Holy Blood, Holy Grail* (New York: Delacorte Press, 1982). According to their hypothesis, Jesus married Mary Magdalene, had several children, was the rightful heir to the Palestinian throne, took part in a mock crucifixion, and then fled to either Kashmir, India, or Alexandria, Egypt. Following the crucifixion, his family sought refuge in southern France where Jesus' bloodline (the true Sangreal of Arthurian legends, the sang real, i.e., "blood royal") became the foundation of the French Merovingian dynasty of kings (5th–8th century) whose heirs have survived to the present.
12. John 15:16.
13. "Higher Ground," Christian hymn: "I'm pressing on the upward way, / New heights I'm gaining every day; / Still praying as I onward bound, / 'Lord, plant my feet on higher ground'. . . " (words by Johnson Oatman, Jr.; music by Charles H. Gabriel).
14. "Go ye into all the world, and preach the gospel to every creature (Mark 16:15). . . . And this gospel of the kingdom shall be preached in all the world for a witness unto all nations; and then shall the end come." (Matt. 24:14) This command of Jesus Christ is being fulfilled through the worldwide stumping tours of Mother and her chelas.
15. My church refers to the International Church of the Foursquare Gospel.
16. Luke 4:16–32; John 8; 10:22–39.
17. Mark 15:34.
18. The 7 o'clock line on the cosmic clock is the point of transition from the seven "outer" rays (12 through 6 o'clock lines) to the five "secret" rays (7 through 11 o'clock lines). Initiations of the secret rays, beginning on the 7 o'clock line under the hierarchy of Leo, are a refinement of the senses of the soul. "The secret rays promote an action of detail," Mighty Cosmos explains, "the final sculpting of the mind and consciousness in the perfect image of the Christ. The secret rays are like the refiner's fire. They purge, they purify." (June 30, 1973) Symbolically and actually, the initiations of the five secret rays take the soul into the white-fire core of being, into the very nucleus of life, into the secret chamber of the heart where the individual stands face-to-face with the inner Guru, the beloved Christ Self, and receives the soul testings that precede the alchemical union with the Christ Self— the marriage of the bride (the soul who becomes the Lamb's wife). The initiations of the five secret rays are described by Saint John of

the Cross as the dark night of the soul and the dark night of the spirit, in his work "The Dark Night."

19. Where John has bidden you for this class. See John the Beloved, 1982 *Pearls of Wisdom,* vol. 25, no. 22, pp. 235–39.

20. John 11:25, 26.

CHAPTER 8: My Altar Call: The One Choice

Prior to this dictation, the messenger read Malachi 4.

1. Mal. 4:2.

2. The messenger and Keepers of the Flame attending the healing service preceding this dictation took part in the ritual of the Creation of the Cloud for the healing of the economy of America. In *Saint Germain On Alchemy,* Saint Germain explains how to magnetize millions of "focal points of light" into a brilliant pulsating "cloud of infinite energy" that can be directed into personal and planetary problems for the healing of specific conditions, such as disease, pollution, crime and war. See also *The Creation of the Cloud* meditation CD and booklet, available at https://Store.SummitLighthouse.org.

CHAPTER 9: The Path of the Avatar

Prior to this dictation, the messenger delivered a sermon on Luke 2:7–20, "The Great Mystery of the Birth of Christ," and on II Kings 4, "Four Miracles of Elisha." Dictation published on the album *The Buddhas in Winter,* 4 DVDs and 1 MP3.

1. Col. 2:9.

2. Gen. 15:17.

3. Heb. 10:7, 9.

4. Jesus Christ was embodied as Seth, third son of Adam and Eve, born after Cain slew Abel and left home. With the coming of Seth, Eve exclaimed, "God hath appointed me another seed instead of Abel, whom Cain slew." (Gen. 4:25) Of him it is written, "Then began men to call upon the name of the LORD." (Gen. 4:26) Jesus was also embodied as Joseph, eleventh and most favored son of Jacob; as Joshua, successor of Moses; as David, king of Judah and Israel; and as Elisha, disciple who received the mantle of the prophet Elijah.

5. Lord Maitreya, who holds the position of the Cosmic Christ, is the Great Initiator of our souls. He was the Guru, referred to as "the LORD GOD," who initiated the twin flames Adam and Eve in the Lemurian mystery school known as the Garden of Eden. (see Gen. 2, 3)

6. See I Kings 19:16–21; II Kings 2–9; 13:14–21.

7. Matt. 6:28, 29; Luke 12:27.

8. See "My Altar Call: The One Choice," chapter 8, this volume.
9. Heb. 13:2.

CHAPTER 10:   The Awakening of the Dweller-on-the-Threshold

Prior to this dictation, the messenger read and delivered teaching on Jeremiah 47 and Luke 21. See "Understanding World Karma in the Light of Prophecy," by Elizabeth Clare Prophet, 1983 *Pearls of Wisdom*, vol. 26, no. 36, pp. 351–82.

1. Dan. 12:2.
2. *Electronic belt:* the negative spiral or forcefield of density that surrounds the lower portion of man's physical form and is created through his misqualification of energy. Extending from the waist to beneath the feet, the electronic belt is similar in shape to a large kettledrum and contains the aggregate records of an individual's negative thoughts and feelings. It is the perversion of the *causal body,* electronic rings of rainbow light surrounding the I AM Presence (the upper figure in the Chart of your Divine Self). This is man's "cosmic bank account" where energy he has positively qualified is stored and becomes a part of his immortal identity. Thus Jesus admonished his disciples to "lay up for yourselves treasures in heaven. . . ." (Matt. 6:20) See Mark and Elizabeth Prophet's teaching on the causal body: "The Sanctuary of the Most High," in *The Path of the Higher Self* (Book 1 of the Climb the Highest Mountain series, pp. 268–77, trade size).
3. Col. 3:3.
4. Rev. 15:2; 12:10, 11.
5. Matt. 25:1–13.
6. Matt. 4:1–11; Luke 4:1–13.
7. See Jesus Christ, "The Final Judgment of Satan," chapter 5, this volume.
8. Rev. 14:1–5.
9. II Cor. 6:14.
10. See the Great Divine Director, October 10, 1971, "Arrest the Cycles," 1983 *Pearls of Wisdom*, vol. 26, no. 36, an excerpt in "The Radiant Word," p. 392.
11. Luke 21:26.
12. Sanat Kumara (Sanskrit, meaning "always a youth") is the Ancient of Days, spoken of in Daniel 7:9, 13, 22.
13. Luke 21:22.
14. Matt. 24:34; Luke 21:32.
15. Rom. 8:1–13.

CHAPTER 11: The Glorification of the Son of God

1. James 1:21.
2. Satans (pronounced seh-tánz): the race of the seed of Satan who long ago rose up against the I AM Race, and "who have infiltrated every corner of this galaxy and beyond." Jesus Christ pronounced their judgment, concurrent with the final judgment of Satan, in a dictation given February 1, 1982. See "The Final Judgment of Satan," chapter 5, this volume.
3. Acts 6:8–15; 7; 8:1–3.
4. Matt. 7:15; Luke 11:39–44.
5. Col. 1:27, 28; 3:1–4, 16; I Cor. 3:16, 17; Gal. 2:20; Eph. 3:16–19; Phil. 1:20; Heb. 10:16–22.
6. John 1:11–13; 3:15–18, 36; 6:40, 47; 11:25, 26; Acts 10:42, 43; 16:31.
7. Matt. 3:9.
8. Matt. 21:42, 44; I Cor. 10:4.
9. Rom. 6:6; Eph. 4:22, 24; Col. 3:9, 10.
10. John 15:1–8.
11. I Sam. 19:9–24; 23:7–29; 24:1–4; 26:1–5.
12. II Kings 19:30, 31; Isa. 10:20–22; 11:11, 16; 37:31, 32; 46:3; Jer. 23:3, 4; 44:28; Ezek. 6:8; 14:22; Joel 2:32; Mic. 2:12; Zech. 8:12; Rom. 9:27; 11:5.
13. Matt. 7:1, 2; Luke 6:37, 38.
14. John 20:23.
15. Jude 11, see also Num. 16.

Scriptural readings at the Easter Sunrise Service:
John 20:1–18; Luke 24:13–35; John 20:19–31; Luke 24:41–53.

CHAPTER 12: The Second Advent:
"The Day of Vengeance of Our God"

Prior to this dictation the messenger gave a sermon on Jer. 1:4–10; Isa. 61; Luke 4:14–19; Jer. 23:1–8; Luke 4:20–32.

1. Ps. 8:1, 9.
2. Acts 1:10, 11.
3. Isa. 61:3–65:24.
4. The Judgment Call. See Jesus Christ, "They Shall Not Pass!" decree no. 20.07 in *Prayers, Meditations and Dynamic Decrees for Personal and World Transformation*.
5. John 8:16; 5:22.

6. Isa. 61:2–62:12, "the day of vengeance of our God . . . "; Luke 4:16–21.

7. Job 19:26.

8. The word of my own heart as David. "As for me, I will behold thy face in righteousness: I shall be satisfied when I awake with thy likeness." Ps. 17:15.

9. Luke 4:29.

10. Elizabeth Clare Prophet, *Forbidden Mysteries of Enoch: The Untold Story of Men and Angels,* now titled *Fallen Angels and the Origins of Evil: Why Church Fathers Suppressed the Book of Enoch and Its Startling Revelations.*

11. Rev. 11:3.

12. Matt. 4:1–11.

13. Matt. 24:22; Mark 13:20.

14. Comet IRAS-Araki-Alcock passed within 3 million miles of earth the week of May 8–15, 1983, making it the second closest comet to enter this solar system in recorded history. (The closest, Comet Lexell, passed within 1.5 million miles of the planet in 1770.) Traveling at about 64,800 mph, IRAS is thought to be composed of frozen dust and gases and believed to have originated in the deep freeze of outer space beyond the orbit of Pluto. According to Cardiff University astronomer Chandra Wickramasinghe, the comet may be depositing microorganisms in earth's atmosphere that could cause deadly epidemics. "Throughout history there has always been a link between plagues like the Black Death and comets," he said, postulating that this comet most likely would cause a flu epidemic that would reach the Northern Hemisphere in January or February 1984.

15. Rev. 12:10.

16. Enoch Rosary: the messenger's responsive readings from the Book of Enoch, with beautiful prayers, songs, and praises to the Ancient of Days.

17. Song of Sol. 2:1.

18. Mal. 4:2.

19. II Cor. 6:14.

20. Rev. 13:1–8; 17:3; 19:20; 20:10, 14, 15; 21:8.

21. John 14:16–18, 26; 15:26; 16:7; Acts 1:8.

22. Return Home with 100 percent of your karma balanced. Lanello, September 9, 1973, and April 8, 1979.

23. For references to earth as Freedom's Star, see Saint Germain, July 4, 1975, "A Confirmation of Freedom," in *The Great White Brotherhood in the Culture, History, and Religion of America,* p. 165; November 23, 1975, "Enshrining the Flame of Freedom in the Capitals of the Nations," in *The Greater Way of Freedom,* pp. 56, 62; July 1, 1983, Omri-Tas and Holy Amethyst, December 29, 1976, "The Lord's

Commission to the Keepers of the Flame," in 1977 *Pearls of Wisdom,*
vol. 20, no. 15, pp. 63, 64.

24. John 14:23.

CHAPTER 13:   The LORD's Rebuke of the Betrayer of the Word

The messenger's sermon preceding this dictation included teaching on
Mark 16:9–20 and Matt. 24:25–51.

1. John 20:21.
2. Luke 2:49.
3. Matt. 10:33; II Tim. 2:12.
4. Matt. 24:35.
5. *Depart* from me, ye *despisers* of the Word! See Jesus Christ, "Father,
   the Hour Is Come," in *Where the Eagles Gather* (1981 *Pearls of
   Wisdom,* vol. 24, no. 24), p. 262.
6. Matt. 24:34.
7. Matt. 21:9; 23:39; Mark 11:9; Luke 13:35; 19:38.
8. Matt. 24:30.
9. Matt. 24:42; 25:13; Luke 12:40, 46; Rev. 3:3.
10. Rev. 13:1–8; 17:3.
11. I John 2:18, 22; 4:3; II John 7.
12. Rev. 12:10.
13. Col. 1:27.
14. Rev. 19:11–16.
15. Matt. 24:30.
16. Mark 16:16; John 1:12; 3:14–18, 36; 6:40, 47; 11:25, 26; Acts
    10:43.
17. Matt. 24:14; Mark 16:15; Rev. 14:6.
18. Rev. 19:17, 18.
19. Luke 4:24; John 4:44.
20. Mal. 3:10.
21. Luke 21:26.
22. Mark 16:16; John 3:18, 36; 8:24.
23. Matt. 24:15–26, 29.
24. See Rose of Light, "Close to Your Heart." 2005 *Pearls of Wisdom,* vol.
    48, no. 44.
25. Rev. 13:8.
26. Isa. 11:9; Hab. 2:14.
27. Matt. 24:13; Mark 13:13; James 5:11.
28. Luke 11:50.
29. Matt. 8:12; 22:13; 25:30; Rev. 20:11–15.
30. Rev. 12:1–5.

31. John 5:22.
32. John 11:25.
33. John 17:12; II Thess. 2:3.
34. John 10:30.
35. Rev. 1:8, 11; 21:6; 22:13.

CHAPTER 14:   **You Can Become a Christ!**

The messenger's sermon, "My Peace I Give unto You . . . , " which preceded this dictation, included the following scriptural readings: Ps. 75; Isa. 2:1–5; Mark 4:26–32, 35–41; John 14:25–31.

1. John 8:28; 13:19.
2. The aura. See Kuthumi, *The Human Aura.*
3. Isa. 40:4; Luke 3:5.
4. Saint Germain was embodied as Sir Francis Bacon (1561–1626), author of the Shakespearean plays. See *The Golden Age Prince: A Lecture on Francis Bacon* by Elizabeth Clare Prophet.
5. John 14:1, 27.
6. Gen. 3:24.
7. Num. 4:15; II Sam. 6:6, 7.
8. Exod. 25:18–22; 37:7–9; II Chron. 5:8.
9. Matt. 24:31; Mark 13:27.
10. Dark Cycle in Pisces. On April 23, 1983, the Dark Cycle entered its fifteenth year, commencing the initiations of the two o'clock line of the cosmic clock under the ascended master Jesus Christ and the solar hierarchy of Pisces. The flame of God-mastery on this line is misqualified through doubt and fear, anxiety, human questioning, and records of death.
11. Isa. 1:18.
12. See Gautama Buddha, "The Torch Is Passed!" 1983 *Pearls of Wisdom,* vol. 26, no. 22, pp. 169–76.
13. On November 20, 1983, the Sunday preceding this dictation, ABC aired *The Day After,* a widely advertised television drama (written by Edward Hume, produced by Robert Papazian, directed by Nicholas Meyer) graphically depicting the nuclear destruction of Kansas City and its devastating aftermath. The film, which stirred national and international debate, was described by *Newsweek* (21 November 1983) as "the single biggest mobilizing point for the antinuclear movement" and as a "two-hour commercial for disarmament. . . . What most explains the unprecedented controversy surrounding the show is the fact that it both coincides with and reinforces a growing nuclear consciousness . . . an upsurge in belief that nuclear Armageddon may

be creeping ever closer." According to ABC officials, *The Day After* was viewed by an estimated 100 million Americans. The messenger's comment was: "This is a film for and by and on the death entity of the planet, the demons of death—the kind that come and wiggle the skeleton in front of your face, you know, on Halloween—just to be sure that you don't forget that one day *'you will die!'* *The Day After* is a last hurrah for the program and platform in defense of death. This is a film in defense of the belief in death on planet Earth, which proposal and platform Jesus Christ resolved 2,000 years ago with his victory over death and hell and the mighty power of the resurrection flame.... We need to realize just how dead-serious is the death entity. It's the most deadly serious entity on the planetary body, and this is its big one-night stand to convince everyone that they're going to die and that death is real." The messengers are staunch proponents of survival and have conducted seminars on total preparedness for cataclysm, economic collapse, or the eventuality of nuclear war. The Royal Teton Ranch is the base provided by Keepers of the Flame for a spiritual retreat and self-sufficient community of devotees prepared to meet the challenges of this century—come what may—physically, mentally, emotionally, and spiritually. Members of Church Universal and Triumphant are dedicated to the principles of survival and have vowed to survive. They have a very thorough understanding of the necessities and precautions which must be taken in the face of the uncertainties of world conditions. They are neither escapists nor espousers of a doomsday consciousness. They are simply willing to face realities and to deal with them out of their own self-knowledge and heart-tie to God. They are not moved by *The Day After* except to keep on doing what they have been doing for 20 years—what the governments of the West have not done for their people and what only a few churches have done: to provide a place of safety for their families and their community and to be ready to face any emergency with calmness and a well-planned and well-rehearsed alternative in the face of life-threatening dangers.

14. See *Laborem Exercens:* Encyclical of Pope John Paul II on Human Work, September 14, 1981.
15. John 14:26.
16. Matt. 7:16, 20.
17. Ps. 149:6; Heb. 4:12; Rev. 1:16.
18. Matt. 26:41; Mark 14:38; Luke 22:40, 46.
19. I Pet. 3:4.
20. Matt. 27:51; Heb. 8; 9.
21. Luke 10:17, 20.

CHAPTER 15:   The Mission of Jesus Christ
Fulfilled in the Seed of the Woman

The service preceding this dictation—dedicated as a prayer vigil for the Middle East—opened with the messenger's scriptural reading of Psalm 72. The congregation viewed newsclips of events in Lebanon (November 5–December 4, 1983) that culminated with reports by President Reagan and Sam Donaldson on the downing of 2 American planes that occurred earlier that day. (The planes were shot down during a U.S. strike on Syrian anti-aircraft positions in Lebanon—a strike performed in retaliation for the attack upon American reconnaissance planes the day before. Hours after the U.S. air strike, 8 Marines were killed and 2 wounded in a massive barrage on their compound in Beirut.) Throughout the service of fiery decrees, songs, and judgment calls, the messenger made specific invocations for the anchoring of light aboard the U.S. battleship *New Jersey,* and for the protection of all U.S. forces and lightbearers in Lebanon and the Middle East.

1. As part of the prayer vigil for the Middle East, the messenger led the congregation in the sacred ritual for the Creation of the Cloud, invoking "the fiery cloud to consume on contact the cause and core of war, to protect the hosts of the LORD and forces of light, and to seal the Middle East from all intervention of 'aliens,' known or unknown." The "cloud," as described by Saint Germain, is an "electronic vibratory action of vital, moving, ineffable light" that can be used for the healing of the nations and the soul of a planet, as well as personal illnesses and other conditions. See also chapter 8, this volume, note 2.

2. The Middle East is the focus of the base-of-the-spine chakra for the planet.

3. Dan. 12:2.

4. Matt. 24:40, 41.

5. II Kings 2:9–15. Jesus was embodied as Elisha, the disciple of the prophet Elijah—who later incarnated as John the Baptist to prepare the way for Jesus' mission as the Nazarene master and avatar of the Piscean age.

6. Heb. 13:2.

7. Matt. 28:20.

8. The *i-niche-i-action* of the Lord Jesus Christ. Initiation begins when that which affirms *I AM,* that which has an awareness of selfhood, secures itself in the *niche* of the All-Eeeing *Eye* of God for the purpose of establishing right *action* on earth as it is in heaven.

9. Matt. 1:23.

CHAPTER 16: The Vow of the Ministering Servant

This was the closing dictation for fall quarter of Summit University, sponsored by Jesus and Kuthumi. The messenger's sermon included teaching on the forces of anti-love, invocations for the magnification of the light of Archangel Chamuel and Charity, scriptural readings and commentary (John 13:34, 35; 14:15; 15:12; Luke 6:17–49; 12:31) on the teachings of Jesus to his disciples concerning divine love, obedience, healing through the Holy Spirit, the law of desire, and forgiveness as the way to displace world condemnation.

1. John 8:23; 3:13.
2. Isa. 55:8, 9.

CHAPTER 17: My Victory, Your Victory

1. Prior to this dictation, at the request of beloved Jesus in order that the world might better understand his message, the messenger read the book of Zephaniah. The prophet rebukes Judah for its moral degeneracy and worship of Baal and other deities. He prophesies the judgment of Judah as well as neighboring heathen nations who have reviled Israel. The immediate fulfillment of this prophecy came in 597 B.C. when Nebuchadnezzar captured Judah and carried its leading citizens into captivity in Babylon. In 587 B.C., Jerusalem was destroyed and all but a few inhabitants were deported.
2. Not all have been delivered or restored, but all have had the opportunity.
3. Jer. 23:5, 6; 33:15, 16.
4. Exod. 3:13–15.
5. Isa. 43:25; Jer. 31:34; Heb. 8:12; 10:17.
6. II Pet. 3:7, 10–12.
7. John 12:28.
8. Enoch 45:3, 4; 50:3, 5; 51:5, 10; 54:5; 60:7, 10–13; 61:1.

CHAPTER 18: The Mystery School of Lord Maitreya

1. Matt. 6:28, 29; Luke 12:27.
2. June 6, 1984, marked the 40th anniversary of D-Day, which commenced the heroic World War II Allied invasion of Europe—also known as Operation Overlord. On June 6, 1944, the combined forces of the Allied armies, commanded by Gen. Dwight D. Eisenhower, launched the first wave of attack upon five Normandy beaches, breaking through the German defenses on the coast of occupied France, in the greatest seaborne invasion in history. This valiant assault against Hitler's Atlantic Wall opened the way for the defeat of

Nazi Germany and the winning of the war. Today, row upon row of graves, marked by white crosses and Stars of David, line the 172-acre U.S. cemetery at Colleville-sur-Mer, above Omaha Beach, Normandy, where 9,386 American servicemen and women are buried.

3. In a dictation given July 6, 1975, Jesus Christ described a vision that he received in his embodiment as David: "As I knelt in prayer long, long ago, serving the children of Israel, and I wrote down the meditations of my heart as the Psalms which have been preserved, I remember the vision which I saw in the starry heavens—a fiery cross of light which God allowed me to see. And I knew that my soul would be perfected, and I declared with the prophets of old, 'Yet in my flesh shall I see God!' That prophecy came to pass in my incarnation in Galilee. And I experienced what you, too, can know as the miracle of the Word incarnate."

4. See Saint Germain's teaching on the threefold flame of life in *Saint Germain On Alchemy: Formulas for Self-Transformation,* Book III, "A Trilogy On the Threefold Flame of Life."

5. In his dictation of October 7, 1962, given in Washington, D.C., the ascended master Hilarion announced: "The messenger that stands before you has had a special anointing of the sacred fire preparatory to this address this day which has caused the very physical atoms of his body to change. And within him an action has taken place in preparation for his own ascension. Yet he shall walk among you for a time."

6. Through a filigree thread of light connecting his heart with the hearts of all God's children, the Lord of the World Gautama Buddha sustains and nourishes the threefold flame, the divine spark, for all children of God on earth. See "Lord of the World," 1983 *Pearls of Wisdom,* vol. 26, no. 9, pp. 75–76.

7. As charted on the cosmic clock by Mother Mary, Capricorn, positioned on the 12 o'clock line, is an earth sign in the fire quadrant, symbolizing the power of the sacred fire in the heart of the mountains and the initiation of the cycles of the Law by the Father as in Horeb. Cancer is a water sign in the water quadrant symbolizing the power of the Mother in the sea as the passive polarity, receiving the light of the Great I AM for her children on the 6 o'clock line. This is a demonstration of the law of interchange through the Alpha-Omega T'ai Chi of cosmic forces.

8. All of the ascended-master dictations given through the messenger Mark L. Prophet have been released under the title *Only Mark,* in 30 albums. Each album contains many dictations on MP3 audio CD format. These can be purchased as individual albums or in two Box

Sets, each containing 15 albums. Available at https://Store.Summit Lighthouse.org.

9. Jer. 31:33; Heb. 10:16.

10. *Manus* [Sanskrit for "progenitors" or "lawgivers"]: The Manus are the sponsors who ensoul the Christic image for a lifewave, or *root race.* According to esoteric tradition, there are seven primary root races— individual groups of souls who embody together and have a unique archetypal pattern, divine plan, and mission to fulfill. For teaching on the golden ages of the first three root races, and on the allegorical Fall during the time of the fourth root race on the continent of Lemuria, see Mark L. Prophet and Elizabeth Clare Prophet, *The Path of the Higher Self,* pp. 60–88 and *The Path to Attainment,* pp. 278–86, 288–89.The fourth, fifth, and sixth root races (the latter not fully descended into physical incarnation) yet remain in embodiment on earth today; the seventh root race is destined to incarnate on the continent of South America in the Aquarian age.

11. As recorded in The Second Book of Adam and Eve, the children of Jared (descendants of Seth) were lured down the Holy Mountain of God by the children of Cain, who committed all manner of abominations and serenaded them with sensual music from the valley below. For the full story, see Elizabeth Clare Prophet, *Fallen Angels and the Origins of Evil,* "Prologue on the Sons of Jared," pp. 395–407.

12. El Morya's program for those who would be "ministering servants" was formally introduced in a dictation by Gautama Buddha on June 30, 1983: "Let, therefore, the disciples of blessed El Morya . . . enter the path of the ministering servant. . . . By this name I call you who would be ordained ministers in the Church Universal and Triumphant, that you might always remember that the minister is the servant of the Christ in souls mounting unto the Shekinah glory of the Mother of Israel." See Gautama Buddha, 2005 *Pearls of Wisdom,* vol. 48, nos. 28 and 29; Jesus and Kuthumi, "The Vow of the Ministering Servant," chapter 16, this volume. See also decree 60.09, "My Vow to Be the Ministering Servant," in *Prayers, Meditations and Dynamic Decrees for Personal and World Transformation.*

13. Gen. 3:24.

14. Gen. 1:29; 2:9, 16, 17; 3:1, 2, 3, 8.

15. Benjamin Creme, British author-lecturer and self-proclaimed representative of Lord Maitreya, announced on May 14, 1982, in Los Angeles, that the Cosmic Christ had entered the modern world and had been living in a Pakistani community in southeast London since July 19, 1977. According to Creme, the master would identify himself within two weeks in an international radio and television

broadcast in which he would communicate telepathically with all
people on earth in their own language.

16. Acts 1:9.

CHAPTER 19:   The Order of the Good Samaritan

1. John 3:13.
2. Rom. 8:15, 23; Gal. 4:5; Eph. 1:5.
3. John 1:12.
4. Gen. 14:18–20; Heb. 7:4. See Elizabeth Clare Prophet, "Teachings
   of the Mother on Morya as Abraham" and "The Story of Our Father
   Abraham and of His Chela and of His Guru," from the *Class of the
   Seven Chohans,* the first conference ever held in the Heart of the Inner
   Retreat, available on DVD and MP3 at https://Store.SummitLight
   house.org.
5. Heb. 13:14.
6. I Cor. 15:47–50.
7. At Jesus' request, prior to the dictation the messenger read Luke
   10:1–37 on the "other seventy" and the Good Samaritan.
8. Mal. 3:10.
9. *calcinated:* term used by chemists to describe a substance that has
   been reduced, through heating or roasting, to a hard and brittle residue or chalklike powder.
10. "Life is a mission. . . . Every existence is an aim." Giuseppe Mazzini
    (Italian patriot, 1805–1872), *Life and Writings.*
11. Deut. 6:5; Lev. 19:18; Matt. 22:36–40; Mark 12:30, 31; Luke
    10:25–28.
12. See El Morya, *A Report,* October 26, 1962, *Pearls of Wisdom,* vol. 5,
    no. 43.
13. Matt. 18:11, 14.
14. Order of the Golden Lily established by the Goddess of Liberty. See
    1984 *Pearls of Wisdom,* Book 1, vol. 27, no. 2, p. 18 n. 5.
15. Luke 22:31.
16. The focus referred to by beloved Jesus is a deep purple/indigo crystal
    cylinder, 12½ inches tall and 3½ inches in diameter—with a ¾-inch
    band of clear crystal 5 inches from the base. It was offered on the altar
    by a chela who had no inkling of its intended use by the Master for
    the visualization of the pillar of purple-blue fire that co-occupies the
    same "time" and "space" as the violet flame within the tube of light.
    The clear band denotes the so-called "line of demarcation" between
    the octaves of Spirit and the octaves of Matter and symbolizes in man
    the plane of the heart.

CHAPTER 21:　**A Torch of Responsibility**

This dictation by Jesus and Magda was delivered by the ascended messenger Lanello through the unascended messenger Elizabeth Clare Prophet. It was the concluding address to the students of Summit University fall quarter 1984, sponsored by Mother Mary, Jesus and Magda.

1. The seven chakras, their colors, rays, and the seven chohans who initiate the light of the Elohim in the seven spiritual centers of their chelas are as follows:

    base-of-the-spine chakra, white, fourth ray, Serapis Bey;
    seat-of-the-soul chakra, violet, seventh ray, Saint Germain;
    solar-plexus chakra, purple and gold, sixth ray, Nada;
    heart chakra, pink, third ray, Paul the Venetian;
    throat chakra, blue, first ray, El Morya;
    third-eye chakra, green, fifth ray, Hilarion;
    crown chakra, yellow, second ray, Lanto.

2. Dan. 9:20–27. See *The Scofield Reference Bible,* p. 914 n. 1.

3. On December 3, 1984, a storage tank containing methyl isocyanate (MIC) at the Union Carbide pesticide plant in Bhopal, Central India, leaked a cloud of noxious gas that spread over the city, killing more than 2,500 people and leaving an estimated 100,000 permanently disabled.

4. Rom. 7:15–25.

5. See Kuthumi, "Remember the Ancient Encounter on Discipleship under Lord Maitreya," 1985 *Pearls of Wisdom,* vol. 28, no. 9, pp. 95–96, on the Order of Saint Francis and Saint Clare in the Aquarian age and the interpretation of the vow of obedience, poverty, and chastity.

6. See Mother Mary, "The Power of God in My Right Hand," 1984 *Pearls of Wisdom,* Book II, vol. 27, no. 51, pp. 437–38.

7. In his June 3, 1960, *Pearl of Wisdom,* (vol. 3, no. 23, p. 3), El Morya announced: "A mighty Temple of Victory is to be built in this nation for all mankind, dedicated to the presence of Almighty God! It shall be called '*I AM' the Temple of Life's Victory*. . . the first temple of the Great White Brotherhood known to the outer world since Atlantean days." Jesus' vision of the building of the temple and the cathedral at the Inner Retreat is an indication that the time is approaching when Victory's Temple is to be built.

8. In November 1983, a team of scientists headed by Professor Richard D. Palmiter of the University of Washington in Seattle reported successful injection of the human growth hormone gene into fertilized mouse eggs, producing mice which grew larger than normal in size,

and which also manufactured the human hormone in several of their organs. See "Metallothionein-Human GH Fusion Genes Stimulate Growth of Mice," *Science* (November 18, 1983), pp. 809–14.

9. Dan. 9:27; 11:31; 12:11; Matt. 24:15; Mark 13:14.
10. See El Morya, "The Pillars of Eternity," 1971 *Pearls of Wisdom,* vol. 14, no. 19, pp. 75–77. Rev. 3:12.
11. Matt. 11:12.
12. Jesus and Kuthumi, *Prayer and Meditation.*
13. Heb. 13:14.

THE
WORD

Mystical Revelations of Jesus Christ through His Two Witnesses

Volume 8 (1993–1998)   372 pp • ISBN 978-1-60988-370-6

Volume 7 (1989–1992)   304 pp • ISBN 978-1-60988-385-0

Volume 6 (1985–1988)   364 pp • ISBN 978-1-60988-403-1

Jesus Christ is the avatar of the ages—the same yesterday, today, and forever. We knew him when he walked the streets of Atlantis and Lemuria. We also knew him in eras of darkness, when he sought to lead men to the light.

His message did not begin with the Bible, nor did it end with the Book of Revelation. He has never stopped speaking to his own.

Two thousand years ago, he foretold a time of tribulation—the end of an age. That time has come. It is the era when the mystery of God should be finished, when the Two Witnesses should prophesy "a thousand two hundred and threescore days."

And so Jesus once more delivers his Word to a world in transition. As always, the message is one of judgment to the fallen angels, admonishment to those who would walk in the light, hope for all who are striving on the path, and the vision of a golden age to come.

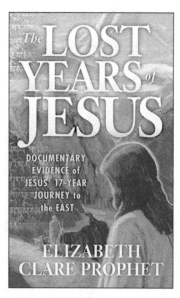

480 pp • ISBN 978-0-916766-87-0

THE LOST YEARS OF JESUS
Documentary Evidence of Jesus' 17-Year Journey to the East

"Reads like a detective thriller! It picks you up and never lets go of you."
—**Jess Stearn,** bestselling author of *Edgar Cayce: The Sleeping Prophet*

Ancient texts reveal that Jesus spent 17 years in the Orient. They say that from age 13 to age 29, Jesus traveled to India, Nepal, Ladakh and Tibet as both student and teacher. For the first time, Elizabeth Clare Prophet brings together the testimony of four eyewitnesses—and three variant translations—of these remarkable documents.

She tells the intriguing story of how Russian journalist Nicolas Notovitch discovered the manuscripts in 1887 in a monastery in Ladakh. Critics "proved" they did not exist—then three distinguished scholars and educators rediscovered them in the twentieth century.

Now you can read for yourself what Jesus said and did prior to his Palestinian mission. It's one of the most revolutionary messages of our time.

"Well-written and provocative.
The research was not only thorough and accurate but very, very careful."
—**Robert S. Ravicz, PhD,** Professor of Anthropology, California State University, Northridge

THE LOST TEACHINGS OF JESUS 1

Missing Texts •
Karma and Reincarnation

Mark L. Prophet and Elizabeth Clare Prophet prove that many of Jesus' original teachings are missing. They show that the New Testament records only a fragment of what Jesus taught—and that what was written down was tampered with by numerous editors or suppressed by "guardians of the faith."

Now, in their landmark series The Lost Teachings of Jesus, the Prophets fill in the gaps with a bold reconstruction of the essence of Jesus' message. They unfold the lost teachings Jesus gave in public to the multitudes and in secret to his closest disciples. And they answer questions that have puzzled readers of the Bible for centuries.

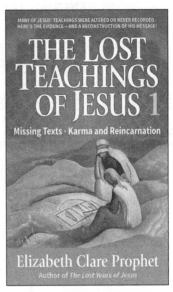

358 pp • ISBN 978-0-916766-90-0

THE LOST TEACHINGS OF JESUS 2

Mysteries of the Higher Self

How Church Fathers suppressed Jesus' original teaching on the Christ within.

This volume reveals how early churchmen distorted Jesus' true teachings and robbed you of what he wanted you to know about the power of your own inner Christ. It recaptures the heart of Jesus' message—that you, like Jesus, can reconnect with your Divine Source to realize your full potential.

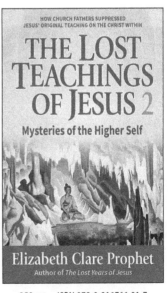

352 pp • ISBN 978-0-916766-91-7

PRAYER AND MEDITATION

A combination of Christian mysticism and Eastern meditation that teaches the art of unceasing communion with God and the way of higher meditation to open the heart. Eighteen Chinese-style prints of great spiritual masters.

302 pp • ISBN 978-0-916766-19-1

CORONA CLASS LESSONS

For Those Who Would Teach Men the Way

Reveals the many treasures to be found on the spiritual path, with rare insights on love, habit, mercy, brotherhood, charity, the soul, vision, mission and faith. Unveils new interpretations of the Bible.

408 pp • ISBN 978-0-916766-65-8

ELIZABETH CLARE PROPHET is a world-renowned author, spiritual teacher, and pioneer in practical spirituality. Her groundbreaking books have been published in more than thirty languages and over three million copies have been sold worldwide.

Among her best-selling titles are *The Human Aura, The Science of the Spoken Word, Your Seven Energy Centers, The Lost Years of Jesus, The Art of Practical Spirituality,* and her successful Pocket Guides to Practical Spirituality series.

The Summit Lighthouse®
63 Summit Way
Gardiner, Montana 59030 USA
1-800-245-5445 / 406-848-9500

Se habla español.

info@SummitUniversityPress.com
SummitLighthouse.org